Pascal's
Lettres Provinciales

Pascal's
Lettres Provinciales

A STUDY IN POLEMIC

RICHARD PARISH

CLARENDON PRESS · OXFORD
1989

Oxford University Press, Walton Street, Oxford OX2 6DP
Oxford New York Toronto
Delhi Bombay Calcutta Madras Karachi
Petaling Jaya Singapore Hong Kong Tokyo
Nairobi Dar es Salaam Cape Town
Melbourne Auckland
and associated companies in
Berlin Ibadan

Oxford is a trade mark of Oxford University Press

Published in the United States
by Oxford University Press, New York

British Library Cataloguing in Publication Data
Parish, Richard
Pascal's Lettres Provinciales.
1. Christian doctrine
I. Title
230
ISBN 0-19-815155-1

Library of Congress Cataloging in Publication Data
Parish, Richard.
Pascal's lettres provinciales.
1. Pascal, Blaise, 1623–1662. Provinciales.
2. Jesuits—Controversial literature—Early works to
1800. 3. Jansenists—Early works to 1800. 4. Port
Royal—Early works to 1800. I. Title.
BX4720.P4P3 1989   271'.53   88–25428
ISBN 0-19-815155-1

Photoset by Rowland Phototypesetting Ltd
Bury St Edmunds, Suffolk.

Printed and bound in
Great Britain by Biddles Ltd
Guildford and King's Lynn

for my parents

Acknowledgements

Of the many friends and colleagues who have helped and encouraged me to work on this book, I should like in particular to thank Mademoiselle Odette Barenne, librarian of the Bibliothèque de la Société de Port-Royal in Paris; Monsieur and Madame Jean Daubigny, for their innumerable kindnesses; and Mrs Alana Davies, Fellows' Secretary at St Catherine's College, Oxford. It is more than a convention to say that, without their help, I could not have completed it.

Contents

Abbreviations

BL British Library, London.
BN Bibliothèque Nationale, Paris.
Bodleian Bodleian Library, Oxford.
BPR Bibliothèque de Port-Royal, Paris.
Cognet Edn. of the *Lettres Provinciales* below, when referring to Introduction, Notes, or other works included in the same volume (notably the *Écrits des Curés de Paris*).
IL Roger Duchêne, *L'Imposture Littéraire*, 2nd edn. (Paris, 1985).
LPs *Les Provinciales ou les lettres écrites par Louis de Montalte à un provincial de ses amis et aux RR. PP. Jésuites*, ed. Louis Cognet (Paris, 1983). I shall identify quotations from the *LPs* by the number of the letter, in Roman numerals, followed by the page number in Cognet's edn.
Pensées I have used the numbering adopted by Louis Lafuma in Pascal, *Œuvres Complètes* (*OC*) (Paris, 1963). I shall identify fragments by the letter L, followed by the number in this edn.
RLPs *Réponses aux Lettres Provinciales publiées par le Secrétaire du Port-Royal contre les PP. de la Compagnie de Jésus, sur la Morale des dits Pères* (Liège, 1657) (see Appendices I and II). I shall identify quotations from the *RLPs* by *RLP*, followed by the page number in the 1st edn. (BN: D 89990). The 2nd edn. adopts a different (consecutive) pagination (see Appendix II).

Chronology

1567   Bull *Ex omnibus afflictionibus* (Pius V) condemns Baïus (Michel de Bay) of the Louvain Faculty of Theology for unorthodox views, grounded in an over-rigorous interpretation of Augustine's anti-pelagian writings.

1588   Molina, *De Concordia liberi arbitrii cum divinae gratiae donis* (Lisbon), primary text of 'Molinism', and perceived by critics as restatement of semi-pelagian position on grace and free will.

1602   Angélique Arnauld becomes Abbess of Port-Royal (-des-Champs).

1612–17   Cornelius Jansenius (Corneille Jansen) and Jean Duvergier de Hauranne study together in Bayonne.

1620   Duvergier becomes Abbé de Saint-Cyran.

1625–6   Nuns of Port-Royal-des-Champs move to Paris.

1627   Agnès Arnauld, *Chapelet secret du Saint-Sacrement*.

1631   Du Moulin, *Le Dénombrement des Traditions Romaines*, Protestant attack on 'unfounded' traditions within Roman orthodoxy.

1633   *Chapelet secret du Saint-Sacrement* denounced by Sorbonne. Saint-Cyran replies with *Apologie du Chapelet*.

1635–6   Saint-Cyran becomes spiritual director of Port-Royal and confessor of Angélique Arnauld.

1637   First 'solitaires' established at Port-Royal-des-Champs.

1638   Death of Jansenius, bishop of Ypres since 1636. Incarceration at Vincennes of Saint-Cyran.

1640   Posthumous publication of *Augustinus* of Jansenius in Louvain. Bauny, *Somme des péchés qui se commettent en tous états* (1634), placed on *Index Librorum Prohibitorum*. Publication of *Imago Primi Saeculi* celebrates first centenary of Society of Jesus.

1641   *Augustinus* published in Paris. Cellot, *De hierarchia et hierarchicis*, containing proposition (censured by the Sorbonne) that, in questions of morality, modern authorities prevail over the Fathers. Sirmond, *La Défense de la Vertu*: 'en plusieurs passages... l'auteur y éludait pratiquement le précepte d'aimer Dieu' (Cognet). Arnauld receives doctorate of Sorbonne (19 December).

1642   Bull *In Eminenti* (Urban VIII, 6 March; published 19 January 1643) condemns *Augustinus*. Alphonse Le Moyne appointed by Richelieu to Sorbonne to combat *Augustinus*.

1642–3 Habert preaches against Jansenius in Notre-Dame-de-Paris.

1643   Arnauld, *De la Fréquente Communion*, published in August: 'une copieuse défense des idées rigoristes de Saint-Cyran sur la pénitence et sur l'eucharistie' (Cognet). Arnauld and Hallier, *La théologie morale des Jésuites extraite fidèlement de leurs livres*. Death of Saint-Cyran (Duvergier), 11 October. His nephew, Barcos, succeeds him as abbot.

1644   Caussin, *Réponse au libelle intitulé 'La Théologie morale des Jésuites'*. Arnauld publishes, anonymously, *Apologie de M. Jansénius*. Lyons edition of Escobar, *Liber Theologiae Moralis*.

1644–5 Arnauld publishes *Seconde Apologie* and *Apologie pour M. de Saint-Cyran* (with Le Maître).

1648   Large part of community returns to Port-Royal-des-Champs.

1649   Seven propositions, of which five (the *Cinq Propositions*) will be retained, condemned by the Sorbonne, at the instigation of the *Syndic de la Faculté*, Nicholas Cornet (1 July). These were not initially identified as being specifically associated with the *Augustinus*, but their close similarity with passages in it was subsequently demonstrated.

1650   Rome asked by Habert to pronounce on first five propositions.

1651   Arnauld, *Apologie pour les Saints Pères*. La Lane, *De la Grâce victorieuse de Jésus-Christ, ou Molina et ses disciples convaincus de l'erreur des pélagiens et des semi-pélagiens*.

1652   Jacqueline Pascal enters convent of Port-Royal.

1653   The *Cinq Propositions* condemned by Innocent X in the bull *Cum Occasione* (31 May): four as heretical, the fifth as false.

1654   Arnauld, while condemning the *Cinq Propositions* in their heretical sense, denies that the *Augustinus* contains this sense. Innocent X specifies, in a reply to Mazarin (29 September), that in condemning the *Cinq Propositions* he had condemned the doctrine of Jansenius. Pascal's 'second conversion' (23 November); the *Mémorial*. Marandé, *Inconvénients d'état procédant du jansénisme*. Nicole becomes Arnauld's secretary at Port-Royal-des-Champs.

1655   Marquis de Liancourt refused absolution at Saint-Sulpice (1 February) on the grounds of his sympathy towards Jansenism. Arnauld, in response, writes his *Lettre d'un Docteur à une personne de condition* (24 February). Assembly of bishops (spring) seeks to impose on all members of clergy signature of *formulaire* condemning the *Cinq Propositions*, 'au sens de Jansénius'. This specification was in distinction to the terms in which the Jansenist party was prepared to condemn the propositions, viz. 'en quelque livre qu'on les puisse trouver sans exception'. Annat, *Réponse à quelques demandes dont l'éclaircissement est nécessaire au temps présent* (26 May), emphatically states heresy of Jansenists. Arnauld writes the *Seconde Lettre à un Duc et Pair* (10 July), to the duc de Luynes. Arnauld retires to Port-Royal-des-Champs (14 October). *Seconde Lettre* examined at Sorbonne by commission hostile to Arnauld (4 November). Arnauld requests hearing from Faculty (24 and 30 November). Commission reports (1 and 2

December), withdrawing from *Seconde Lettre* five statements considered worthy of condemnation—four on matters of substance (*question de droit*) and one on the question of accuracy (*question de fait*). Arnauld considers the conditions under which the Faculty would be prepared to receive him are unacceptable. Therefore he defends (in writing) his position on grace (7 December) and on 'fait' (10 December).

1656   In January Pascal goes on retreat to Port-Royal-des-Champs. Arnauld censured on *question de fait* (14 January). The vote contested on the grounds that an irregularly large number of those present were monks for mendicant orders. First *Lettre Provinciale*, 23 January (published 27 January). Doctors sympathetic to Arnauld withdraw from Sorbonne debate (25 January). Arnauld contests legitimacy of assembly (27 January). Arnauld censured on *question de droit*. Second *Lettre Provinciale*, 29 January (published 5 February). Third *Lettre Provinciale*, 9 February (published 12 February). Arnauld expelled from the Sorbonne, 15 February. Earliest reply: *Lettre écrite à un abbé par un Docteur*, 22 February. Fourth *Lettre Provinciale*, 25 February (published early March). Fifth *Lettre Provinciale*, 20 March (published 28 March). Marandé, *Considérations sur un libelle de Port-Royal*. Pascal's niece, Marguerite Périer, cured at Port-Royal of a lachrymal fistula, by the application of a relic from the Crown of Thorns (24 March). First four *Lettres Provinciales* reprinted (30 March).

Sixth *Lettre Provinciale*, 10 April (published 15 April). Seventh *Lettre Provinciale*, 15 April. April–May: *Réponse et remerciement. Lettre de Philarque. Lettre d'un Provincial au Secrétaire de Port-Royal. Première Réponse aux lettres que les jansénistes publient contre les jésuites.* May: Meynier, *Port-Royal et Genève d'intelligence contre le très-saint sacrement de l'autel.* Eighth *Lettre Provinciale*, 28 May. *Lettre écrite à une personne de condition sur le sujet de celles que les jansénistes publient contre les jésuites* (June). Ninth *Lettre Provinciale* (3 July). July: *Lettre écrite à une personne de condition sur la conformité des reproches*; Alexander VII disallows 'fait'/'droit' distinction as reason for refusing to condemn *Cinq Propositions*. Tenth *Lettre Provinciale*, 2 August (published 15 August). Eleventh *Lettre Provinciale*, 18 August (published 23 August). August: Nouet, *Réponse aux lettres que les jansénistes publient contre les jésuites*; Annat, *Rabat-Joie des Jansénistes*; Lemaître, *Réponse à un écrit publié sur le sujet des miracles qu'il a plu à Dieu de faire au Port-Royal* (published November); Nouet, *Réponse à la onzième lettre des jansénistes*.

Assemblée du clergé draws up *formulaire* condemning *Augustinus*, for signature by all members of clergy (1 September). Twelfth *Lettre Provinciale*, 9 September. September: Nouet, *Réponse à la douzième lettre*; *Réfutation de la réponse à la douzième lettre*; Nouet, *Continuation des impostures que les jansénistes publient*; Thirteenth *Lettre Provinciale*, 30 September (published ?10 October). Nouet, *Réponse à la treizième lettre* (late October). Fourteenth *Lettre Provinciale*, 23 October. October–November: *Réponse à la quatorzième lettre*; *Seconde partie des impostures*; Morel, *Réponse générale à l'auteur des lettres*. Fifteenth *Lettre Provinciale*, 25 November (published 12 December). Sixteenth *Lettre Provinciale*, 4 December (published 26 December). Nouet, *Réponse à la quinzième lettre*. Annat, *La Bonne Foi des Jansénistes* (9 December). Annat, *Défense de la vérité catholique touchant les miracles* (30 December). *Justification du procédé des Catholiques contre les Jansénistes tirée de Saint-Augustin. Réponse d'un théologien aux propositions extraites des lettres des Jansénistes par quelques curés de Rouen.*

1657   *Lettre au Père Annat sur son écrit* (15 January). Seventeenth *Lettre Provinciale*, 23 January (published 19 February). First sixteen *Lettres Provinciales* condemned by *Parlement d'Aix* (9 February). Bull of Alexander VII, *Ad sacram beati Petri sedem* (11 March; dated 16 October 1656), condemns *Cinq Propositions* in the sense of Jansenius, and affirms his authorship of them. *Assemblée du clergé* (17 March) imposes on clergy signature of *formulaire* condemning Jansenius. Annat, *Réponse à la plainte que font les jansénistes de ce qu'on les appelle hérétiques.* Eighteenth *Lettre Provinciale*, 24 March (published ?10 April). Early months. *Lettres Provinciales* published as a *recueil* in-4°, with title: *Les Provinciales ou les lettres écrites par Louis de Montalte à un Provincial de ses amis et aux R R. PP. Jésuites, sur le sujet de la morale et de la politique de ces Pères.* This collection also contains the first version of Nicole's *Avertissement*, dealing with the first 17 letters. The complete version, together with the date of 5 May 1657, occurs only in the 1659 edition. Pascal begins nineteenth *Lettre Provinciale* (?April–May). Publication of *Lettres Provinciales* in-12°, 'A Cologne, chez Pierre de la Vallée' (? July). *Lettres Provinciales* placed on *Index Librorum Prohibitorum* (6 September). English translation published in September. Autumn: Pirot, *Apologie pour les Casuistes; Réponses aux Lettres Provinciales* published in Liège (reprinted in 1658). Winter: Second in-12° edition of *Lettres Provinciales*.

1658   *Premier Ecrit des Curés de Paris* (25 January). Latin edition of *Provinciales*, translated and amended by Nicole, and published (spring) under pseudonym of Wendrock: *Ludovici Montaltii litterae provinciales de morali et politica jesuitarum disciplina, a Willelmo Wendrockio.* This edition will in turn be translated into French by Mademoiselle de Joncoux in the 1699 edition. *Second Ecrit des Curés de Paris* (2 April). Nicole, *Troisième* and *Quatrième Ecrits des Curés de Paris* (May). *Cinquième Ecrit des Curés de Paris* (11 June). *Sixième Ecrit des Curés de Paris* (24 July).

1659   New (revised) in-8° edition of *Lettres Provinciales* appears. *Apologie pour les casuistes* placed on *Index Librorum Prohibitorum* (21 August).

1661   Certain nuns of Port-Royal sign *formulaire* with appended reservation on 'fait'/'droit' distinction.

1664   August. Archbishop of Paris initiates purge of Port-Royal-des-Champs.

1665   Arnauld and Nicole, *Apologie pour les religieuses de Port-Royal*. Bull *Regiminis apostolici* (Alexander VII) again condemns heresy of Jansenism, and demands signature of *formulaire* by all French clergy (15 February). Nuns who had not signed confined to Port-Royal-des-Champs (July).

1668   'Paix de l'Eglise', or 'Paix Clémentine', after compromise allows submission to Clement IX of four French bishops favourable to Port-Royal (23 October).

1669   Clement IX ratifies 'Paix de l'Eglise' (14 January). Remaining nuns sign *formulaire* (15 Feburary) inaugurating decade of relative prosperity at Port-Royal-des-Champs. Separation of the two monasteries. Restoration of Arnauld as *docteur de Sorbonne*.

1669–74   Arnauld and Nicole, *La Perpétuité de la foi de l'Eglise catholique touchant l'Eucharistie*.

1670   January. First edition of *Pensées*.

1671   First edition of Quesnel, *Réflexions morales*. First edition of Nicole, *Essais de Morale*.

1679   Persecutions of Port-Royal-des-Champs by Archbishop of Paris recommence (16 May). In June Arnauld goes into exile to Brussels, initially accompanied by Nicole.

1683   May. Nicole returns to Paris.

1694   Daniel, *Entretiens de Cléandre et d'Eudoxe sur les 'Lettres au Provincial'*.

1705   Bull *Vineam Domini Sabaoth* (Clement XI) condemns option of 'silence respectueux' in face of demands for assertion of orthodoxy (16 July). The nuns remaining at Port-Royal-des-Champs refuse to accede.

1709   Renewed persecutions and dispersal of nuns from Port-Royal-des-Champs (29 October), followed by destruction of buildings on orders of Louis XIV.

1713   Condemnation (8 September) of propositions drawn from Quesnel's *Réflexions morales* in bull *Unigenitus Dei Filius* (Clement XI). 'Le choix et le groupement de ces propositions tendait visiblement à en faire une sorte de somme de ce que l'on considérait comme la doctrine janséniste' (Cognet).

1773   Suppression of Society of Jesus by Clement XIV.

Note

I have modernized spelling throughout. In certain quotations from works for which no modern edition exists, I have also slightly amended punctuation and capitalization.

Introduction

'*La polémique, c'est beaucoup d'affirmations injurieuses appuyées sur deux ou trois faits précis*'

(Jules Romains)

M Y purpose in writing this book is at least to reflect and, I hope, to add a small amount to the very stimulating revival of interest which has been apparent in recent French publication on Pascal's *Lettres Provinciales*. The succession of articles (which I have listed in the bibliography), together with the books of Roger Duchêne and Gérard Ferreyrolles (and the fascinating *débat* appended to the second edition of the former) seem to have confirmed, or perhaps reaffirmed, the central place of this text in the Pascalian canon, and in French literary studies as a whole. English writing, in particular that of Patricia Topliss, Walter Rex, and Jan Miel, has also been influential. And my debt to this recent work, especially to Duchêne, is considerable.

I have approached my reading from two related angles. First of all, I have attended to formal or structural questions within the text, particularly to relationships between the different parts of the series, to the fictional apparatus—epistolary form, vulgarization of arguments, play of ingenuousness, development of personae—to stylistic features, and to argumentational tactics. I must straightaway make one general remark to try to pre-empt a false impression which such an investigation may give. The *Lettres Provinciales* can be described in a variety of numerical patterns: they can be seen as eighteen quasi-independent pieces; as two quite distinct series, one satirical, one direct, with the break coming at the eleventh letter; or as divisible in other ways within the arbitrarily abandoned work seen as an entity. It is perhaps worth noting immediately therefore that in a good many of my remarks I am taking it for granted that we may attend to the work with the perspective that hindsight allows. I do not thereby seek to question the, virtually indisputable, view of the letters which places greater emphasis on their evolution in the course of composition. Nothing allows us to assume that the *Lettres Provinciales* were conceived of as an entity, nor that Pascal knew, when he began writing, what the ultimate direction of the series would be, or indeed that he even envisaged it as a series. The incompleteness (to which I have given a certain amount of consideration), the changes of direction, and the introduction of external events, either political or literary, all point to a generally aleatory development, even though there are motifs which group certain sequences.

The reason for stating this rather obvious point will perhaps become clear as I develop my argument, since it is difficult at the same time, in my view, not to be aware of degrees and kinds of coherence that the series presents—in its overall structure, in relationships between the different parts, in the developments of themes, tactics, and patterns of argument. The perspective which the last letters provide on the first cannot fully allow us to take an evolutionary view of the series as the sole focus of interpretation. This may just be inevitable, since after all the letters are all broadly speaking related to the same dispute or disputes. Or it may stem from a particularly developed sense in Pascal of how to get an argument off the ground, or to initiate a tactic in such a way as to be able to introduce further developments from the same starting-point (supremely true of the invention of the persona of the Jesuit). Or it may be a matter of trial and error, of pursuing some lines of argument that are fruitful, before adapting or abandoning them under the influence of external circumstances or internal exhaustion, yet without ever losing a sense of the broad direction of the text.

All these elements no doubt contribute; I enumerate them less in order to suggest that I expect to be able to attribute to each its degree of influence in the work, than to acknowledge the existence of facets of the work's evolution that my readings may tend to underplay. I am trying to say something about how the series works, as much as about how its mechanisms came into being, or fell from use.[1] In so doing, I have nevertheless followed very broadly the sequence's order, beginning with the first letter of the series, and ending with the last.

Interplaying with this kind of investigation, I have examined the text in the light of two other texts, or series of texts, which are, I consider, inextricably bound up with it: the sequence of replies which constitute what I have called the counter-polemic, and the *Pensées*. In both cases there exists, as I shall hope to show, a relationship of independence and complementarity.

The counter-polemic is little known and rarely quoted. As the abbé Maynard wrote in 1851: 'Presque personne ne consulte les réfutations... tous préfèrent la lecture exclusive de l'œuvre'.[2] I have therefore provided in the Appendices a full bibliography (substantially drawn from Cognet), and a copy of the 'Table des Matières' of the collected *Réponses aux Lettres Provinciales*, since so much is brought together in this volume. I also provide a small amount of bibliographical information when I first mention a counter-polemical work, and, when discussing it, use occasionally quite lengthy quotation or, unashamedly, paraphrase or summarize arguments from it. Although its direct interaction with the *Lettres Provinciales* only takes its full effect from the eleventh letter onwards, I introduce quotation from it in certain contexts from the outset. Whatever its inaccessibility or (arguably) mediocrity, its examination has seemed to throw light on a variety of aspects, both thematic and formal, of the complementary text; and the two series together tell us more about the common as well as the divergent features of polemic than could one taken in isolation.[3]

As for the *Pensées*, and while concentrating my treatment of juxtaposed aspects of the two major Pascalian works in a couple

[1] The most comprehensive repository of source materials is still the edn. of the *Lettres Provinciales* by F. Gazier, vols. 4–7 in the Grands Ecrivains de la France edn. by L. Brunschvicg *et al.* (Paris, 1904–49). Of more modern edns. the most fully documented are those of L. Cognet (Paris, 1983) and M. Le Guern (Paris, 1987).

[2] M. -U. Maynard, *Les Lettres Provinciales... et leur réfutation* (Paris, 1851), i, p. xxv.

[3] There is, I am convinced, room for a whole work devoted to this corpus of writing, allowing for more detail than I have been able to provide.

of chapters, I have again introduced certain fragments I consider germane to my argument at stages throughout the book. The tendency has been too strong to view the *Pensées* as a work of enduring significance, with the *Provinciales* relegated to the status of a period piece of only stylistic curiosity. What I have therefore aimed to show is how the *Provinciales* are related to the project contained in the apologetic (and other) fragments which we call the *Pensées*, and what this connection demonstrates in terms of the characteristics of apologetics and polemics. The fragments from the *Pensées* apparently related to the *Provinciales* in a more direct way also interlock with the completed letters, in much the same way as do the shorter apologetic fragments with the longer ones within the same collection. Many of them are just *brouillons* (Cognet identifies these where germane *au fur et à mesure* in the notes to his edition); but some are long enough to add a certain angle on or emphasis to the arguments. I hope that my evidence will support Cognet's contestation that 'jamais Pascal n'a songé qu'il pût y avoir entre les *Provinciales* et les *Pensées* cette "rupture idéologique" dont on a parfois affirmé la réalité' (Cognet, pp. xvi–xvii).

I have thus, in short, tried to propose a reading which does not ignore the substance of the *Provinciales*, whilst giving full attention to formal questions. The broader context which I have considered seems to me to be reflected in the work itself, and thus to endow it with a density of significance lying not far beneath the superficial impression of an entertainingly presented internecine quibble.

★

Each of the parties involved in the dispute we are about to examine accused the other of heresy; each believed itself to promote, indeed to exemplify, orthodoxy. Looking from a distance at such (no doubt deeply committed) posturing, we may feel happier to interpret the positions adopted in terms of emphases: after all neither Jansenists nor Jesuits made that kind of radical formal break with Rome that, in the previous century, had

made it possible to identify distinct and autonomous com-
munions (even if, at various points in their history, both were to
be condemned by Rome). And yet each contained a subversive
potential that strained at the limits of a credal system dependent
on some kind of balance. The balance was, in this case, that
between grace and free will, examined in terms of its implications
in the fields of doctrine and ethics. Tension in their interpretation
had found its earliest expression in the Augustine–Pelagius controversy, (early fifth century AD), and our disputants indeed still
used that model as a nominal point of reference (the *Augustinus*,
the 'nouveaux pélagiens'). Certain of the historical assumptions
underlying such labels must, furthermore, remain intact for the
pragmatic purposes of our enquiry. It is not possible here to
consider how far it is in fact historically correct to endorse
Augustine's status as 'le docteur de la grâce'. Nor, on the other
hand, is there room to examine how far the Council of Trent and
elements in the post-tridentine Church, notably the Society of
Jesus, encouraged an implicit or explicit movement towards a
semi-pelagian ethos within Roman orthodoxy. It must be suf-
ficient to note that these two potential directions found, in the
two component texts of our dispute, their most polarized public
expression, and at the same time (no doubt for this very reason)
their most accessible one.

The form in which the debate is conducted is twofold. In the
framing letters of the *LPs* (i–iii; xvii and xviii), and in the
aggressive replies, the issue under discussion is the doctrinal
orthodoxy of Arnauld, and by implication of Port-Royal; and the
burden of the argument concerns the accusation of heresy levelled
against Arnauld by the Sorbonne, on the grounds of a denial of
the role of free will. In the central series of letters (iv–xvi
inclusive), and in the defensive replies, the issue under discussion
is the moral orthodoxy of the Society of Jesus; and the burden
of the argument concerns the accusation of heresy levelled
against it by the writer of the *Provinciales*, on the grounds of a
denial of the role of grace. Thus although the issues constituting
the respective parts of the two series are situated in different
illustrative areas, and although they have a different historical

status, they still attend, compositely, to the two poles of the broader question.

Furthermore, they do so by reference to two, albeit very dissimilar, documents or sets of documents. The *texte de base* of the doctrinal accusations against Arnauld is the *Augustinus* (1640) of Cornelius Jansenius (gallicized as Corneille Jansen), from which five statements, the *Cinq Propositions*, had been extracted as evidence of its heretical content. In order to suppress the elements within the Church which favoured the Jansenist tendency, the condemnation of these statements had been required of the clergy, and notably those whose allegiance was suspect. In 1656, Arnauld, in his *Seconde Lettre à un Duc et Pair*, both contested that the assumptions they contained were heretical, and denied that they were accurately transcribed from the *Augustinus*. On these two assertions (themselves a summary of five statements extracted by the Sorbonne from Arnauld's text), the censure of Arnauld was based, with the distinction made between the substantive matters of belief, and the technical matters of accuracy—in other words the *question de droit* and the *question de fait* which are initially in dispute in the *LPs*. The writings which form the basis of the counter-accusation of Jesuit moral laxity are more diverse. Principally they are the manuals of moral theology and of confessional practice intended to serve as guidance to clergy in the resolution of moral dilemmas encountered in penitential counselling and in the granting of absolution. Both sets of writing are, in their primary manifestations, distinguished therefore by being technical theological treatises, of which the *LPs* and *RLPs* give little or no accurate impression. At the same time our texts refer continually to these fundamental expressions of divergent Christian tendencies, and cannot, in any serious respect, be separated from the questions underlying the tension which they both record and enhance.

It is still noteworthy that the limits of the matters in dispute remain somewhat indistinct; thus, for the largely polemical reasons that I shall examine, neither the writer of the *LPs* nor those of the *RLPs* spend a great deal of time attending explicitly to the primary theological difficulties surrounding the roles of grace and free will. However, the associated questions which are dealt with may be related either directly to this problem—Christian morality, spirituality, penitential and eucharistic beliefs and practices, the universality of salvation, respect for tradition and authority; or, to a variety of degrees, indirectly—accuracy of quotation from primary sources, political motivation and relations with the state, individual and corporate answerability, connections with other Christian bodies (within or beyond Roman orthodoxy), and the implications for proselytizing.

Two further, and interrelated, points should perhaps be added here. First, given the chronology of the broader debate, it is obvious that the *LPs* and *RLPs* are not situated in the early stages of a dispute—indeed they are preceded by a whole range of publications which, in various ways, examine related facets of the primary question: the *Dénombrement des traditions* of Du Moulin; the *Somme des péchés* of Bauny; the *Fréquente Communion* of Arnauld, and so on. These earlier pieces will be mentioned where relevant in my remarks on the later polemical exchange. Secondly, it cannot be denied that the question of orthodoxy and the role of ecclesiastical authority is, in the contemporary context of an absolute monarchy, intimately bound up with the role of obedience to political authority. Writers of distinguished socio-political studies have amply explored this question, and I cannot hope to add much here to their conclusions.[4] Suffice it then to underline, at a very simple level, the potential on the one hand for departure from agreement with the dominant forces within the recognized confession of the state to become a focus for dissentient political elements (Port-Royal, Protestants); and on the other to signal the opportunity for those dominant forces (the Society of Jesus, the Sorbonne) to blur and at worst to exploit the overlap between the spiritual and the temporal.

Some of the detail of such a summary will be treated in the course of the remarks that follow. To attempt any further historical reappraisal of the event of the *LPs* within the scope of

---

[4] P. Bénichou, *Morales du grand siècle* (Paris, 1948); and L. Goldmann, *Le Dieu caché* (Paris, 1959).

this study would run the risk of embarking on what could only be an amateurish reassessment; and the chronological table at the beginning of the book is intended simply as an *aide-mémoire*. For a brief list of fuller historical examinations which amplify the broader context, I therefore refer the reader to the bibliography.

I

The Opening Letters: Themes and Tactics

'NOUS étions bien abusés. Je ne suis détrompé que d'hier' (i. 3). In view of the nature of much of the material which it serves to introduce, the first paragraph of the first *LP* is at one level a bluff; it functions as a mechanism to permit the eventual development of the argument away from its apparent *point de départ*; it suggests by its succinct statement of resolution that a simple clarification will suffice to demystify, to correct an error. It is misleading because it implies that an explanation will ensue which, by its evidencing of an insubstantial problem, will minimize, indeed negate, the obligation that Montalte and his 'ami provincial' had previously felt to concern themselves with the 'disputes présentes de la Sorbonne'; they will learn things which will allow them to withhold their concern. And so will every other reader. And that will be an end to the matter.

Nicole, indeed, in the *Avertissement sur les dix-huit lettres*, further reinforces this disingenuously simple impression. He writes of the first four letters:

Comme l'obscurité des termes scholastiques, dont on les [= disputes] couvrait à dessein, n'en laissait l'intelligence qu'aux théologiens, les autres personnes, en étant exclues, demeuraient dans une curiosité inutile et dans l'étonnement de voir tant de préparations qui paraissaient à tout le monde, pour des questions qui ne paraissaient à personne. Ce fut alors que ces Lettres furent publiées, et qu'on eut la satisfaction d'y voir l'éclaircissement de toutes ces difficultés. (Cognet, p. 470)[1]

A useful point of contrast may immediately by provided by the tone of the opening of the *Premier Ecrit des Curés de*

---

[1] *Avertissement sur les dix-huit lettres, où sont expliqués les sujets qui sont traités dans chacune*. This prefatory piece, attributed to Nicole, introduced the 1657 edns. of the *LPs*, and was reproduced in the 1659 edn. See Cognet, pp. lxx–lxxii (background), and pp. 469–78 (text).

Paris,[2] in which the substantial nature of the ensuing moral debate is unequivocally stated: 'Notre cause est la cause de la morale chrétienne: nos parties sont les casuistes qui la corrompent. L'intérêt que nous y avons est celui des consciences dont nous sommes chargés' (Cognet, p. 404). And indeed much of the interest of the first ten letters consists in charting the evolution between these two kinds of utterance.

Taken at face value, however, the simple satirical level at which the opening of the *LPs* functions is then developed by means of the various examples of semantic conjuring that so enliven the early letters as a whole: crisp, informative sentences describe the terms of an easily dismissable dispute, and after the briefest of résumés Montalte concludes on the *question de fait*: 'Voilà comment s'est terminé la question de fait, dont je ne me mets guère en peine; car, que M. Arnauld soit téméraire ou non, ma conscience n'y est pas intéressée' (i. 7). 'Témérité', the 'ami provincial' is led to conclude, may offend good manners; it does not offend orthodoxy. The critique that is carried by the reiterated emphasis on the insubstantial nature of the dispute surrounding the *question de fait*, and which is quickly extended to include the *question de droit*, is, like the dispute to which it refers, presented simply as a personal one, centring on individuals not doctrines: 'Ce sont des disputes de théologiens, et non pas de théologie' (iii. 52). Arnauld is characterized as the victim of a political and legal intrigue marked by semantic obfuscation and the exploitation of numerical supremacy, 'parce qu'il leur est bien plus aisé de trouver des moines que des raisons' (iii. 46)—an irregularly large number of monks from mendicant orders having voted for the censure. The 'ami provincial' is thereby brought to consider the means and implications of the isolation of Arnauld as a trouble-maker, a demonstration which, as Duchêne points out, will tend to gain him public support: 'On se détournerait d'un hérétique; on aura de la sympathie pour la victime d'un règlement de compte' (*IL* 6). The critique of the way in which he is presented as a threat,

---

[2] *Factum pour les curés de Paris, contre un livre intitulé: Apologie pour les Casuistes, contre les calomnies des Jansénistes, et contre ceux qui l'ont composé, imprimé et débité.* This work, generally known as the *Premier Ecrit des Curés de Paris*, dates from Jan. 1658. See Cognet, pp. lxvi–lxvii (background), and pp. 404–17 (text).

and of the measures taken against him, is therefore for the time being expressed by the emphasis placed on the debate's insignificance, with semantic and numerical factors kept in high relief: the Molinists,

étant tous unis dans le dessein de perdre M. Arnauld. . . se sont avisés de s'accorder de ce terme de *prochain*, que les uns et les autres diraient ensemble, quoiqu'ils l'entendissent diversement, afin de parler un même langage, et que, par cette conformité apparente, ils pussent former un corps considérable, et composer le plus grand nombre, pour l'opprimer avec assurance. (i. 12–13)

And a fragment of the *Pensées* would develop and generalize this accusation: 'Vous corrompez la religion ou en faveur de vos amis ou contre vos ennemis; vous en disposez à votre gré' (L 836).

The first point that is here being made in the first *LP* is that the majority is taking a word and giving it a private meaning, separate from the accepted 'common-sense' meaning (which is in turn for the time being (and essentially for the tone of the letter) undistinguished from the more technical theological meanings). The immediate effect of this is to imply that, as Robert Nelson points out, 'there are no antecedent realities upon which words depend for their meaning. Words refer only to one another',[3] creating a climate conducive to what Ferreyrolles refers to as 'une idolâtrie du signifiant'.[4] The recognition of this semantic process still leaves no more than implicit, however, the suggestion that the 'antecedent realities', the meanings behind the words which politics have reduced to sounds, may eventually reassert themselves. In this way the appeal to common sense still remains primary; the serious theological discussion has yet to emerge.

---

[3] R. Nelson, *Pascal, Adversary and Advocate* (Harvard, 1981), 188. D. Jaymes writes: 'The Jesuits had . . . cleverly transformed their inability to clarify Arnauld's heresy into something akin to sacred mystery in the minds of the uninformed' ('Pascal's Ironic Silence in *Les Provinciales*', in J. -J. Demorest and L. Leibacher-Ouvrard (eds.), *Pascal, Corneille: Désert, retraite, engagement* (Paris, etc. 1984), 47).
[4] G. Ferreyrolles, *Blaise Pascal: Les Provinciales* (Paris, 1984), 55.

The political charge and the associated critique of the obfuscation surrounding the *question de fait* will be forcefully reasserted in the last two completed *LPs*; what this initial satirical ploy both supports and conceals however is a deeper critique, to the effect that serious questions are being trivialized. This is closely bound up with the question of the Montalte persona (which I shall examine shortly in more detail). Suffice it to say here that the figure who is 'détrompé' at the end of the first sentence is writing, in terms of the epistolary fiction, with only the degree of enlightenment that the contents of that letter will reveal. He is thus, as Montalte, rather easily brought to conclude that there is no substance in the debate at this stage; it is Montalte who, at his most ingenuous, carries the politico-semantic points which compose the first three letters. Consonant with this, however, but at the same time anticipating the eventual development (education, and finally defictionalization) of Montalte, is the underlying critique of the debasement of the central concerns of theology; and the pointers to this second emphasis coincide with the pointers to the still (superficially) ambivalent outburst which opens the fourth letter and begins to shift the terrain of debate: 'Il n'est rien tel que les Jésuites' (iv. 53). In other words as Montalte educates himself towards his emergence as a figure I shall call 'the polemicist' in the eleventh letter (anonymity necessarily replaces pseudonymity), so gradually the underlying critique, anticipating and reflecting the charges which the polemicist-'je' will in due course explicitly articulate, comes to the surface. Montalte stays firmly within his persona when he states that: 'Je ne suis détrompé que d'hier', because that persona is the condition of the political satire, however heavy the irony which the remark will be seen to carry in the light of the ensuing developments; as he concludes the first letter, however, he effects by a semantic shift of emphasis the first intrusion of the polemicist-'je', the burden of whose argument will be fundamental, will interest consciences, will concern theology, and will implicate the Christian reader alongside the uncommitted one. Dominique Descotes makes, I think, the same point in different terms: 'Il faut bien distinguer Montalte personnage comique de Montalte épistolier, dont la fonction est celle du narrateur. Entre ces deux Montalte, il y a la découverte progressive de la morale et de la politique des Jésuites. Les dix premières *Provinciales* sont l'histoire d'un désabusement'.[5]

It is of course with the pun on '(pouvoir) prochain' that the shift is first made. In the course of the letter, 'prochain' has progressively been deprived of a referent and thus, as the satirical investigation has continued, lost its power to signify; as the 'disciple de M. Le Moyne' reproaches the over-eager Dominican: 'Ne sommes-nous pas demeurés d'accord de ne point expliquer ce mot de *prochain*, et de le dire de part et d'autre sans dire ce qu'il signifie?' (i. 18). Then a further devaluation is (dis)ingenuously suggested by Montalte: 'il faut prononcer ce mot des lèvres, de peur d'être hérétique de nom'; and finally, just before the concluding paragraph, 'il n'y a plus que le mot de *prochain* sans aucun sens qui court risque' (i. 18–19). The matter is then clinched at the beginning of the last paragraph: initially and superficially the opening phrase, 'Je vous laisse cependant dans la liberté de tenir pour le mot *prochain*, ou non' maintains the fiction of the Montalte-'je' and the illusion of resolution; but the ensuing, and climactic, semantic rehabilitation—'car j'aime trop mon prochain [*not italic*] pour le persécuter sous ce prétexte'— endowed as it is not just with common-sense meaning but also with biblical resonance and thus theological significance (and could it not in addition correspond to the persecuted Arnauld?), this rehabilitation is the first glimpse of the fictionality and thus eventual transformation of Montalte, of the burden of the central series of letters, of the implied coincidence between evangelic orthodoxy and common sense, and thus also, retrospectively, of the ironic status of the opening. In addition, this procedure looks forward to the presentation of a Jesuit language which functions by the twin processes of removal and reversal of meaning as dictated by subjective requirements, and which will be illustrated as the letters gradually reveal the semantic principles which are attributed to the Society's utterances.

For the time being the linguistic remarks contain no specific foreshadowing of these principles, nor any explicit degree of

---

[5] D. Descotes, 'Fonction argumentative de la satire dans les *Provinciales*', in H. Baader (ed.), *Onze études sur l'esprit de la satire* (Tübingen and Paris, 1978), 53–4.

attack; indeed, in the first letter, the play of *naïveté* depends on the mode of functioning of the language remaining mysterious. Furthermore in the short term the linguistic attack is displaced by the assault on moral laxity. At the same time, a great deal of the future material of the *LPs* is initiated as early as the end of this first letter, and the density of implication of such an apparently simple piece endows it with a dynamic force which will carry through to later parts of the series; and these in turn will often send us back to its embryonic and ironic statement of the questions in play. Finally, further attention is given to the letter's closure in a recent article by Philip Lewis,[6] and his helpful conclusion also stresses the way in which the play on 'prochain' heralds formal as well as ideological developments later in the series:

At the close of a letter in which the narrator's recurrently abortive attempts at dialogue with the adversary are prefigured and elucidated, the salient contrast of *le mot prochain* and *mon prochain*—of the adjectival sign of a lack and the substantive sign of a human presence—resumes the diacritical opposition of the improper use of the word as a vehicle of power . . . to its proper use as the vehicle of unambiguous meaning.

It would first be appropriate however to move straight to the early stages of the counter-polemic, and to the reply of Marandé[7] of which the fourth section in particular attends to this question of semantics. He first accuses the writer of the first four letters (whom he considers to be Arnauld) of trying to 'énerver ou affaiblir la *Censure* de la Faculté, sous prétexte... que toute la dispute n'aboutit qu'au sens et à l'interprétation d'un seul terme formé de deux syllabes' (p. 82). He then quotes, first, Tertullian against the heretic Hermogenes: ' "Les pointilles et subtilités des

---

[6] P. Lewis, 'Dialogic Impasse in Pascal's *Provinciales*', *Canadian Review of Comparative Literature* (Winter 1976), 37–8.

[7] *Considérations sur un libelle de Port-Royal intitulé Défense de la Constitution d'Innocent X etc, sur la retraite des docteurs jansénistes, sur la protestation de Monsieur Arnauld, et sur les Lettres qu'il a fait courir dans Paris, depuis la Censure de Sorbonne.* 'Par le sieur [Léonard] de Marandé Conseiller du Roi en ses Conseils, et Aumônier de Sa Majesté' (Paris, 1656). Marandé assumes the writer of the *LPs* to be Arnauld. See Appendix I. viii. Marandé had earlier been responsible, in 1654, for a pamphlet entitled *Inconvénients d'état procédant du jansénisme*.

hérétiques sont si raffinées en malice, qu'elles forment des questions sur les paroles les plus communes et les plus simples"' (p. 84), and then St Ambrose: '"Ce n'est pas merveille si des esprits emportés et hors d'eux-mêmes émeuvent des troubles et des riottes sur des mots, puisqu'ils en font même sur les syllabes"' (p. 84). There follows a substantial defence of lexical innovation, accompanied by the insistence that the Church introduces new terms to combat the heretical understanding of doctrine:

Ainsi dans la naissance des hérésies de notre siècle, l'Eglise pour les condamner et les interdire s'est trouvée obligée d'introduire le terme de *transsubstantiation* contre l'hérésie de Luther, non pas pour faire une chose nouvelle dans la foi, mais pour expliquer nouvellement le sentiment ancien et uniforme de l'Ecriture, de la tradition, et des Pères contre les hérétiques. (p. 87)

The same difficulty arises, Marandé explains, with the Arian heresy surrounding the terms 'substance' and 'consubstantiel'; and he reports against (as he believes) Arnauld the conclusion on that subject of the *Epître Synodale du Concile d'Alexandrie*, throwing back the rehabilitated 'prochain' as he does so: '"Ceux qui s'amusaient à susciter des querelles et des riottes dans l'Eglise sur des petites paroles de cette qualité, ne faisaient autre chose en vérité que de présenter une boisson vénéneuse à leurs prochains, capable de leur renverser la cervelle, comme ennemis, et amateurs des troubles et des schismes"' (p. 89). This does not disguise a point that will be made repeatedly in the counter-polemic, namely that such terms may well conceal technical disagreements, but rather asserts that the Catholic laity should be prepared to acknowledge these terms as they stand. Likewise, therefore, it should accept the phrase 'pouvoir prochain', 'sans embarrasser son esprit dans les subtilités différentes de l'Ecole, pour l'accord de la liberté et de la grâce, jusques à ce que l'Eglise en ait déterminé quelque chose à l'avantage de l'un ou de l'autre parti des docteurs Catholiques' (pp. 88–9). Thus Marandé identifies the likelihood that theology will make use of a word in a specialized way, which may involve a technical distinction (and without necessarily introducing a neologism). Montalte's confusion would stem from a failure to distinguish between the two functions. Duchêne, although without reference to the counter-polemic, also remarks:

Refusant de considérer qu'il peut y avoir en ces matières un double registre de vocabulaire, celui des docteurs et celui du monde, il ne se demande pas si le langage des honnêtes gens est capable de rendre compte des disputes sur la grâce sans les trahir. Appeler le public à en juger, c'est nier qu'elles relèvent d'un domaine technique dont seuls des spécialistes peuvent décider. (*IL* 69, and cf. 71).

The related and vital distinction to emerge from the fifth section of Marandé's work (devoted to the second *LP*) is that between 'doctrine de la foi' and 'doctrine de l'Ecole' (p. 93), a distinction allegedly unrecognized by the writer of the *LPs*, but one to which we shall frequently have cause to return. It articulates a difference between the broad issues of belief essential to a basic understanding of the faith, and a technical theological dimension, exclusively the domain of the expert, in which the tenets of belief are submitted to the analysis of reason. What will in due course emerge from the *LPs* in contradistinction to this definition is the capacity of Pascal to unite the levels of faith and (common) sense, morally, linguistically, and doctrinally, and to exclude the intellectual exploration of both doctrine and ethics. He thereby places all substantial questions of belief in the realm of 'doctrine de la foi', reducing 'doctrine de l'Ecole' to a subsidiary, and irrelevant status. By thus negating the Jesuit marriage of the supernatural and the intellectual he erects a framework which progressively isolates the terms of his adversaries. (Furthermore if the Jesuit position is arguably the more Catholic (it is certainly the more clerical), it is at the same time polemically the more difficult, because the arguments, if not the material, are less susceptible to vulgarization.) The full impact of this hierarchization will not however be evident until the end of the series. For the time being, and whatever light Marandé's distinction sheds on the lexical, semantic, and indeed theological arguments, the political accusation (over the use to which these innovations and distinctions may be put) remains unanswered.

We may notice too from these remarks certain features which will recur throughout the counter-polemic: the accusation of heresy (and comparison with other heretics); the distinction between technical/scholastic theology and the needs of the majority of the laity; and the feature shared with the *LPs* themselves, albeit with different emphases, of the appeal to antiquity in the defence of particular procedures or definitions. Returning to the *LPs*, we may summarize our first remarks. We have noted the emergent appeal to the point at which common sense and orthodoxy overlap, and also seen initiated the discussion of linguistic and political tactics, and of the *question de fait* and the *question de droit*. We have also identified the inception of a rhetorical pattern which draws attention, with hindsight, to the ironic status of previous discourse. This pattern will accompany, albeit with an ever increasing degree of simultaneity, the evolution of Montalte. The opening of the last paragraph of the first letter points immediately if embryonically to all the accusations which will become more explicit as the letters progress; but in so doing it disables the ensuing letters from employing the full tone of flippant disregard which predominantly characterizes the opening piece. At the same time, it is his receptiveness to this tone that commits the 'ami provincial' to an acceptance of the serious implications which will subsequently be examined. He is, like the interlocutor of the wager fragment, 'embarqué' by his initial receptiveness.

Similar insights into the full purport of the letters then multiply in the second piece—the impassioned outcry, 'Où en sommes-nous donc? m'écriai-je, et quel parti dois-je ici prendre?' (ii. 27), also closely reminiscent of the wager; the pseudo-evangelic image of the Church as a wounded man: 'Voulez-vous voir une peinture de l'Eglise dans ces différents avis? Je la considère comme un homme qui, partant de son pays pour faire un voyage, est recontré par des voleurs qui le blessent de plusieurs coups et le laissent à demi mort' (ii. 29);[8] and above all the combative intensity of the interventions of 'mon second', 'l'ami janséniste'. Thus its conclusion advances considerably on that of the first letter, even if, as Duchêne shows, 'tout ce qu'exprime la seconde *Provinciale* était déjà contenu en puissance dans la précédente' (*IL* 44).

---

[8] Morel counters this parable with a parallel one in his *Réponse générale à l'auteur des lettres qui se publient depuis quelque temps contre la doctrine des Jésuites*, p. 10 (see Appendix I. xviii). See also J. Leprun, 'La Parabole de la seconde *Provinciale*', in *Méthodes chez Pascal* (Paris, 1979), 241–52.

Montalte may then seem to have been *détrompé* at the stage at which he writes his first letter, at least partially; but the fact that the person who is *détrompé* is subsequently identified as a naïve person, and ultimately as a *faux naïf* persona, indicates the grounds both for the elucidation of a simple point and the elaboration of a far more complex and profound one. Very simply, Montalte is not *détrompé* until he stops being Montalte; as the argument is rehabilitated, so the fiction is dropped. The apparent enlightenment of Montalte at the beginning of the series is seen to be precisely apparent as the deceiving fiction of Montalte, the real 'tromperie', is abandoned. While that is happening, the two levels of critique may function, to a lessening degree, simultaneously, although the device of disingenuousness at the service of political arguments is in fact relatively quickly exhausted. The closing remark of the third letter, 'Nous, qui ne sommes point docteurs, n'avons que faire à leurs démêlés' (iii. 52), is thus identifiably ironic in a way in which the opening was not; it carries the self-conscious irony that will furnish much of the comic interest of the ensuing letters, and which the first three have served to make possible.

It is at the same time, and in spite of its heavily ironic tone, a vulnerable admission, and was not to go unnoticed by the counter-polemicists. Thus in the *Préface* of the *Deuxième Réponse* of the *RLP*[9] we find: 'C'est merveille qu'un homme, qui n'est ni prêtre, ni ecclésiastique, ni docteur, soit devenu en deux jours le théologien des femmes' (*RLP* xliv). Then, a little later, he is described as 'un homme laïque, qui prenait la qualité de réformateur de la morale, et de directeur des consciences, avant que d'avoir acquis celle de prêtre et de docteur' (*RLP* li). And again, in the *Lettre écrite à une personne de condition*,[10] the position is parodied:

Qui ne voit clairement par là combien il est avantageux d'avoir commerce avec ces savants disciples de Saint Augustin, qui ont des grâces

---

[9] See Appendix II.

[10] *Lettre écrite à une personne de condition sur la conformité des reproches et des calomnies que les Jansénistes publient contre les Pères de la Compagnie de Jésus avec celle que le ministre Du Moulin a publiées devant eux.* Contained in the *Réponses aux Lettres Provinciales.* See Appendix I. x.

du Ciel si efficaces et si extraordinaires, qu'ils peuvent diriger les consciences sans être ecclésiastiques, discerner la lèpre spirituelle des âmes sans être prêtres, [et] enseigner la doctrine des mœurs sans être docteurs. (*RLP* lviii)

Such reactions are of course right to break through the irony, and yet understandably slow in seeing how that irony was in fact increasingly drawing attention to itself. Superficially the conclusion of the third letter is also the closure of the first series in that it provides the counterpoint to the opening of the first letter; it actually announces the fuller treatment of the underlying themes which have increasingly shown through the surface triviality. The resolution is thus perfectly elegant and utterly false, as the surface calm now draws attention to its own superficiality by means of self-conscious irony. There will not really be any doubt as to the meaning of the fourth letter's opening flourish: 'Il n'est rien tel que les Jésuites', or as to its potential for development.

2

Question(s) de Fait *and* Question(s) de Droit

IT becomes increasingly clear on reading the various polemical (and critical) works associated with the dispute of which the *LPs* were a manifestation that, whilst the terms *question de fait* and *question de droit* seem to describe a simple and quite obvious distinction (are the *Cinq Propositions* in the *Augustinus*? are they heretical?), they are at the same time open to, and indeed in need of, a good deal of clarification. It is equally evident that the ability to provide the most convincing terms for such a clarification will be decisive in the establishment of argumentational supremacy. It is almost, it might appear, as if the dispute is less about the resolution of the *question de fait* and *question de droit* than about what constitutes these two questions. For this reason, there is something shadowy about the whole polemic, with each side providing its own, often implicit, definition of the terms in dispute: the *question de droit* for Pascal will increasingly define itself in terms of morality; for the Jesuits it remains a matter of doctrine, but with the issues extended beyond the original bounds. Thus although it is not surprising that both parties prefer the attack to the defence, it is difficult a good deal of the time, for this very reason, to say exactly within what limits the dispute is being conducted. Both parties move onto their own preferred territory; they deflect the debate to a greater (Pascal) or lesser (Jesuits) extent, before returning to the original *question de fait*. (It is at the same time the Jesuits who are consistently more anxious to return to it, since it is more immediately related to the particular *question de droit* with which they are initially concerned in their attack). Yet whilst they move away from the simple question introduced at the outset, neither explicitly recognizes (nor perhaps perceives), the full implications of the variety of questions undertaken in its stead. There is thus a primitive understanding of the two terms, which does not fully reach a definition until the last letters of the series (and even then it is not an agreed one); and an implicit broadening out of the *question de droit* to embrace the major areas of Christian concern in the interim. What informs the debate at the deepest level, and constitutes the broadest *question de droit* of all, is the problem of how to articulate the Christian revelation in the related areas of theoretical/doctrinal and pratical/moral language. But this primary question remains largely unacknowledged.

By thus preferring to keep to their own more limited *questions de droit*, Pascal's moral, the Jesuits' doctrinal, both parties implicitly deny the existence of a common, inclusive definition in which they would be able to concede and to win certain particular arguments. There is eventually a concession by Pascal in his return to the original *question de fait/droit* dispute in the seventeenth and eighteenth letters, but once the debate has been broadened out in the preceding series, the two lines of argument function in more and more separated parallelism. Thus at the same time as the final (superficial) thematic *rapprochement*, there is an unconcluded dispute about fundamentals still in play, expressed and effected by the ever greater distancing of the intervening letters and replies. Let us consider the detail.

At one level, that of the Montalte-'je', the *question de fait* is dismissed about a third of the way into the first letter—'ce point-là est peu important, puisqu'il ne s'y agit point de la foi' (i. 8)—not to be examined again until the seventeenth. However, what follows is telling: 'Pour la question de droit, elle semble bien plus considérable, en ce qu'elle touche la foi... Mais vous serez bien satisfait de voir que c'est une chose aussi peu importante que la première' (i. 8). As Duchêne remarks, 'la question de droit devient elle aussi une sorte de question de fait dont tout le monde peut juger' (*IL* 35), and therefore gives rise to a reiteration of the same satirical points, that the apparently substantial charges are in fact also politico-semantic ones, and thus, by implication, that the real dispute is as yet unidentified (even if it exists)—and indeed to some extent it remains unidentified throughout. The first three letters move at this level in different ways towards the elaboration and dismissal of a succession of what are increasingly identified as imaginary *questions de fait*, since every time the *question de droit* is apparently being touched upon, it eludes Montalte, and another point of personal or semantic ambiguity, explicable (and satirizable) without recourse to God or conscience, takes its place. As the writer of the *Réponse à la douzième lettre* rightly observes (of this stage of the exchange): 'Vous fuyez sans cesse à la question de droit, en quoi vous manquez à votre promesse; et vous ne répondez point à la question de fait, en quoi vous péchez contre votre devoir' (*RLP* 211). These terms are rather used at the outset by Pascal as *entrées en matière*, as satirical rather than theological pretexts, whose serious examination will not be undertaken until the seventeenth and eighteenth letters.[1] The role of counsel for the defence of Arnauld as undertaken by Montalte (as distinct from that undertaken later by the polemicist and then by Pascal) is thus conducted at the level of the satirical dismissal of the issues; it would seem to emerge from the first *LPs* that there is no real *question de fait* any more than there is a real *question de droit*; there are only, in the current dispute, *questions de majorités*, *personnalités*, and so on. As the *question de droit* progressively becomes identified by Pascal however, it is as something far more fundamental than the relatively narrow sense given at the outset by the Sorbonne.

There is furthermore a manifestly convenient coincidence between the frivolous, vulgarizing tone of the first letters and the avoidance of the detailed examination of ultimately serious questions; by the time they are examined more fully the epistolary context will have evolved in such a way as to make their

---

[1] H. Davidson introduces a substantial discussion of *question de fait* and *question de droit ou de foi* in his *Audience, Words, and Art* (Ohio, 1965). In my own, somewhat more speculative, examination of their meaning and development, I do not dissent from his analysis of their eventual epistemological status. Since however he suggests that they do not reach it until the end of the series, I will take Davidson's argument in that context. With regard to the terms of the original dispute, two points should be noted: first, that neither the laity nor indeed the clergy were considered to be at liberty to discuss the theological implications surrounding the question of grace and free will, until such time as Rome had made a definitive pronouncement on the matter: the very examination of the problem thus constituted an initial act of disobedience; and secondly, and relatedly, that the questioning of the terms of any statement endorsed by the Church's authority would also have invariably been seen as constituting some kind of disrespectful act, irrespective of the status of the differences involved.

resolution at a serious level appear more urgent, as the intervening letters will have accumulated complementary, but far more incriminating evidence against the accusers. The *LPs* are a reply to an inaccessible, because theologically technical, accusation. They reply by returning, in a more attractive form, an alternative accusation. In other words, the weakness on paper of the Jesuit position must be attributed to the fact that they are all the time trying to take the old *question de fait/droit* argument academically backwards, while Pascal takes the new one readably forwards.

No snappy answer can be given on the *question de fait* in the tone of the first letters, let alone on the *question de droit*; the most that can be done at this stage is to make a fairly crude case for Arnauld's victimization (and therefore implicitly his orthodoxy), whilst letting it be understood that technical ambiguities may still prevail. This is achieved by the foil persona of Monsieur N., a 'docteur de Navarre' and 'des plus zélés contre les Jansénistes' (i. 8). He informs Montalte that there remain genuine difficulties of interpretation concerning the universality of grace: 'les examinateurs mêmes avaient dit en pleine Sorbonne que cette opinion est *problématique*' (i. 9), but that on the central questions the statements of Arnauld are sound: 'ce n'est pas là une hérésie; c'est une opinion orthodoxe' (i. 9–10). The kind of subtlety and intellectual seriousness required to elaborate on this problem would however be quite inappropriate in the context, and so, vitally, the debate is shifted into the related areas (what Cognet (p. vii) in another context calls 'terrains annexes') of ethical and, later, spiritual practices.

This is of course where Pascal's argumentational preferences part company with the Jesuits', since they continue to insist on the centrality of the questions as understood in the context of the *Cinq Propositions*, and to argue within the detailed terms which Pascal eschews. And it is arguably Pascal's most felicitous departure, achieving as it does a maximal popularity of 'forme' and seriousness of 'fond' to which the counter-polemical effort will never be able to attain. The Society of Jesus, having conceded the initial impact to Pascal's epistolary invention, now sees emerging from within the same fictional *entrée en matière* the even more damaging series of comic dialogues, whose emotive subject-matter will in turn bring about the introduction of the serious register. None of the counter-polemic ever fully recovers from the primary failure to initiate an effective counter-fiction (despite various imitations),[2] let alone one with such potential for internal development.

The new material then ideally allows the evolution of Montalte to continue within a framework of example and illustration, before the theoretical consideration of all aspects of the dispute is undertaken in the second half of the work. Before returning to the defence, Pascal moves on to the attack; in response to a theoretical charge (which Montalte has demonstrated to be purely political) he will erect a practical charge against a system which, it is claimed, constitutes a major departure from orthodoxy. The *question de droit* of the Jesuit accusation has been reduced to nothing; the *questions de fait* that he will now introduce amount to a new *question de droit*, a matter of far greater substance and discernment and one which takes as its starting-point the definition found in the fourth letter: '*l'ignorance du... droit*, c'est-à-dire... l'ignorance du bien et du mal qui est en l'action' (iv. 69). This question will be shown to have wide-reaching implications, since it is portrayed as at least constitutive of a threat to the authority of the Church's teaching, and, ultimately, to the credibility of Christianity *tout court*.

The terms of the attack, like those of the defence, are provided by the perennial postlapsarian tension between nature and grace, whose relationship constitutes an element of the broader *question de droit*, understood now in both its dimensions and thus potential deformations (the narrower *question de droit* on which Arnauld is accused only takes into account the possibility of error by over-emphasis on grace): 'Tous les fidèles demandent aux théologiens quel est le véritable état de la nature depuis sa corruption' (ii. 29). It is not, the 'ami provincial' is finally to be persuaded in reply, a series of *questions de fait* loosely and inexactly related to an

---

[2] The major work produced by the Jesuits to have such an overall fictional framework was the *Entretiens de Cléandre et d'Eudoxe*, by the Jesuit Père Gabriel Daniel, which was not published until 1694. Because of its distinct status as a retrospective examination of the whole dispute I have not taken it into account in my remarks on the counter-polemic.

over-emphasis on grace that will pose the threat, but a different *question de droit* which relates to the complementary over-emphasis on human nature. Or, as the 'ami janséniste' predicts in a phrase linking the first and second series of letters:

> Vous remarquerez aisément, dans le relâchement de leur morale, la cause de leur doctrine touchant la grâce... Vous ne trouverez plus étrange qu'ils soutiennent que tous les hommes ont toujours assez de grâce pour vivre dans la piété de la manière qu'ils l'entendent. Comme leur morale est toute païenne, la nature suffit pour l'observer. (v. 78)

The charges against Arnauld, in so far as they are expressed in terms of a suppression of the role of nature in his doctrine, are dismissed by Montalte; it is the complementary charge against the Jesuits that will be taken up by Pascal, the charge of denying any role to grace in their ethics. This will also be accompanied by a polarization of the disparity: the defence of Arnauld is at this stage conducted by Montalte in terms of minimalization; the attack against the Jesuits (who are explicitly introduced in the second letter) will amplify the emphasis on nature to the point at which it challenges both the fundamental tenets of Christianity and the dictates of common sense.

The very terms into which the debate is shifted furthermore enhance the position of Pascal: in so far as Montalte argues from what he presents as concrete ethical dilemmas, his argument takes the practical/moral domain as its starting-point (the multitude of extracts from manuals are the 'faits' building up his evidence on the *question de droit*); the investigation of orthodoxy on matters of grace and free will, however, lies in the theoretical/doctrinal sphere. Within the terms of the earlier *LP*s, therefore, the Jesuits define orthodoxy by speech and writing; Pascal by actions. The fact that each party chooses the other's weakness for attack paradoxically gives the polemical advantage to Pascal; his mastery of the moral debate stems from its capacity for illustration. His argument is principally successful because it is descriptive and concrete; the signifiers and signifieds seem to have a simple relationship. The Jesuits' chosen domain of doctrine, however, by virtue of being abstract and to some degree speculative, translates less easily into relatively simple signs and arguments, as imponderables lend themselves readily to semantic confusion. By initially moving on to the attack, Pascal thus effects a transferal of the advantages of the Jesuit material in terms of its capacity for popularization; he takes the Jesuit appeal to the practical and employs it satirically in the polemical realm. It will only be later in the series that the full implications of these moral questions will in turn be explicitly related to the doctrinal fundamentals.

The impression given by the move onto the moral questions is also one of a rehabilitation of the dispute. As Pascal writes in another context, 'il faut que nous nous servions du lieu même où nous sommes tombés pour nous relever de notre chute'.[3] The debate has vulgarized itself, the reader is led to understand, and the level of Montalte's starting-point is thus consonant with the status of the quarrel. (Duchêne writes of 'le glissement qui s'est, selon les Jansénistes, produit de l'essentiel à l'accessoire' (*IL* 34).) Just as, in the eleventh letter, the polemicist will hold the Jesuits responsible for the use he has made of 'raillerie' in his work, so at the outset the responsibility is placed implicitly with the ecclesiastical authorities for the triviality of the questions to which it superficially attends. Cognet remarks, quoting Nicole, that 'le conflit est ramené à "une question de nom, qui ne convient nullement à la gravité des théologiens"' (p. 23 n. 3). And Le Guern, in *IL*, adds:

La note qui accompagne la traduction de Mlle de Joncoux [*of the Preface of Wendrock (Nicole)'s edition of the* LPs] rétablit les faits: 'Ce fut Mr Arnauld lui-même qui dit que la chose ne méritait pas d'être traitée sérieusement aux yeux du public. Il ajouta qu'il n'y avait que Mr Pascal qui fût capable d'en faire le sujet d'un agréable badinage' (t. I, p. 8 de l'édition des *Provinciales* de 1739). (*IL* 312 n. 1)

Duchêne has, on the other hand, proposed that the debate was taken seriously: 'La méthode des *Provinciales*, c'est précisément, dans une querelle qui était sérieuse et grave, de donner un nouveau ton, et de donner un ton... galant'.[4] But Philippe Sellier,

---

[3] *Lettre de Pascal et de sa sœur Jacqueline à Madame Périer, leur sœur*, 1 Apr. 1648, in *OC* 272–3.

[4] R. Duchêne, in *débat* following D. Jaymes, 'La Méthode d'ironie dans les *Provinciales*', in *Méthodes chez Pascal* (Paris, 1979), p. 210.

again in *IL*, discussing the importance of the 'débats en Sorbonne', suggests: 'Le volume de la discussion sur un sujet ne signifie pas forcément qu'on va au fond des choses. . . . Ce fond des choses était: "Est-ce que l'Eglise catholique va renoncer à la théologie augustinienne de la grâce qu'elle suit depuis douze cents ans?"' (*IL* 377). He then adds: 'Ce qu'a senti Port-Royal (et c'est un très grand débat), c'est qu'on trahissait la pensée d'Augustin et que par conséquent, selon lui, l'Eglise se détruisait elle-même' (*IL* 378). And Duchêne himself remarks:

> Il n'y a pas tellement lieu de se demander s'il [Pascal] savait ou s'il ne savait pas ce qu'était le pouvoir prochain. Le thème est que l'on n'a pas traité les vrais problèmes. Pascal peut donc, à son gré, inventer le sujet qu'on y aurait selon lui débattu, et il a choisi le pouvoir prochain, parce qu'il lui fournissait l'occasion d'un épisode comique... Ce dont il veut persuader son lecteur, c'est qu'on s'est refusé à traiter des vrais problèmes et qu'on continuera à le faire. (*IL* 326–7)

In other words the debate is seen to have lost sight of fundamentals, thereby affording Pascal the opportunity to reintroduce them in his own terms. Thus, whether or not we attribute this emphasis solely to Pascal's party, or accept that some of the blame must lie with the authorities, the capacity for rehabilitation within the terms of the *LPs* remains the same. Or, as Duchêne again puts it, 'il a dès lors toute latitude pour remplir à sa guise le vide qu'il a lui-même créé' (*IL* 42). The space is filled by the two series of letters on 'la morale relâchée', which precede and follow the eleventh, so that when the (theoretical) defence of Arnauld is eventually restated it has been reinforced by the (practical) attack on the Jesuits. (The Jesuits will of course in turn argue that it is Pascal who has trivialized the debate, and that the substantial questions that remain to be answered are still those surrounding the *Cinq Propositions*.) Pascal thus rehabilitates the complementary debate to the one that is considered to have been degraded, and only attends to a rehabilitation of the initial debate in the last letters of the series, within a radically different epistolary convention. The new *question de droit* is argued out in the terrain of Pascal's choosing.

He has therefore moved his reader imperceptibly from the tone of the first letter some way towards the more vehement satire of the middle series. The move is made from the theoretical/ doctrinal to the practical/moral, from the defence to the attack, from the dismantled *question(s) de fait* to a reconstructed *question de droit*; the context has been erected for the first ironic and then serious examination of the Jesuit code of morality and case ethics. The tone of assumed *naïveté* has become more self-conscious again, as the expectation of a disillusionment has grown both within Montalte's own utterances and by virtue of his interaction with the 'ami janséniste'. And finally the 'dispute de théologie' is revealed as separate from, yet in the current debate inescapably bound up with, the 'dispute de théologiens'; if the particular doctrinal advantage is conceded historically, as it seemed to have been by virtue of the censure of the Sorbonne with which the second letter ends, then the general moral principles must come to the surface as the terrain of war. The real 'sujet bien extraordinaire' of the first letter is now embarked upon, and it is Pascal who has determined the kind of enquiry it will involve. The shift has however established the preconditions for the *dialogue de sourds* which the two polemics will forthwith constitute.

3

Dramatis Personae

WE must first return to Montalte. The satirical advantages of the *faux naïf* persona are manifold, and have been thoroughly examined.[1] However, a related aspect of Montalte, his mobility in the early letters, can perhaps be elucidated further, and certain implications suggested. He is, as Duchêne illustrates (especially at *IL* 26 and 34), most strikingly mobile, literally and figuratively, introducing and reporting on his meetings with other figures, before settling down to the sustained series of encounters with the Jesuit in letters v–x. He is thus enabled initially, by his assumed independence, affability, and access to the well-connected clerical milieu, to ascertain the views of a variety of spokesmen in a persuasive yet civilized sequence. The key contributors in the first two letters are, however, slightly distanced, either from the vital sources of power and opinion, (Monsieur N., 'docteur de Navarre' (Sorbonne); Monsieur N., 'notre ancien ami' (Jesuits)), or from Montalte (the brother-in-law of Monsieur N., 'qui se porte de mieux en mieux' (Jansenists)), and so for the time being lack either or both of the aspects of personal *engagement* which will characterize the participants in later exchanges, fictional dialogic or actual epistolary. Montalte's encounters, then, gradually increase in intensity proportionately to his own growing *parti pris*, thereby heightening the whole tone of the correspondence as it progresses.

Some attempt is made at an imitation of this opening style in one part of the *RLP*, the *Autre Lettre sur la conformité des reproches*

---

[1] See e.g. D. Descotes, 'Fonction argumentative'; R. Duchêne, *IL* 192–200; G. Ferreyrolles, *Blaise Pascal: Les Provinciales*, pp. 45–52; P. Kuentz, 'Un discours nommé Montalte', *RHL* 71 (1971), 195–206; M. Reisler, 'Persuasion through Antithesis: An Analysis of the Dominant Rhetorical Structure of Pascal's *Lettres Provinciales*', *Romanic Review*, 69 (1978), 172–85.

(i.e. those made by Port-Royal and Protestants).[2] We notice in
particular the report of a friendly and wide-ranging conversation:
'Je m'approchai de lui pour le saluer, car il est de ma connaissance,
et après quelques civilités je lui dis...' (*RLP* lxviii). This letter
also features a Monsieur N. (who reads out the 'lettres morales' at
Charenton where they are received 'comme un second Evangile'
(*RLP* lxvii)) and a fictional Jesuit, the equivalent to, and fulfilling
the same role as the 'ami janséniste', who initiates in this piece an
important element of the counter-polemical argument, the comparison between the *LPs* and Du Moulin's *Traditions* (*RLP* lxx),
to which we shall return.[3] This kind of imitation only exists in
one instance, however, and is not carried on into any of the
remainder of the series.

   Through the intermediary role of Montalte the early letters
thus transmit a variety of points of view, and provide a contemporary context, a background of opinion, against which the
longer Jesuit encounter of v–x is foregrounded. The first letter, as
I have said, makes no mention of the Society, concentrating
rather on the allegation of political agreement between otherwise
rival groups, who are telescoped thereby into a kind of composite
opposition. The Jesuits 'enter' abruptly in the first paragraph of
the second letter, represented initially by a related but not implicated figure, who gives the first account of the Society's theology
and ethos: 'Je fus visité par M. N., notre ancien ami... il est très
informé des questions du temps, et il sait parfaitement le secret
des Jésuites, chez qui il est à toute heure, et avec les principaux' (ii.
21). Clearly the eventual emergence of the Jesuit position will
provide the focus for the remainder of the series; but equally
clearly the preliminary attention given to other parties by
Montalte proposes an infiltration of Jesuit doctrine and ethics into
a broader ecclesiastical context, into which a part of the more
specific critique is implicitly carried. The attack expressed in

---

[2] *Autre Lettre du même auteur* [as the *Lettre écrite à une personne de condition*
(Appendix I. x)] *sur la conformité des reproches et des calomnies que les Jansénistes
publient contre les Pères de la Compagnie de Jésus avec celles que le Ministre du Moulin a
publiées devant eux contre l'Eglise Romaine, dans son livre des Traditions, imprimée à
Genève en l'année 1632.* See Appendix II.
[3] Chapter 6.

terms of the 'morale relâchée' crystallizes therefore a more general exposure of the Church's debased orthodoxy, symbolized initially by the adherence of other non-Jesuit groups within the Church to a common point of view: the Dominicans are already shown in the first *LP* to be in league with the 'disciples de M. Le Moyne', the anti-Jansenist 'docteur de Sorbonne', on *pouvoir prochain*; thereafter, on *grâce efficace*, 'Ils s'unissent aux Jésuites. Ils font par cette union le plus grand nombre' (ii. 29). And then immediately afterwards the whole Church, by the implications of the parable of the wounded man, is shown to have fallen into their hands as well. Furthermore the historical background deployed by the Dominican of the second *LP* shows the achievements of the Jesuits in leading the reaction against Luther and Calvin, whereby 'on les vit bientôt maîtres de la créance des peuples' (ii. 32). These examples provide an initial demonstration of their exercise of power by virtue of a numerical, as opposed to an apostolic, authority; and an illustration of how the danger of an implied association with the Protestant view obliges another order (here the Dominicans) to submit, at least nominally, to the Jesuit position—a consideration not, as we shall see, unrelated to the counter-polemical effort.

When the final status of the Jesuits is established at the outset of the fourth letter: 'Il n'est rien tel que les Jésuites... Les autres ne font que les copier. Les choses valent toujours mieux à leur source' (iv. 53), it is thus increasingly understood that the critique of the Society can be extended both to their collaborators and indeed to the Church as a whole (their influence on Le Moyne, and thus on the Sorbonne, also being explicitly brought out in this letter). But though other groups are shown to contribute to the disorder, the Jesuits are identified as the primary offenders. They are situated at one end of a spectrum, which in the satirical context they are deemed the best to exemplify.

If we look forward briefly to later letters, and to other writing, we find these insinuations confirmed. The tendency of the Church to be assumed (by the Society) to subscribe to Jesuit teaching is explicitly stated in the sixth letter, where the principle of inertia is described: '[Une opinion nouvelle] se trouve autorisée par la tacite approbation de l'Eglise, selon cette grande maxime du Père Bauny : "Qu'une opinion étant avancée par quelques casuistes, et l'Eglise ne s'y étant point opposée, c'est un témoignage qu'elle l'approuve"' (vi. 102). More obliquely in the eleventh: 'Qu'ils [= gullible disciples] considèrent donc devant Dieu combien la morale que vos casuistes répandent de toutes parts est honteuse et pernicieuse à l'Eglise' (xi. 203). And fragments of the *Pensées* also support the accusations of the *LPs*:

Non seulement ils veulent être soufferts dans l'église mais comme s'ils étaient devenus les plus forts ils en veulent chasser ceux qui n'en sont pas...

Qui eût dit à vos généraux qu'un temps était si proche qu'ils donneraient ces mœurs à l'église universelle et appeleraient guerre le refus de ces désordres. (L 700)

Ils font toute l'Eglise corrompue afin qu'ils soient saints. (L 707)

Montalte's adopted role as the searcher after orthodoxy in this variety of opinions leads him to the expression of the kind of rhetorical uncertainty characteristic of the searchers in the *Pensées*, adding urgency to the need felt to discern the truth, and anticipating the intensity of his later contributions. The dilemma demands a personal response:

Où en sommes-nous donc? m'écriai-je, et quel parti dois-je ici prendre? Si je nie la grâce suffisante, je suis Janséniste; si je l'admets comme les Jésuites, en sorte que la grâce efficace ne soit pas nécessaire, je serai *hérétique*, dites-vous. Et si je l'admets comme vous... je pèche contre le sens commun, et je suis *extravagant*, disent les Jésuites. Que dois-je donc faire dans cette nécessité inévitable d'être ou extravagant, ou hérétique, ou Janséniste? (ii. 27)

The parallels in tone are clear between such an expression and the words of the interlocutor of the 'pari': 'J'ai les mains liées et la bouche muette, on me force à parier, et je ne suis pas en liberté, on ne me relâche pas et je suis fait d'une telle sorte que je ne puis croire. Que voulez-vous donc que je fasse?' (L 418). Or the words of the first person in other 'seeker' fragments: 'Je regarde de toutes parts, et je ne vois partout qu'obscurité. La nature ne m'offre rien qui ne soit matière de doute et d'inquiétude.... Voyant trop pour nier et trop peu pour m'assurer, je suis dans un état à plaindre' (L 429). All these figures, from their respective starting-points,[4] then move towards the expression of the same degree, and kind, of certainty. As Montalte's mobility decreases, so does his open-mindedness; but the satirical purpose it has served is more than one of simple preparation.

The existence of multiple dialogue in the early *LPs* obviously endows other voices with first-person utterance, most notably that of the 'ami janséniste'. This figure makes his initial appearance in the second letter, and serves generally to advance the combative quality of the dialogues, particularly in the later parts of the second and fourth letters, and to predict some of the more direct challenges of the later series. He holds the (with hindsight) ironic, indeed paradoxical, position of being both at one further fictional remove from the author than Montalte, but also more exactly expressive of the authorial position as it will in due course emerge (even though the polemicist will deny membership of Port-Royal). It is this status that allows the vital coexistence of emergence and concealment, and makes the satirical purport of the work unmistakable.

The 'ami janséniste' precipitates the movement of Montalte towards a siding with the Jansenist cause, and it is to him, rather than to Montalte, that the first intense expression of aggression is given at the end of the second letter. For Duchêne, 'il économise en quelque sorte le personnage principal des *Provinciales*, prenant sur lui tout ce qui sentirait le parti-pris' (*IL* 93). The 'Montalte-ami janséniste-nouveau Thomiste [= Dominican]' trio is then taken a stage further in intensity in the fourth letter's elaboration of a 'Montalte-ami janséniste-Jésuite' trio, since this allows the first (fictional) direct confrontation between Jansenist and Jesuit, announcing both the Montalte–Jesuit series and the concluding Pascal–Annat exchanges. The 'ami janséniste' is, in both these letters, but especially the fourth, contrasted with Montalte by virtue of his greater degree of *engagement*, preparedness, and eventually hostility. He is described in the second letter in

[4] I would make a working distinction between (hypothetical) initial positions of a seeker and a non-seeker persona in the *Pensées*. See R. Parish, 'Mais qui parle? Voice and Persona in the *Pensées*', *Seventeenth Century French Studies*, 8 (1986), 23–40.

editions prior to 1659 as 'mon ami, plus sérieux que moi' (ii. (33))[5] and the following descriptions reinforce this in the fourth letter: 'Mais mon second, soutenant mon discours, lui dit. . . Mais mon Janséniste, se tenant dans les termes que le Père avait prescrits, lui dit. . . Mais mon second, qui avait, à ce que je crois, étudié toute cette question le matin même, tant il était prêt sur tout, lui répondit' (iv. 61–4). He is furthermore significantly pitted against the Jesuit of the fourth letter, 'un des plus habiles' (iv. 53), rather than the more affable 'bon casuiste de la Société. . . une de mes anciennes connaissances' (v. 79) of the fifth and subsequent letters, thus reinforcing the impression of a sharp doctrinal confrontation at a secondary fictional level, preceding the much more gradual and (initially at least) amicable exchange at a primary level of the following series.

The final role he is given is to discuss Jesuit practices and principles with Montalte, who is becoming increasingly persuaded by his position, in the first part of the fifth letter, which Duchêne sees as the introduction to the whole series on 'la morale relâchée' (*IL* 119). His contribution is concluded by a fervent statement in favour of the power of grace, which stands immediately before, and prejudicially sets the tone for, the first encounter between Montalte and the second Jesuit:

Il est aussi peu raisonnable de prétendre que l'on a toujours un plein pouvoir, qu'il le serait de nier que ces vertus, destituées d'amour de Dieu, lesquelles ces bons Pères confondent avec les vertus chrétiennes, ne sont pas en notre puissance.

Voilà comment il me parla, et avec beaucoup de douleur; car il s'afflige sérieusement de tous ces désordres. Pour moi. . . je fus, selon son conseil, trouver un bon casuiste de la Société. (v. 79)

A particularly striking effect of juxtaposition is thereby achieved, and a strong case made for the Jansenist position in advance of the major series of satirical letters. (The juxtaposition of expressions

---

[5] The 1657 in-4° ed. is reproduced in Pascal, *Œuvres Complètes*, ed. L. Lafuma (Paris, 1963). M. Le Guern remarks of the 1659 edn.: 'Cette version définitive est moins l'œuvre de Pascal, et davantage celle de Port-Royal' (*IL* 309). Since the differences are in fact relatively slight, I have kept to the widely respected critical edn. of Cognet, and referred to variants only in so far as this seemed relevant. There has recently been published an edn. (by M. Le Guern) of the second 1657 in-12° text (Paris, 1987).

of extreme opinion is common throughout the series—and reflects the 'for or against' ideology that will be articulated in the later letters, and particularly the fourteenth: 'On ne peut être que d'un parti ou de l'autre, il n'y a point de milieu' (xiv. 271).) The final statement of the 'ami janséniste' also occurs immediately after the (fourth) letter in which the Jesuits are established as epitomizing the alternative theology. The first stage of the definition of the terms has thus taken place, and the case for a confrontation been built up; and all the developments in the ensuing letters further polarize the positions from which the debate is conducted. Initially the dispute is narrowed down by the exclusion of all factions other than the Jesuits, who thereby assume a representative function. Then, once the background has become sharper and more honed down, the same development occurs in the foreground, as the examples taken from the Jesuits are pushed to the extreme.

In addition, however, we see in the contribution of the 'ami janséniste' at the beginning of the fifth letter a powerfully expressed indication of what is more and more to be perceived as orthodoxy, preluding the apparently free-ranging, though increasingly unambiguous satirical letters; a touchstone is implicitly set up from which the degree of aberration will thereafter be measured, all the more so since the association of intensity of expression with credibility is already established in the figure of the 'beau-frère janséniste' of the first piece: 'Mon homme s'échauffa là-dessus, mais d'un zèle dévot... Il m'en parla si sérieusement, que je n'en pus douter' (i. 11). Finally we might note the, albeit deleted, remark to be found in the *Pensées*: 'Qu'on voie les discours de la 2, 4 et 5 du janséniste. Cela est haut et sérieux' (L 610). The 'ami janséniste' thus represents, by both the tone and content of his contributions, the end point to which Montalte will accede.

Confronting him in the fourth letter is the first Jesuit, less fully developed than his successor, but with the same readiness to explain, consulting his authorities as he does so. The more aggressive tone results however in his more rapid discountenancing—'Le bon Père... commenca à lâcher le pied' (iv. 64)—until he is finally released only by a jibe at the expense of the Society's 'mondanité': 'comme il pensait à ce qu'il devait dire, on vint l'avertir que Madame la Maréchale de... et Madame la Marquise de... le demandaient' (iv. 70). It is perhaps then that Pascal perceives the potential for Jesuit self-incrimination which Montalte's greater restraint and indulgence in the ensuing series will release. For this to happen, however, a fresh start has to be made with a second, unruffled representative of the Society who can, at far greater leisure, satisfy Montalte's curiosity.

The other sustained first-person contribution, the counterpart of the role fulfilled by the 'ami janséniste', is provided in the third letter by 'un de ceux qui, par politique, furent neutres dans la première question' (that of *pouvoir prochain*) (iii. 45). Here we find a voice evolving alongside that of Montalte, that of an involved, but impartial figure, shedding a complementary light to those partial figures who are however at one remove from the proceedings. His function, nominally more independent, is made more accusatory for that reason; the blandness of his quotation of Le Moyne is thus all the more efficaciously followed by an intense, and intensely placed, response from Montalte:

... les inventions nouvelles qu'on fabrique tous les jours à notre vue passent pour l'ancienne foi de l'Eglise. Sur cela il me quitta.
    Cette instruction m'a servi [ouvert les yeux *in editions prior to 1659*]. J'y ai compris que c'est ici une hérésie d'une nouvelle espèce. Ce ne sont pas les sentiments de M. Arnauld qui sont hérétiques; ce n'est que sa personne. (iii. 51)

The remaining first-person interventions are briefer, or at least less sustained, and contribute, in the dialogues of the first letter, to the aim of establishing the nature of the politico-semantic victimization. However already here Pascal establishes, by the juxtaposition of the first Monsieur N. ('docteur de Navarre') and the brother-in-law of the second ('qui se porte de mieux en mieux'), contrasts in the frivolous setting between a voice who is 'des plus zélés contre les Jansénistes' and one 'qui est Janséniste s'il y en eut jamais'. Two such figures will of course conclude the whole series, but with the fictions removed and the seriousness restored. These early figures thus seem like unconscious heralds of the debate's thematic progress, just as Montalte and the 'ami provincial' are of its formal development. In other words, the four fictional personae of the beginning of the first letter become compressed into the two historical personages of the last two, as the fictionally required diffuseness is contracted into the bluntness of direct confrontation.

4

Arenas of Debate and Readerships

IT is a critical commonplace to point out that Montalte has his Jesuits condemn themselves out of their own mouths, and it is indisputable, as Duchêne has demonstrated,[1] that Pascal has adapted his raw material to fulfil this satirical function. What we see in the letters on the 'morale relâchée' is how that material is put to effect.

Montalte is, in these satirical letters, not so much uninformed as incredulous: 'J'avais peine à croire cela, et je priai le Père de me le montrer dans l'original' (vi. 98). They serve the purpose less of educating a figure who is completely unversed in his subject as of confirming at first hand (against what is *vraisemblable*), and indeed extending, what he in fact half knew or suspected. The 'ami janséniste' has already indicated the nature and scope of Jesuit aberration to him—'il me dit de si étranges choses, que j'avais peine à le croire' (v. 72)[2]—and so 'Je ne me suis pas fié à ce que notre ami m'en avait appris. J'ai voulu les voir eux-mêmes' (v. 73–4). The ensuing letters (v–x) render actual and detailed what is vaguely and unspecifically hinted at; thus we see an exposition of the Jesuit mentality in the first half of the fifth letter, followed by an illustration of it in those following, two presentations of similar material in different fictional elaborations. The distinguishing characteristics of individual pieces diminish however to virtual non-existence and, even if certain epistolary conventions (what Duchêne calls 'signes épistolaires') continue to be used, connections between letters are made perfunctorily, and with

---

[1] This is the major burden of Duchêne's argument in *IL*, esp. 'Le bricolage pascalien' (pp. 160–70) and 'Citation, trahison' (pp. 171–84). It is also considered by Cognet (pp. xli–xlii and notes *passim*) and by W. Rex, *Pascal's Provincial Letters: An Introduction* (London, etc., 1977), 61–3.

[2] In edns. prior to that of 1659 this sentence reads: 'il me dit de si plaisantes choses... '.

little or no incidental material. At the same time, their thematic and satirical unity is considerable.

In these letters, Montalte takes his interlocutor progressively into the arena of debate in which the principles of his exposition of 'opinions probables' are negated. The introductory phrase of the fifth letter is taken from the work published to celebrate the first hundred years of the Society, the *Imago Primi Saeculi* of 1640. But its application (as is the case with the later observation on the *Querelle des Rites* to which we shall return) extends into the whole letter: '*Ils ont changé la face de la Chrétienté. Il le faut croire puisqu'ils le disent. Et vous l'allez bien voir dans la suite de ce discours, qui vous apprendra leurs maximes*' (v. 73). This immediately establishes the tone and themes of the following letters, and the governing satirical device which is to be employed is identified: '*Vous pensez peut-être que je raille: je le dis sérieusement, ou plutôt ce sont eux-mêmes qui le disent... je ne fais que copier leurs paroles*' (v. 72–3).

The first counter-polemicists apparently recognized the skill with which this tactic was initiated. In the *Réponse et remerciement*[3] we find the following remark concerning the fifth letter: '*il semble que vous triomphez, avant même que d'être entré au combat*' (p. 2), and, although he is more grudging, the writer of the *Lettre de Philarque*[4] similarly acknowledges the techniques employed: '*C'est montrer, et l'hypocrisie des mœurs et le désespoir de la cause, que de changer ainsi de quartier et de batterie, d'attaquer au lieu de continuer à défendre, et recourir aux médisances confites dans le sucre de ces plumes dorées qui s'est enfin aigri sur le feu et tourné en raillerie*' (p. 3).

The ensuing satirical development consists in the movement towards *cas-limite* problems of Christian moral judgement, and the first specific question to be broached, in the fifth letter, is that of fasting, introduced by the disingenuous enquiry: '*Je pris occasion du temps où nous sommes [= Lent] pour apprendre de lui quelque chose sur le jeûne, afin d'entrer insensiblement en*

---

[3] *Réponse et remerciement d'un Provincial à Monsieur EAABPFDEPA sur le sujet de ses lettres et particulièrement de la cinquième*. See Appendix I. i.

[4] *Lettre de Philarque à un de ses amis*. See Appendix I. ii. This and the *Réponse* (above) are two of the earliest replies.

matière. Je lui témoignai donc que j'avais de la peine à le sup-
porter' (v. 79–80). Once this kind of reasoning has been
embarked upon the movement towards the more extreme
examples is rapid. Montalte needs to provide little more than this
initial impetus in order to unleash, 'insensiblement', the whole
scandal. This is also made psychologically plausible by the readiness of the second fictional Jesuit (aptly described by Derôme as
'l'homme de bonne foi dans un parti malhonnête')[5] to show off
his versatility and skill. As Descotes points out: 'Le Jésuite est
d'abord un personnage de naïf... Le lecteur s'amuse de son
émerveillement devant la finesse des casuistes... Plus encore,
c'est cette naïveté qui l'engage si avant dans la doctrine des
casuistes qu'il ne mesure plus lui-même le poids de ses paroles'.[6]

All clear distinctions concerning the frequency and gravity of
sins, or the moral status of the penitent, are necessarily left
inexplicit by Montalte in the section that follows, which fore-
shadows much of the series. Of course in the system of simple
absolutes which will emerge no such distinctions need to be
made; the satirical advantage at which the *meneur du jeu* places
himself is evident. Equally, the disadvantage at which the advocate of the relative system finds himself stems from the fact that
abuses are in one sense logical extensions of legitimate uses
(differences of degree not kind)—and it is for precisely that
reason that Pascal shifts the argument as quickly as possible into
the domain where an absolute moral system must prevail. He
applies the perspective of simplicity against the arguments of
complexity in precisely that area where it is most efficacious and
they are most implausible. What is true in the twelfth letter is also
true here: 'je vous ferai des questions si simples, qu'elles ne seront
point sujettes au *distinguo*' (xii. 227). It is by extending the means
of judgement appropriate to the grey areas into those cases where
black and white are the only possible colours that he gives the
maximum discredit to the Jesuit position on the practice of
'opinions probables'. As Duchêne comments, 'la probabilité,

---

[5] *Lettres Provinciales*, ed. L. Derôme (Paris, 1885–6), i, Introduction, p. clxiii.
[6] D. Descotes, 'Fonction argumentative', pp. 48–9. Descotes goes on to argue
(p. 62) that this self-incrimination continues in the various Jesuit replies, and
indeed beyond the conclusion of the *LPs* into the *Apologie pour les Casuistes* (see
n. 7).

dans son principe, ne cherche pas à encourager le caprice ou la cupidité; elle reconnaît seulement la diversité des solutions quand il y en a plus d'une qui puisse être fondée sur des arguments raisonnables' (*IL* 142). But the advocate of inspirationalist belief suggested in the *Pensées*, and particularly the *Mémorial*, is able to promote a much simpler kind of doctrinal certainty and (related) moral inflexibility (consonant with 'doctrine de la foi') than is available to the academic theologian and (related) spiritual director and exponent of 'doctrine de l'Ecole'. Pirot draws attention to this stance when he writes in the *Apologie pour les Casuistes*: 'Il n'appartient qu'à des esprits superbes, qui présument de connaître toutes les vérités, ou à des âmes abusées, qui se persuadent d'avoir des révélations de tout, de blâmer les opinions probables' (p. 40).[7]

But the alleged abuses go further than this, since the Jesuits are shown to be erecting their practice of relative morality into a system of absolutes of a different kind; instead of the role of circumstance playing a central part in the definition of ethical solutions, what, paradoxically, is deemed to emerge is a rigid system of relative values: 'Un docteur étant consulté peut donner un conseil, non seulement probable selon son opinion, mais contraire à son opinion, s'il est estimé probable par d'autres, lorsque cet avis contraire au sien se rencontre plus favorable et plus agréable á celui qui le consulte' (v. 88). In other words, an orthodoxy of the majority and expediency is shown to be emerging against an orthodoxy of antiquity and authority, as a means of resolving the clash when a relative system comes into conflict with an absolute imperative. Complexity resolves itself thereby into an anarchic simplicity, diametrically opposed to the simplicity of the Gospel. Or, as Hugh Davidson puts it: 'What happens is not the accommodation of new opinions to authoritative doctrine (which Pascal could not object to); instead, that doctrine is subordinated to the basically skeptical devices of the new probabilities'.[8] Certain fragments in the *Pensées* apparently also comment on this tendency:

---

[7] Père Georges Pirot, *Apologie pour les Casuistes contre les calomnies des jansénistes* (1657). This work, to which the *Ecrits des Curés* were a reply, was placed on the Index in 1659. See Appendix I. xxiv, and Cognet, pp. lxv–lxx.
[8] *Audience, Words, and Art*, p. 127.

Ils font de l'exception la règle. Les anciens ont donné l'absolution avant la pénitence? Faites-le en esprit d'exception. Mais de l'exception vous faites une règle sans exception; en sorte que vous ne voulez plus même que la règle soit en exception. (L 727) Que serait-ce que les Jésuites sans la probabilité et que la probabilité sans les Jésuites? . . . Autrefois, il était difficile d'éviter les péchés, et difficile de les expier; maintenant, il est facile de les éviter par mille tours et facile de les expier. (L 981, cf. L 956)

And the following is found in the *Premier Ecrit des Curés de Paris*: 'Ce qu'il y a de plus pernicieux dans ces nouvelles morales, est qu'elles ne vont pas seulement à corrompre les mœurs, mais à corrompre la règle des mœurs' (Cognet, p. 405). We notice too the advantage for Pascal's polemical methods of this development; just as the position of (Jansenist) orthodoxy has hardened, so the position of error is intensified and then systematized in order to stand in the most efficacious contrast to it.

Moving from practice to theory, and turning at greater length to the counter-polemic, we find a Jesuit definition and defence of 'opinions probables' provided in the *XXᵉ Imposture* of the *RLP*, taken from the reply by the Père Caussin to the *Théologie Morale des Jésuites*.[9] In the case of 'les [maximes] probables' (and in distinction to those on which there is universal agreement, 'parce que l'Ecriture Sainte, ou le consentement des Pères et des Docteurs les a rendues certaines et indubitables'), four conditions must be fulfilled:

La première, qu'elle ne choque point les vérités universellement reçues dans l'Eglise. La seconde, qu'elle ne blesse point le sens commun. La troisième, qu'elle soit fondée en raison, et appuyée d'une autorité sans reproche. La quatrième, que si elle n'a pas la voix générale de tous les docteurs, elle n'en soit pas aussi généralement abandonnée. (*RLP* 95)

The piece concludes: 'Ce qu'il appelle *la source de leurs désordres, et la base de leurs dérèglements*, est une pratique innocente, que

---

[9] See C. Sommervogel, *Bibliothèque de la Compagnie de Jésus* (Brussels, etc., 1890–1960), ii. 921 (18). Nicholas Caussin's *Réponse au libelle intitulé la Théologie Morale des Jésuites* (1644) was a reply to the anonymous *Théologie morale des Jésuites extraite fidèlement de leurs livres* of 1643. Cognet attributes this to a collaboration between Arnauld and 'le docteur de Sorbonne François Hallier, polémiste très au courant de ces problèmes' (p. x). He adds: 'A n'en pas douter, ce factum marque, dans la polémique, un tournant que les *Provinciales* ne feront qu'accentuer' (p. xi).

l'Eglise permet, que toutes les Universités observent, qui exerce les plus beaux esprits, qui forme les plus sages directeurs, et qui les rend capables de gouverner les consciences' (*RLP* 98). The role of the negative in this definition, and also of the relative, is necessarily considerable; it is curious however to note that the first two conditions, the 'vérités universellement reçues dans l'Eglise' and 'le sens commun', recall the major appeals to orthodoxy and common sense which characterize the *LP*s; it is no doubt the introduction of 'une autorité sans reproche' and, above all, the appeal to a negative consensus in the last two conditions which potentially endow them with the capacity to subvert the first two.

Such a difficulty seems tacitly to be acknowledged as the question is turned back in the next *Impostures*, and particularly in the *XXIIe Imposture*, where the polemicist is asked exactly how he would resolve difficult cases: 'S'il n'est pas permis de se servir de la raison, comment veut-il qu'un docteur examine les choses qui ne sont point évidentes par elles-mêmes, ni certaines par aucun principe de foi, ni déterminés par les lois ecclésiastiques ou civiles, et qui demeurent dans la probabilité simple?' (*RLP* 108). The question is developed: 'Vous m'objecterez peut-être que vous ne serez jamais assuré de la vérité... mais voulez-vous aussi que les casuistes changent la nature des choses, et qu'ils fassent que ce qui est seulement probable soit évident et indubitable?' (*RLP* 109) —taunting the polemicist precisely with his own objection, as hyperbolically developed in the satirical context. Here again, the freedom for this argument to be used aggressively by both parties stems partly from its deformation, but also from its capacity for deformation. The Jesuit case rests on a need to apply discernment in matters of faith in the practice of the direction of conscience; their morality is an applied one, with all the potential for qualification, ambiguity, and thus for abuse that that status implies. This flexibility and applicability is of course the very *raison d'être* of the procedure; the importance of casuistry, and its relationship to auricular confession, emanates from the need to make practical distinctions between categories and cases of sin. But it is also what allows its deformation, be it satirical or actual, as must be true of any relative system dependent on individual judgement.

The purity of the case with which Pascal opposes it, whereby any departure from moral perfection is tantamount to a heresy, is exempt from such considerations (and it is perhaps noteworthy that there is a lack of any serious positive attention given to the resolution of moral dilemma in Pascal's writing as a whole).[10] The aggressive purity and comprehensiveness of his profession of faith leaves no room for a distinction between statement and practice; its enactment is a perpetual commentary on its doctrines, and the kind of statement a Christian makes by his life will have distinguished itself from that made by an unbeliever. For the Jesuits, the distinction is not, and cannot be, as clear. The Jesuit theory functions in the space between ideal and actualization and, while never losing sight of the former, insists that the latter can only be a pale reflection of it. In the *débat* in *IL*, the R. P. Pontet remarks: 'L'équivoque fondamentale des *Provinciales*, c'est... de confondre morale et casuistique: la seconde relève de la miséricorde et la première de la perfection' (*IL* 315); furthermore, and as is emotively expressed in the *XXIIIᵉ Imposture*: 'l'empire que Jésus-Christ a donné aux confesseurs n'est point un empire tyrannique: c'est un empire d'amour, qui s'est établi par miséricorde, et qui subsiste par la douceur' (*RLP* 118). The kind of guidance which ensures the means for differentiation between such statements and Pascal's parodic extrapolation from them is incapable of any clearer general formulation beyond that provided in the *Réponse*. The only way it may be amplified is seen in the manuals of direction. But they too are susceptible to satirical exploitation.

Moving on to the counter-attack, the position of Port-Royal is challenged in the reply to the thirteenth letter:

Si vous ne le croyez pas [qu'il y a des opinions probables], vous allez contre le sens commun. Car s'il est vrai, comme dit le Philosophe [= Aristotle], qu'il n'y a point de science où il y ait plus de probabilité et moins d'évidence que dans la morale, n'est-il pas absurde d'y penser trouver ce qui n'y est pas? (*RLP* 263)

Furthermore the refusal of any role for reasoning in such matters is said by the Jesuits to be held in common by Port-Royal and the

[10] This question is studied in A. Baird, *Studies in Pascal's Ethics* (The Hague, 1975), esp. ch. 2.

Calvinists, and Saint-Cyran is quoted as writing (to the abbé de Prières) that 'St. Thomas même avait ravagé la vraie théologie par le raisonnement humain, et les principes d'Aristote' (*XXIVᵉ Imposture, RLP* 128). The theory of 'opinions probables' is also turned ironically back against the writer of the *LPs*: in the *XXIᵉ Avertissement*, it is suggested that the definition of 'opinions probables' should perhaps have been extended to include heresies (*RLP* 106); and in the following one, the idea is developed thus: 'Faites réflexion sur les auteurs de votre secte, et voyez si un docteur particulier peut en conscience s'attacher opiniâtrement à son sentiment, quand il est condamné d'hérésie par le Pape et par les Evêques' (*RLP* 113).

The terms of reference of casuistry pertain most convincingly therefore within a framework of relativism, a framework in other words where Christian imperatives are assimilated to natural ideas of acceptable behaviour. So Pascal brings the methodology of casuistry to bear in precisely the arena of debate where its mode of functioning offends human nature, by shocking the very 'sens commun' to which it should appeal; he illustrates a system nominally answerable to grace, but in fact more 'natural' than nature, and so against nature. The Jesuits of the letters are endowed with a self-subverting ethical code in which nature defeats its own claims, by applying them *ad absurdum*.

The way in which the extreme cases are introduced is easy to identify in such phrases as: 'Cela me parut si horrible, que j'eus peine à me retenir; mais, pour savoir le reste, je le laissai continuer ainsi' (vii. 124); 'mais pour voir jusqu'où irait une si damnable doctrine' (vii. 125); 'je me retins, afin de le laisser aller jusqu'au bout' (x. 181); 'ne s'ensuit-il pas de là qu'on pourra... être sauvé sans avoir jamais aimé Dieu en sa vie?' (x. 187). Spirituality, although less fully treated, is handled in the same way in the satirical letters. On the question of 'dévotions aisées', the Jesuit is invited: 'Apprenez-m'en donc quelqu'une des plus faciles', introducing a section which concludes 'Voilà, mon Père... l'extrême facilité' (ix. 154–5). And again, in the later series, 'que s'ensuit-il de tout cela ensemble, sinon que nous avons une entière liberté de conscience' (xiii. 252); 'Voilà comment les opinions s'élèvent peu à peu jusqu'au comble de la probabilité' (xiii. 242). Such a

procedure furthermore, and vitally for the dynamic of his argument, exempts Pascal from attending to all the intervening (and
for the reader tiresome) detail. Just as the reader/interlocutor of
the *Pensées* is moving/moved towards a particular kind of self-
perception (to which a specific doctrine is applicable and from
which all others are debarred), so the casuist of the *LPs* is
moving/moved towards a particular set of ethical dilemmas, to
which a specific ethical code is applicable, and from which all
others are debarred. The polemicist indeed draws attention to his
use of *cas-limites* in an important passage in the thirteenth letter:
'C'est ainsi que vous faites croître peu à peu vos opinions. Si elles
paraissaient tout à coup dans leur dernier excès, elles causeraient
de l'horreur; mais ce progrès lent et insensible y accoutume
doucement les hommes, et en ôte le scandale' (xiii. 246). A further
point is added in the same letter (on the subject of two phrases
which, if taken together, are likely to be interpreted as authoriz-
ing homicide): 'il ne faut, pour votre condamnation, que ras-
sembler ces maximes que vous séparez pour votre justification'
(xiii. 252). It is in just these ways that the twin effects of
qualitative isolation and quantitative concentration are made to
throw into relief and falsify the limits of a system whose sense and
utility depend on context and gradation.

    The ethical system of the Jesuits of the *LPs* is thus defeated by
its hyperbolically expressed tolerance of abuses that even unre-
generate human nature would condemn. If the structures of
Christianity are a 'renversement' of the natural order of things,
the Jesuits overthrow that 'renversement' in a return to nature,
but then transgress the bounds of natural justice, and even, on
occasion, civil laws. (Thus, on the question of the duel, Montalte
exclaims: 'J'admirai sur ces passages de voir que la piété du roi
emploie sa puissance à défendre et à abolir le duel dans ses états, et
que la piété des Jésuites occupe leur subtilité à le permettre et à
l'autoriser dans l'Eglise' (vii. 121)). The process is represented
diagrammatically in Fig. 1, in which the divine and the natural
perspectives meet in *cas-limites*. It is therefore this appeal to
human nature, at the level of common sense, that is brought
devastatingly to bear in the letters, and by which the Jesuits are
isolated on their own territory. Two pertinent comments in the

Pensées also resume this evolution. The first shows how the apparently worldly is able to appear more unattractive than the apparently unworldly: 'Les opinions relâchées plaisent tant aux hommes qu'il est étrange que les leurs déplaisent. C'est qu'ils ont excédé toute borne' (L 692). And the second, albeit from a different angle, charts the Jesuits' failure to appeal to the two polarized value systems by the erection of a false synthesis: 'Les Jésuites ont voulu joindre Dieu au monde, et n'ont gagné que le mépris de Dieu et du monde. Car, du côté de la conscience, cela est évident; et, du côté du monde, ils ne sont pas de bons cabalistes' (L 989).

It is perhaps therefore worth pointing here to a further parallel with the *Pensées*, in support of the idea that the *LPs* would have shared with a part of the anticipated readership of the apology a *point de repère* in an appeal to common sense. In fragment L 427 the 'unnatural' non-seeker is held up to common sense for the same sort of ridicule as are the Jesuits: 'S'ils y pensaient sérieusement, ils verraient que cela est si mal pris, si contraire au bon sens, si opposé à l'honnêteté, et si éloigné en toutes manières de ce bon air qu'ils cherchent, qu'ils seraient plutôt capables de redresser que de corrompre ceux qui auraient quelque inclination à les suivre.' Or, more snappily, 'Si vous continuez à discourir de la sorte... en vérité vous me convertirez' (L 427, and cf. L 428: 'La

divine perspective/simplicity of Gospel

|

Christian imperatives,
'contre nature'

|

human nature/common sense

|

Jesuit aberration, against natural and Christian values

|

anarchy/simplicity of disorder

FIG. 1

conduite des hommes est tout à fait déraisonnable, s'ils ne prennent une autre voie [que la négligence]'). The two works are united at this level, therefore, by what is 'raisonnable' (again in the broad sense of what is commonly and socially acceptable). It is 'raisonnable' for the non-believer to interest himself in Christianity; and good sense, as well as faith, will recognize the errors of the Jesuits.[11]

This coexistence of worldly common sense and orthodoxy also underlines two levels on which the *LPs* can be read, or rather on which an appeal is made to idealized readers. Such a union finds its most extreme expression in the third volume of *La Philosophie de Pascal* (*Pascal et la Casuistique*),[12] where Emile Baudin suggests an unexpected liaison: 'L'alliance des libertins et des jansénistes . . . réconcilia, contre la puissance des Jésuites d'abord, puis peu à peu contre l'autorité royale et contre l'autorité ecclésiastique, à mesure que celles-ci se montrèrent hostiles à Port-Royal, des esprits à doctrines et à tendances radicalement opposées.' He thus argues that the *LPs* are imbued with 'la morale mondaine'. Sellier too, if more moderately, suggests that, 'contrairement à ce qu'on serait tenté d'imaginer, il existe, au cours des années 1650, une véritable osmose entre le groupe de Port-Royal et les salons' (*IL* 334), and specific references do indeed periodically appear to 'mondain' opinion, not least in the intercalated reply to the second *LP*. Or, as the 'ami janséniste' points out to the Dominican of the second letter, 'Votre explication serait odieuse dans le monde; on y parle plus sincèrement des choses moins importantes' (ii. 33). So even if we do not necessarily want to draw Baudin's conclusion that '[les] intuitions morales [du libertin] sont encore les intuitions d'un cœur chrétien', it is still manifest that the early *LPs* are in large part addressed to, and accessible to, a society readership.

Yet Marc Fumaroli states: 'On parle toujours du public mondain des *Provinciales*. Il est certain que Pascal y a songé. Mais il s'adresse surtout, et avant tout, à ce public de chrétiens sévères, qui est de toute façon la plus grande garantie de Port-Royal'.[13]

---

[11] The extreme point at which common sense and orthodoxy meet is in the judgement of miracles, a topic to which we shall return in Ch. 12.

[12] E. Baudin, *Etudes historiques et critiques* (Neuchâtel, 1946–7), iii. 37, 69.

[13] M. Fumaroli, in *débat* following J. Morel, 'Pascal et la doctrine du rire grave', in *Méthodes chez Pascal*, p. 219.

Taking Fumaroli's point, we must therefore go further than Descotes, who considers that the reader can only identify with the 'ami provincial': 'La place du lecteur est donc bien définie, il doit s'identifier au Provincial. . . Le Provincial représente, comme par délégation, le lecteur à l'intérieur du texte'.[14] While not denying the great interest of his discussion of this function and of the role played in it by Montalte, it is nevertheless not the only possible focus of identity. Polemic aims to reinforce the conviction of sympathizers just as strongly as (or perhaps more strongly than) it aims to appeal to the uncommitted observer, as may be illustrated from the double function identified in the fictional reply to the second letter: 'elle [the second *LP*] instruit même ceux qui ne savent pas bien les choses; elle redouble le plaisir de ceux qui les entendent' ((ii). 37–8). The *LPs* thus carry throughout an overlapping and evolving appeal to orthodoxy/grace/sympathizers and to common sense/nature/uncommitted observers, and so to two categories of idealized reader which are, initially at least, strongly differentiated, but which converge gradually as the series progresses. These two groups are exemplified by the two 'amis' of the work, the 'ami janséniste' epitomizing the response at the level of the Christian imperative, the 'ami provincial' that of secular, but not necessarily unconcerned, common sense. (The 'mondain' aspect of this figure is evident in the tone of the reply to the second letter, but at the same time we must recall the initial assumption that he has been interested in the 'disputes présentes de la Sorbonne'.) Duchêne considers that the 'ami provincial' should remain a shadowy figure therefore: 'Il ne faut pas qu'il prenne trop d'importance. Comme il n'est là que pour symboliser le lecteur, il doit être suffisamment indifférencié pour que chacun puisse se projeter en lui' (*IL* 116), and it is certainly true that he must provide a broad focus. In his first edition, however, Duchêne proposes that 'à mesure que progresse leur publication, les *Provinciales* tendent à devenir une œuvre pour initiés'.[15] This apparent conflict must presumably be resolved by the assumption that there is some development in the

---

[14] 'Fonction argumentative', p. 47.
[15] This remark only occurs in the 1st edn. of Duchêne's study (Paris, 1984). It is altered in the 2nd.

position of the 'ami provincial', and thus of the idealized reader he symbolizes, a development towards the acknowledgment of Jansenist orthodoxy that begins as soon as the pun on 'prochain' has been made. The 'ami provincial' moves therefore from a position of secular indifference or marginal curiosity to one of rigid (Jansenist) conviction. At no stage is he allowed to represent an intermediate identification with a more subtle intra-Christian position, an option that is indeed excluded throughout the series, for obvious polemical reasons, since it substantially describes the Jesuit constituency. Thus, although there are two ideal focuses, the evolution of the 'ami provincial' increasingly brings them together, so that by the eleventh letter they have become identical. It is fitting that the fictional epistolary 'destinataire' should disappear at this point.

The committed reader, on the other hand, is not initially given a focus of identification; and yet he is accorded a privileged insight into the rapidly emerging self-awareness with which the irony functions and into the gradual vindication of the 'ami janséniste', once he has made his appearance in the second letter. So from two divergent starting-points, a unity of focus is achieved; and in this way too the perspectives of Jansenist orthodoxy and common sense are brought together. There is of course a third friend, the 'bon casuiste de la Société... une de mes anciennes connaissances [... qui] m'aime toujours' (v. 79). But any potential for an associative focus in this case is very short-lived; the putative sympathetic reader is increasingly forced to identify with an outrageous, and furthermore a losing, point of view, and so rapidly withdraws or transfers his allegiance.

Two distinctions must be made in conclusion. First, to recognise the distinction in fictional status between the 'ami provincial', as recipient of the letters, and the other 'amis', who simply contribute internally to the dialogues. The 'ami janséniste' and the 'ami jésuite' are intra-epistolary (just as they are intra-ecclesial). The 'ami provincial' is, in both respects, outside, and therefore uniquely combines the functions of idealized reader *and* fictional recipient.[16] The second distinction is between the ideal-

[16] It is perhaps worth pointing here to evidence for the role of an epistolary friendship in the *Pensées*, as seen in such fragments as L 5: 'Une lettre d'exhortation à un ami pour le porter à chercher'. See also Parish, 'Mais qui parle?', p. 38.

ized readers, represented by the sympathetic 'amis', and the unknown empirical reader. It is this distinction that allows for the persistence of a double appeal after the fusion of the two perspectives within the 'ami provincial'. Thus in the fourteenth letter, when this has occurred, we still find the doubling of '[les] sentiments de l'Eglise, et même de la nature' and 'les principes les plus simples de la religion et du sens commun' (xiv. 255–6), recognizing both the idealized unification of perspectives and the potential need to maintain one emphasis against the other in specific readers.

In these various ways, therefore, different categories of reader are acknowledged at different stages of the work. Some readers will already be convinced of the rightness of the Jansenist cause and stand within the most rigorous confines of evangelic orthodoxy; some will, throughout the series, only be willing to offer a critique at the level of the outsiders whose sense of natural justice is offended—these might be described as the privileged empirical readers; but the ideal response of the uncommitted reader remains that of the 'ami provincial' who, whatever his position so far, is to reject this abuse of compromise in the name of nature, and to concede in theological terms the role of the absolute. The reader whose focus of identification is parodied out of existence is the one that stands within, asking difficult moral questions. In this way the effect is achieved of which Marsha Reisler writes: 'Pascal draws the [idealized/'ami provincial'] reader quite irresistably towards the side advocated by the author [Montalte]' because of the 'premise. . . that the reader shares with him a universal ideal of moderation, clarity, simplicity and nature'. Thus, 'through a clever manipulation of his data, Pascal manages to align his enemies with heresy and irrationality, and the Jansenists with faith and reason'.[17] In this way, too, the *Provinciales* are the story of a conversion.[18]

---

[17] Reisler, 'Persuasion through Antithesis', pp. 173 and 181.
[18] I am inclined to stress this function with reference to the 'ami provincial', in his status as idealized reader, over and above the parallel conversion of Montalte (cf. *IL* 192).

5

The Counter-polemic: Defence

IF certain of the values to which an appeal is made, notably orthodoxy and common sense, are shared by the two polemics, the fundamental points of divergence between the two parties lie in the kinds of area in which this appeal is exploited.

The Jesuits have in fact to fight two battles, one in response to the accusations levelled against them over the 'morale relâchée'; and the other in order to try to steer the debate back onto the question of Arnauld's orthodoxy (and that of Port-Royal) with which it had started. Their most effective way of fighting on both fronts at once will be by reiterating the charge of heresy against Port-Royal, and identifying as characteristic of heretical behaviour the excessive desire to reform morals. They will thereby keep in focus the original charge, which Pascal has displaced from the centre of the dispute, and emphasize the doctrinal fundamentals (or the Society's *question de droit*) asserted against the teachings of Jansenius and his disciples; and they will strengthen their own position by associating their penitential practices with the enduring teaching of the Church. Many replies were however more narrowly defensive, and it is to these that we turn first.

As Jan Miel points out,[1] and as Duchêne develops in considerable detail (*IL* 128 ff.), Pascal is vulgarizing specialist material:

The permission to perform[2] these pernicious deeds was not proclaimed by the Jesuits to the general public, but distributed to 'directeurs de conscience' for use in difficult individual cases . . . Pascal, in discovering the Jesuits' intentions to the general public, also altered them in a way that the sincere theologians in the Company must have found not only unfair but most unfortunate for the faithful.

---

[1] J. Miel, *Pascal and Theology* (Baltimore and London, 1969), 140.
[2] 'Permission to perform' is in the context a misleading phrase; 'provision for the absolution of' would perhaps reflect more accurately the aims of the Society.

Thus the full title, for example, of Bauny's *Somme des péchés* is: *Somme des péchés qui se commettent en tous états; de leurs conditions et qualités, en quelles occurrences ils sont mortels ou véniels, et en quelle façon le confesseur doit interroger son pénitent.* This charge of vulgarization is in fact the second made in the *Première Réponse* (following on from the accusation of changing ground). The Jesuit works at issue 'ne sont connus que des savants et des docteurs' (*RLP* ix–x),[3] whereas Montalte 'les assemble en un lieu, les expose aux yeux des ignorants, et en langue vulgaire, et à des personnes qui ne peuvent discerner le faux d'avec le vrai, l'utile d'avec le dommageable, le recevable d'avec ce qui ne l'est pas' (*RLP* x). Montalte's denial of any status as doctor or theologian is therefore taken up repeatedly, and he will later be accused, by combating 'des opinions reçues dans l'Ecole, et approuvées par les plus célèbres docteurs', of giving 'une marque visible... de son ignorance et de la faiblesse de son esprit, qui s'égare du sens commun, et ne sait pas former un solide jugement sur les différends qui naissent parmi les savants' (*RLP* 91). This is also illustrated in the *Xe Imposture* ('le droit des parents à garder la pudicité de leurs filles'): 'Jugez par là de l'ignorance de ce calomniateur, qui rapporte cette question comme une question extraordinaire, quoiqu'il n'y ait rien de plus commun dans l'Ecole' (*RLP* 53).

Morel for his part makes the charge that Montalte's expression of shock comes from the fact that he is not of the profession (just as a man who blanches at the sight of a sword or at the sound of a canon is not a soldier), and thus is too susceptible: 'Les difficultés à l'égard des consciences, dont l'Ecole retentit tout le jour, vous impriment des terreurs paniques' (p. 3).[4] (And Duchêne also notes: 'le scandale saute aux yeux du mondain alors qu'il échappe au théologien' (*IL* 167).) Morel then charges him with a lack of the caution that would be expected of a theologian: 'La théologie a ses formes, et son style, dont il ne paraît aucune trace dans vos Lettres' (p. 5), and later adds: 'Vous y traitez des choses de la

---

[3] *Première Réponse aux Lettres que les Jansénistes publient contre les Jésuites (Pères de la Compagnie de Jésus* in *RLP*). See Appendix I. vii and Appendix II.
[4] *Réponse générale à l'auteur des lettres qui se publient depuis quelque temps contre la doctrine des jésuites.* See Appendix I. xix.

conscience, comme si vous interprétiez Esope' (pp. 39–40). The idea of professionalism also recurs elsewhere in Morel's piece on the specific question of 'opinions probables'. Since, for example, 'un malade s'abandonne entièrement à son médecin', 'pourquoi donc à proportion n'aurai-je pas créance à un homme de savoir et de probité?' (p. 47). He goes on:

S'il n'y a point d'imprudence à se tenir aux sentiments d'un avocat, d'un médecin, et d'un architecte, parce qu'il est raisonnable de croire des hommes qui sont habiles en leur métier... ce ne sera pas aussi une chose répugnante à la prudence chrétienne d'embrasser les avis d'un docteur plein d'intelligence et de piété, et à qui l'Eglise confie le soin de nous instruire. (p. 48)

Morel also introduces a jibe on the strength of a Latin quotation: 'c'est le seul mot latin que je mettrai en ce discours, puisque vous professez de n'être pas docteur' (p. 10), but in fact gives a further two Latin quotations, and in the context of the last, seems to have modified his scorn somewhat, conceding that 'je sais bien que la langue française n'est pas l'unique que vous savez [*sic*]' (p. 64) (or could this rather be a suggestion that he is more familiar with the languages spoken by heretics, such as English or Dutch?) And the question of Latin is also taken up in the *VIe Avertissement*: 'C'était une action de sagesse à St. Thomas et à St. Antonin d'écrire en une langue qui n'est pas connue au peuple ces décisions que vous appellez extravagantes; mais c'est une horrible malice à vous de les avoir publiées en des termes vulgaires' (*RLP* 29).

This observation opens up again the vital distinction between the clerical/scholastic 'doctrine de l'Ecole' and the lay/patristic 'doctrine de la foi', a further example of which would be found in the detail of the reply to the tenth letter, on the question of whether the love of God is necessary for salvation. Sirmond, on whose *Défense de la Vertu* (1641) the dispute centres, is here, according to the writer of the *XXVIIIe Imposture* which deals with the accusation, '[chicané] sur une proposition conditionnée et mal entendue, qui ne ruine pas le grand commandement de Dieu' (*RLP* 159). This gives rise in due course to the question: 'Pourquoi le quereller sur une subtilité qui n'a lieu que dans les disputes de l'Ecole, et dont le peuple n'est nullement capable?' (*RLP* 161). The writer then goes on to specify the distinction

between 'nécessité de moyen' and 'nécessité de précepte', show
its origins in that between two types of love ('l'un effectif, l'autre
affectif' (*RLP* 161–2)), and attribute this to St Bernard, with the
question: 'Pourquoi sont-elles [paroles] saintes dans les écrits de
St. Bernard, et criminelles dans le livre du Père Sirmond?' (*RLP*
162).[5] As Jean Mesnard remarks, concluding the *débat* in *IL* (385):

Il y a deux formes susceptibles d'exprimer les idées religieuses, une
forme qu'on peut appeler plutôt philosophique et une forme que l'on
appellera plutôt littéraire. La forme philosophique ou technique ou
savante, c'est celle de Saint Thomas d'Aquin, celle des thomistes, celle
des scholastiques... Et il y a une forme d'expression que j'ai appelée
littéraire, qui est destinée à l'homme en général, à l'homme qui est
homme, considéré d'abord comme homme — c'est celle de l'Evangile,
de la Bible en général, des Pères de l'Eglise.

Although Mesnard gives examples of both tendencies in both
parties, the primary stylistic affiliation seems to be the one I have
suggested, at least within the context of the dispute. The *LPs*
appeal to a lay understanding, far less attached to the clerical
establishment than to secular enthusiasm; and they root that
understanding in patristic and Scriptural authority. From both
these angles, then, scholastic professionalism has been attacked.
And, in reply, the Jesuits take up the amateurism of Pascal in
particular, hesitating, for the time being, to challenge too
aggressively the patristic emphasis.

The need then to introduce the framework of judgement
within which the Jesuit (and other) moral writings are intended to
be read is paramount in the counter-polemic. The claim is made
in the *Première Réponse* that:

L'auteur falsifie la plupart des lieux qu'il allègue, et ment souvent avec
effronterie et impudence; il fait dire aux auteurs ce qu'ils n'ont jamais dit;
il tronçonne et mutile les passages, et ne les produit pas entiers, afin

---

[5] Baudin explains the difference between these two types of love as between
'affectif', being 'l'amour de cœur' and 'effectif', 'l'amour dont témoigne l'obéiss-
ance aux commandements de Dieu'. He goes on: 'Les jansénistes reprochaient au
P. Sirmond de tenir pour suffisant l'amour effectif, et de réduire, selon le mot de
Pascal, le précepte de l'amour de Dieu à une "dispense d'aimer Dieu"'. Baudin
also points out that this view was 'l'opinion particulière du P. Sirmond,
combattue et réfutée par la grande majorité des jésuites' (*Etudes historiques et
critiques*, II. i. 23 n. 1).

qu'on n'en connaisse pas le sens; il omet à dessein les modifications et les limitations qu'ils apportent, pour les rendre ridicules ou monstrueux dans leurs sentiments; il s'imagine, qu'ayant cité les endroits, coté les livres, et écrit quelques mots de l'auteur, on lui ajoutera foi, bien que l'auteur de la *Théologie Morale* [Arnauld] ait été convaincu de fausseté en la plupart de ses allégations. (*RLP* xiv–xv)

It is then illustrated thus in the *IXe Imposture* ('Que les Jésuites excusent ceux qui cherchent les occasions de pécher'):

Pour rendre cette doctrine criminelle, il l'explique indifféremment de toutes sortes d'occasions, comme si ces auteurs estimaient que chacun pût, pour des considérations légères, se jeter dans le péril d'offenser Dieu; au lieu que Basile Ponce ne parle que des cas extraordinaires, où il s'agit de l'intérêt de l'Etat ou de la religion. (*RLP* 44)

Equally in the matter of homicide (*XIVe Imposture*) the Jesuit case is addressed to the circumstances 'où l'on se trouve dans la nécessité de périr, ou de tuer celui qui nous attaque injustement' (*RLP* 72), and not to other conditions. And at the end of this series, in the XVIIIe *Imposture*, Pascal is shown to omit the vital phrase: 'Ce cas est si rare, qu'il n'arrive presque jamais' (*RLP* 82). We shall shortly return to such points.

The format of much of the counter-polemic also supports the insistence that the context has been improperly vulgarized, by its careful provision of substantial sections of original Latin texts (accompanied by translations) for all disputed quotations, with their precise identification. Cognet makes the point that both Arnauld and Nicole are also much more precise: 'C'est dans l'ensemble une méthode de techniciens; tandis que celle de Pascal est beaucoup plus celle d'un publiciste' (Cognet, p. xli). No doubt this tendency has also contributed to the relative obscurity of the counter-polemicists against the popularity of their adversary, but it is fundamental to the serious, detailed, and relatively complex academic approach which the Society and its advocates were bound to adopt—both in the face of real life dilemmas and *cas-limite* simplifications in terms of 'fond', and in the face of frivolity in terms of 'forme'. It is perhaps surprising that Cognet should insist, apropos of the writings attributed to Nouet, that:

On peut regretter qu'il se soit fourvoyé dans cette galère, car il fera dériver les réponses aux *Provinciales* sur un terrain qu'il eût mieux valu éviter, celui des discussions sur le détail des textes, au lieu de passer sur un plan plus vrai et plus vaste, celui de la valeur de la Compagnie de Jésus et son action. Il y eut là une grave erreur. (Cognet, p. lii)

It is difficult to see how the material could have lent itself to another sort of defence. As I have argued, Pascal's capacity for making readable argument out of his material is distinctly, but also pre-emptively superior to that of his Jesuit adversaries, an advantage of which he shows himself aware in the abridged quotation from St Augustine in the eleventh letter: 'Qui oserait dire que la vérité doit demeurer désarmée contre le mensonge, et qu'il sera permis aux ennemis de la foi d'effrayer les fidèles par des paroles fortes, et de les réjouir par des rencontres d'esprit agréables; mais que les catholiques ne doivent écrire qu'avec une froideur de style qui endorme les lecteurs?' (xi. 201). Or, as Descotes puts it: 'Pascal avait préparé méthodiquement sa stratégie; ses adversaires, réduits à la défensive, ont improvisé tant bien que mal' (*IL* 362). Yet what is important in their case, on the other hand, is both the accuracy of the detail and the existence of the detail. Thus the Jesuits, for their defence, had to move the debate into the very considerations excluded by Pascal, in order to show the kind of apparatus required for the elaboration of a moral theology and by the direction of conscience, and to illustrate it by providing a small additional amount of the context from which Pascal's satirical material was taken. They had to undo his work of hostile vulgarization, but in so doing necessarily also lessened their own appeal.

Pascal then, to take up Marandé's distinction again, is concerned to make everything into a debate on 'doctrine de la foi'; the Society of Jesus on 'doctrine de l'Ecole'. If Pascal can thus argue in broad, grandiose terms, the Jesuits must challenge them. By far the largest amount of defensive material used against the *LPs* attends therefore to their alleged inaccuracy and deformation of arguments and it is obliged to do so painstakingly and specifically. Cognet, in his notes, is an invaluable guide to the exact degree of alteration for which Pascal was responsible: it is perhaps also worth noticing that, as he shows, Nicole remedied the tendency, to some extent, in his Latin edition of the *LPs*.[6] However, there is no doubt that the burden of accusation in the counter-polemic is correct in so far as the kinds of alteration are concerned, as Cognet's footnotes bear out. It is perhaps also worth mentioning the sheer quantity of Jesuit, and other, moral theology from which Pascal selects a few phrases—as the *Premier Ecrit des Curés* puts it: 'L'Eglise gémit aujourd'hui sous cette monstrueuse charge de volumes' (Cognet, p. 408). No informed reader can however avoid some feeling of disquiet at Pascal's advice to Annat in the eighteenth letter: 'Que ne preniez-vous la même voie que j'ai tenue dans mes lettres pour découvrir tant de mauvaises maximes de vos auteurs, qui est de citer fidèlement les lieux d'où elles sont tirées', and later: 'Voilà une manière bien facile et bien prompte de vider les questions de fait où l'on a raison' (xviii. 368). Pascal's approximations may perhaps better be summed up in the masterly understatement of Cognet: 'Citation absolument littérale, ce qui correspond peu aux habitudes de Pascal' (Cognet, p. 307 n. 4). As Duchêne rather astutely summarizes: 'On a condamné Arnauld sur des phrases qu'on a détournées de leur sens; on a condamné les casuistes sur des phrases qu'on a détournées de leur sens' (*IL*, *débat*, p. 324).

In addition to the twenty-nine *Impostures* of the *RLP* (which deal with the first ten *LPs*), and even more methodical in its presentation, is the *Bonne Foi des Jansénistes* of Annat,[7] which challenges in the most precise terms seventeen questions included in the *LPs*, and which appeared shortly before the seventeenth *LP*. It will perhaps best serve therefore to illustrate the kind of evidence that most characteristically was being produced.

---

[6] This edn., published under the psuedonym of Wendrock, appeared in 1658. See Cognet, pp. lxxiii–lxxvii.

[7] *La Bonne Foi des Jansénistes en la citation des auteurs reconnue dans les lettres que le secrétaire de Port-Royal a fait courir depuis Pâques*. See Appendix I. xxi. The works to which reference is made are: Léonard Lessuis (Leys), *De justitia et jure caeterisque virtutibus cardinale* (Louvain, 1605; Paris 1606), and Thomas Sanchez, *Opus morale in praecepta decalogi* (Madrid, 1613; Lyons, 1615). See C. Sommer-vogel, *Bibliothèque de la Compagnie de Jésus*, iv. 1729. 5, and vii. 534. 2. I have not been able to trace the work mentioned by Cognet (p. 118) and attributed to Lessius, the *De justitia et jure actionum humanarum*. It would appear to be a confusion of two titles. The few references to Layman make no particular additional points. References to Sanchez and Lessius in roman numerals are to the respective parts of the works quoted.

The accusations throughout centre on all kinds of inaccuracy, but most consistently mistranslation, misquotation (material added, omitted, falsely attributed), or disparate quotations randomly made into a sequence or used in isolation without their context (what Duchêne calls 'bricolage' (see *IL* 160 ff.)). It would be laborious to illustrate all these tendencies exhaustively, but it is easy enough to demonstrate something of each one. The writer says in his *Préface au Lecteur*, referring to Pascal, as he does throughout, as 'Le Secrétaire du Port-Royal': 'il est visible que ce Secrétaire a joué sa réputation, exposant son crédit au hasard d'une vérification où la conviction de son infidélité est inévitable'. He has not, he explains, checked all quotations (he has only looked at references to Lessius, Sanchez, and Layman), but is sure that 'cet échantillon suffit pour former le jugement que mérite toute la pièce' (p. vii). Some examples follow.

Mistranslation. Sanchez I (*LP* v): Pascal translates 'in re morali dubia' as 'dans un doute de morale' instead of 'dans les choses morales qui sont douteuses', thus extending the context (p. 21).

Lessius II (*LP* vii): Pascal translates 'in quibus videtur concessa defensio' as 'la défense paraît très juste' instead of 'qu'il semble que la défense est permise', thus altering the emphasis (p. 5).

Adding material. Lessius II (*LP* viii): Pascal adds 'ex sententia omnium' to make a view seem corporately rather than individually held (p. 4). Lessius II (*LP* viii): Pascal adds colour and emphasis by specifying, or rather inventing, 'mauvaises actions', instead of leaving the term general (p. 13).

Omitting material. Lessius II (*LP* vii): Lessius specifies 'qu'il est permis de tuer un *larron*' (to defend one's property); Pascal omits to do so (p. 8). Indeed, if he had looked harder, and wished to be accurate, 'il eût trouvé toutes les précautions qu'on peut souhaiter pour empêcher le mauvais usage de ce droit de défense' and in particular 'pour faire appréhender aux ecclésiastiques et aux religieux ce qui est de plus grande perfection et plus convenable à leur état' (p. 9).

Lessius II (*LP* viii): Lessius specifies that in certain circumstances ('de maladie, de faim, de nudité'), and if 'celui qui est dans la nécessité n'a point d'autre moyen d'y pourvoir', he can steal from the wealthy, 'ab opulentis'; Pascal omits all qualifications (p. 11).

Sanchez I (*LP* v): Pascal again omits the caution, and definition, that for an opinion to be probable, 'il faut *qu'on tienne communément qu'elle ne contient point d'erreur, et qu'elle ne soit point décréditée*' (p. 22).

Lessius II (*LP* viii): '[Pascal] a dissimulé toutes les raisons que Lessius a proposées pour dissuader l'usage du Mohatra, et pour faire appréhender le danger d'offenser Dieu pour ceux qui s'en servent' (p. 10). In the most extreme cases such omission conveys precisely the opposite intention to that contained in the terms of the original passage. One such example would be the conclusion of Sanchez's advice on the duel, which Annat gives as follows:

Sanchez II (*LP* vii): 'Sanchez nie *qu'on puisse accepter le duel pour défendre sa vie . . .* Sanchez enseigne *que le prétexte de l'honneur ou de l'infamie* qu'on appréhende si on refuse le duel est un vain prétexte, et que c'est *un péché mortel* d'accepter pour cela le duel' (p. 26).

False attribution. This takes two forms: first of all there is the attribution to a cited authority of words that are Pascal's, simply by the extension of italicization, so giving to understand Pascal's interpretation of a view as being its unadapted quotation; thus in Sanchez II (*LP* viii) 'il met en Latin et lettres italiques, comme si c'étaient paroles de Sanchez, *si sit artis diabolicae ignarus*, paroles qui ne se trouvent point dans le texte de Sanchez' (p. 29); and secondly the attribution to one Jesuit of what is in fact the view of one or more other authorities, Jesuit and non-Jesuit, thus Lessius II (*LP* vii), where Lessius is quoting Victoria (pp. 2–3); or Lessius II (*LP* vii), where the opinion of Popes, Saints, and Doctors would support that of Lessius (p. 8).

Change of emphasis. Lessius II (*LP* viii): Lessius speaks of an 'opinion probable'; Pascal transcribes: 'il l'assure' (pp. 10–11).

Lessius IV (*LP* vii): Lessius accepts the right 'que Dieu et la nature donnent à un chacun de se défendre' but rejects the use of the maxim 'qu'il est loisible de tuer les faux accusateurs';

Pascal claims that Lessius defends 'l'usage de la maxime' (pp. 6–7).

Composed quotation. Lessius II (*LP* viii): Pascal uses 'une composition des paroles de Lessius éparses çà et là, et des siennes qu'il ajoute' (p. 13); and the same accusation is made in more detail in Sanchez III (*LP* ix) (p. 33).

Duchêne also treats certain of these tendencies, notably omission, change of emphasis, and composed quotation (*IL* 174–8). To these he would add what he calls 'grossissement' (*IL* 162), because of the change in scale of the context: 'D'origine et d'esprit juridique, la casuistique série et sépare les faits pour les apprécier un à un. Pascal place quelques décisions choisies dans un discours continu qui les dénature' (*IL* 163).

If we turn to other counter-polemical writing, we find that Pirot too draws attention to the contextual nature of Jesuit moral teaching by reference particularly to its practical dimension; Scripture and the Fathers cannot always be taken literally, and some rule of thumb must prevail in cases of moral ambiguity. Pirot is however distinguished from the *RLP* by his emphasis less on the inaccuracy of Pascal than on the justifiability of the casuists. Cognet writes of the *Apologie pour les Casuistes*: 'Sur d'autres [points], et parmi les plus importants, elle admettait pleinement le sens incriminé par Pascal et revendiquait hautement la légitimité de certaines solutions des plus scabreuses formulées par les Casuistes : c'était le cas, en particulier, de propositions particulièrement discutables sur l'homicide' (Cognet, p. lxvi). And in the first *Ecrit des Curés*, which is a direct reply to it, we find: 'On soutient dans ce livre les plus abominables propositions des casuistes . . . On ne s'y défend plus comme autrefois, en disant que ce sont des propositions qu'on leur impute' (Cognet, p. 411). Finally Descotes resumes the two kinds of response as (*i*) that of Annat and Nouet, '[qui] consistait à récuser les attaques de Montalte, en affirmant que les propositions de morale relâchée qu'il citait ne se trouvaient pas effectivement dans les ouvrages des casuistes, et que la Compagnie n'avait jamais approuvé de telles maximes' and (*ii*) that of Pirot, 'd'accepter certaines accusations de Montalte, de revendiquer les propositions citées, mais en affirmant . . . qu'elles étaient conformes à la morale chrétienne'.[8]

It is Pirot who provides the greatest amount of exemplary evidence, showing thereby the vast size of the iceberg of which Pascal exposes the tip (and perhaps also thereby giving some idea of the fastidiousness of manuals of moral theology). He mentions, for example, that Sanchez, in his *De Matrimonio*, examines around 480 disputes (p. 143), and thus quotes a lot of very ordinary problems, which he scrutinizes in the light of Pascal's absolutist moral standpoint (just as Pascal scrutinizes absolute problems in the light of a relative moral standpoint). For instance, in the section replying to the objection 'que les serviteurs et servantes peuvent rendre à leurs maîtres et maîtresses des services qui sont d'eux-mêmes indifférents, quoiqu'ils sachent que les maîtres et maîtresses les exigent pour une mauvaise fin' (p. 50), he cites: 'Les cochers . . . et les porteurs de chaises seraient tenus de quitter leurs maîtres, lorsqu'ils les conduisent en des lieux où ils pèchent' (p. 51). As Duchêne writes: 'Ce qui apparaît chez Pascal comme une méthode destinée à tout permettre n'est qu'une permission de respecter les bienséances définies par le temps, le lieu et le sexe' (*IL* 156). Pirot also accuses Pascal of choosing tiresome details and improbable cases: 'je vois clairement en toutes les lettres de ce Secrétaire, qu'il se montre peu judicieux en toutes matières' (p. 53). Elsewhere on the question of hearing a part of four masses to fulfil one obligation, he objects (having suggested that it would in fact probably take longer to do so!) that 'Escobar avait assez de questions d'importance à traiter, sans s'amuser à ces cas inutiles' (p. 154).

Indeed the whole tone of Pirot's writing is discursive and hostile to simplification; he tackles issues as problems capable, in some cases, of only partial solutions, rather than as questions permitting of a correct answer. Morel too desimplifies on the question of 'opinions probables' thus: 'La probabilité d'une opinion... se prend ou de quelque raison considérable, ou de la conformité des sentiments de quelques bons esprits.' Pascal can therefore say of an 'opinion probable' that 'l'opinion contraire

---

[8] Descotes, 'Fonction argumentative', p. 59.

paraît plus sûre, et plus séante à l'exacte piété' (p. 4), but he should not condemn it out of hand for that reason. Morel is here entering into yet another kind of detail (circumspection), though still one entirely at odds with Pascal's satirical vulgarization. The strongest argument is found in the long *Préface au Lecteur* which precedes the *Bonne Foi des Jansénistes*, where it is deemed characteristic of heretics to challenge the Church's moral teaching, a central facet, as I have suggested, of any Jesuit counter-polemic, combining as it does moral defence with doctrinal attack: thus Tertullian, having fallen into error, 's'imagina que la morale de l'Eglise s'était relâchée, écrivant contre les Catholiques, comme contre des hommes *sensuels et matériels*' (p. iv).[9] Annat goes on to assert: 'On trouvera presque dans tous les hérétiques des rigueurs affectées en la morale et en la discipline de l'Eglise' (p. iv). A related point made here contains the implication that the Jesuits are held exclusively responsible for views that are not in fact exclusively held by them. Annat thus fails deliberately to distinguish between 'morale des Jésuites' and 'morale des Catholiques', the Jesuits 'n'ayant aucune opinion importante... qui ne trouve des auteurs dans toutes ces Ecoles [Sorbonnistes, Thomistes, Scotistes, Théatins]' (p. vi). He then speculates that the ultimate attack of the Jansenists will be on Thomas Aquinas: 'On voit bien que c'est là où ils veulent aller. Mais nous les arrêterons devant qu'ils y arrivent' (p. vi). Indeed the whole debate, as Pirot also points out in the *Apologie des Casuistes*, could be expressed in terms of the disciples of Augustine against those of Thomas Aquinas. And Baudin too, characteristically, develops this hypothesis: 'C'est finalement et principalement à saint Thomas qu'il [Pascal] en a sans le savoir; c'est saint Thomas qu'il contredit le plus hautainement, aussi bien dans les *Provinciales* que dans les *Pensées*'.[10] (Much of the argument in this part of Baudin's work centres on Pascal's alleged anti-thomism.) It is however worth noting how often St Thomas, 'l'Ange de l'Ecole' is saliently coupled with St Augustine, 'le Docteur de la Grâce', by

---

[9] The pagination is in fact in arabic numerals, which are also used (beginning again at 1) for the text. In order to simplify reference, I have used roman numerals to indicate quotations from the *Préface*.

[10] Baudin, *Etudes historiques et critiques*, II. i. 123.

Pascal in his profession of orthodoxy in the eighteenth letter
(e.g. xviii. 360, 367, 375).[11]

Returning to the *RLP* we find here too that the identification
of a tendency to attribute too exclusively to the Society of Jesus
occurs already in the *Première Réponse*: 'l'on attribue aux Jésuites
des opinions et des sentiments, comme s'ils en étaient les premiers
auteurs ou les seuls défenseurs... l'on appelle opinions et maximes des Jésuites ce qui a été enseigné par d'autres que par eux'
(*RLP* xx). Complementing this, though to the detriment of the
broader argument, it is claimed that Pascal 'souvent attribue à
tout le corps des Jésuites ce qu'aucun d'eux n'aura dit, ou ce qui
aura échappé à un seul de leur Compagnie, quoique les autres
aient écrit le contraire'; 'qui a jamais vu', the writer goes on to ask,
'que d'un particulier l'on conclue l'universel?' (*RLP* xviii). And
Descotes makes the point (*IL* 350) that 'C'est un reproche
constamment répété... que l'auteur des *Provinciales* a eu tort de
présenter les jésuites comme "un vaste corps dans lequel il n'y
avait nulle distinction à faire"'. These remarks are concluded in
the *RLP* by a summary of the objections:

L'auteur des *Lettres* ne reproche aucune maxime, décision, ou réponse
aux Jésuites, qui ne soit ou faussement alléguée par cet imposteur, ou
falsifiée et déguisée en partie, ou tellement séparée de son lieu, de ses
modifications et limitations, qu'elle n'est plus la même: et si elle est
enseignée par quelqu'un d'eux, qu'elle ne soit combattue par plusieurs
autres du même corps. (*RLP* xxi–xxii)

Much play is therefore made of the conformity between Jesuit
moral teaching and the continuing tradition of the Church.
Indeed the Jesuits throughout the counter-polemic see themselves as singled out for abuse, and are at pains to show that they
have the support of the Church as an argument in favour of their
position and teaching. The authorities most commonly quoted in
justification of the Society in the *Impostures* are St Antoninus, St
Thomas Aquinas, and St Ambrose, as well as non-Jesuit writers

[11] P. Sellier remarks (*Pascal et saint Augustin* (Paris, 1970), 338): 'Cet accord de
saint Augustin et de saint Thomas sur de nombreux points est souligné de plus en
plus nettement dans les *Provinciales* et la formule "saint Augustin et saint
Thomas" constitue une sorte de refrain dans la *Dix-huitième Lettre*, où le
controversiste a précisé avec une extraordinaire rigueur la façon dont Dieu meut
efficacement le libre arbitre sans le violenter'.

(when an accusation is made specifically against the Jesuits) and other writers (when it is made against an individual). In other words, an attempt is made to broaden the spectrum of those implicated, suggesting a belief in numerical justification, but also challenging the isolated Jansenist voice with as great a representation of ecclesiastical authorities as is available. The fact that both parties should, albeit inexplicitly in the *LPs,* imply that the Jesuits are representative of the Church as a whole should not however conceal their entirely different motives: Pascal lets it be understood that the Church is gradually being corrupted thanks to the Society; the Society insists that its doctrines and practices are consonant with the Church's historic teaching. The indirect nature of the critique levelled at the Church in the *LPs* therefore allows the Society to use the reflection of its own doctrine in Roman orthodoxy as an argument against, rather than a point to be conceded to, the Jansenist position.

Finally, Augustine is from time to time ostentatiously quoted throughout the counter-polemic, and indeed one whole work of refutation is entirely devoted to evidence taken from him, the *Justification du Procédé des Catholiques contre les Jansénistes tirée de Saint-Augustin* (1656; not mentioned by Cognet). On the other hand Pascal quotes, as we have seen, St Thomas Aquinas in the eighteenth letter, and also, in the same piece, cites St Robert Bellarmine, a Jesuit, in support of his argument on the *question de fait* (Cognet, p. 343 n. 1).

The defensive Jesuit writing suffers overall from its diffuseness, from its complexity, and from the lack of any dynamic fictional elaboration. It may also seem inconsistent: in one sense, the combination of refutation on grounds of inaccuracy and justification on grounds of comprehensiveness is, to say the least, infelicitous; yet, in another, it is simply the result of two different sorts of defence of detail, one insisting on its quality, the other on its quantity. The juxtaposition of denials of corporate responsibility with protestations of ecclesiastical authority may also appear awkward. But, here again, it is by the defence of the historical status of a more speculative system that these statements are united. At the same time there will, predictably, be some more room for inventiveness in the attack.

6

The Counter-polemic: Attack

THE second purpose of the counter-polemic is naturally enough, alongside the material centred on the defence of the Jesuits, to attack Port-Royal. The background is laid out in the *Première Réponse* of the *RLP*, which speaks of how the 'premières Lettres défendent la doctrine de Jansénius, condamnée sous ce nom, du crime infâme d'hérésie, par le S. Père' and 'les suivantes attaquent les Jésuites, qu'ils blâment d'avoir été les premiers qui ont découvert et attaqué les intolérables erreurs qui composent le livre de Jansénius' (*RLP* iv). Revenge is identified as the principal motive of Pascal: 'Sous le prétexte d'attaquer la mauvaise morale des Jésuites, il se veut venger d'eux... de ce qu'ils ont combattu la doctrine de Jansénius, qui a été condamnée comme hérétique' (*RLP* xxiv), a theme which recurs in the *IVᵉ Avertissement*: 'Avouez la vérité, n'est-ce pas la honte que vous avez reçue, lorsque vos maîtres ont été condamnés d'hérésie...qui vous a porté violemment à la vengeance?' (*RLP* 19). Morel considers it also to be characteristic of heretics, 'au milieu même de nos victoires, de charger d'injures et d'opprobres ceux qui les attaquent généreusement, et qui les vainquent avec gloire' (p. 21), and attributes to Pascal the political aim that Pascal had attributed to the Society: 'Vous avez une politique, qui par des principes bruyants et pompeux veut mettre en crédit le Port-Royal et acquérir aux Jansénistes l'estime et la vénération de toute la France, et... pour cela vous faites mine de fuir les maximes tant soit peu relâchées, et d'embrasser toutes les sévères' (p. 49). The simple accusation against the Jansenists is therefore that they are heretics, expressed both in so many words, and by implication. As Annat writes in the *Préface au Lecteur* of *La Bonne Foi des Jansénistes*: 'Après leurs quinze Lettres il y avait de quoi se contenter quand nous n'eussions fait autre chose que dire quinze fois, *ce sont des hérétiques*' (p. iii). The Jesuits, on the other hand, are a byword for orthodoxy: 'comme l'on croit communément, qu'être des sentiments des Jésuites, c'est être orthodoxe' (*RLP* xi–xii)—a *sententia* which finds its polemical counterpoint in the simile: 'pour dire un impudent menteur, l'on dit qu'il ne l'est pas moins qu'un Janséniste', since 'le mensonge ne quitte jamais l'hérésie' (*RLP* xv). The accusation of heresy is characterized by two principal devices: first, by parallels of substance and approach with both ancient and modern heretics, and among the latter most frequently with the Protestant minister Du Moulin; and secondly, more particularly in the later *RLPs*, by a return to the discussion of both the original and related issues raised by the *Cinq Propositions* (and I will deal with the individual *Réponses*, which follow the *Impostures*, at a later stage). And of course these two perspectives are frequently brought together.

It is in the interests of the Jesuit case to bring out the doctrinally heretical dimensions of the argument. This is after all the basis of the initial condemnation, and therefore the ground on which Port-Royal (whatever its exact relationship with the *LPs*) is most susceptible to attack. Indeed, the *Préface* to the *Deuxième Réponse* proposes that the 'je ne me mets guère en peine' of the first letter already betokens that its writer 'reconnaît que Monsieur Arnauld est à la fin condamné comme téméraire par la Sorbonne' (and is thus legitimately suspected of heresy) (*RLP* xli).[1] Shortly afterwards, there occurs the accusation: 'Il n'a point de honte d'employer contre la grâce suffisante, qui est reçue de tous les fidèles, les chicaneries de Du Moulin, le plus impie sans contredit de tous les hérétiques de France' (*RLP* xlii). This theme is then developed in the second letter, entitled *Autre lettre du même auteur, sur la conformité des reproches et des calomnies que les Jansénistes publient contre les Pères de la Compagnie de Jésus avec celles que le ministre Du Moulin a publiées devant eux contre l'Eglise Romaine, dans son livre des*

---

[1] The accusation of 'témérité' is not, as is given to understand in the opening letter, simply a question of lack of respect or of due submission to authority. A contemporary definition (*Dictionnaire de l'Académie Française*, 1694) of 'téméraire' is: 'En matière de doctrine, et principalement en matière de morale et de théologie, on appelle *proposition téméraire* une proposition qui choque les principes de la doctrine reçue, une proposition dont on peut tirer de mauvaises inductions'.

Traditions, imprimé à Genève en l'année 1632. Parallels are systematically drawn between the two positions, and the effect enhanced by juxtaposing Pascal and the Protestant authorities, on the one hand, with the Jesuits, backed up by both patristic and scholastic traditions, on the other.

In the *Impostures* such accusations abound. The aim of the work is outlined as follows: 'La fin que je me propose est de montrer que le casuiste du Port-Royal, ayant emprunté ses reproches du Ministre de Charenton,... est tombé honteusement dans ses défauts' (*RLP* 3). The accusations are then enumerated, and defence and attack come together. He is charged with:

altérant le sens et les paroles des auteurs jésuites... condamnant sans jugement des opinions probables, que les plus savants théologiens enseignent dedans l'Ecole... attaquant avec une insolente témérité les maximes de la Foi, que l'Eglise tient pour constantes et indubitables... [et] se moquant avec impiété des pratiques familières de la dévotion, que l'on enseigne ordinairement au peuple, pour l'attirer peu à peu par la facilité de ces exercices spirituels à l'amour de la vertu et au soin de son salut. (*RLP* 3)

And a general comparison is found in the *IVe Imposture*: 'Ce que le Janséniste reproche à notre Compagnie, le Ministre Du Moulin l'a reproché devant lui à toute l'Eglise' (*RLP* 16), this, no doubt, because Pascal, described as 'ce Calviniste déguisé', 'n'a lu les anciens Pères que par les yeux de Calvin', and 'ne lit aussi les nouveaux casuistes que par les yeux du Ministre Du Moulin' (*VIe Imposture, RLP* 26). More aggressively again, an ironic point is scored at Pascal's expense in the *Avertissement* of the *XIe Imposture* ('que les Jésuites favorisent les duels'): 'La main de ce Secrétaire qui feint d'avoir tant de peur qu'on n'épanche le sang humain, ne craint-elle point de renouveler les hérésies, qui l'ont tiré avec inhumanité de toutes les veines de la France?' (*RLP* 57).

It is worth attending briefly to the comparison with Du Moulin. The work in question is entitled: *Des Traditions et de la perfection et suffisance de l'Ecriture Sainte... Avec un catalogue on dénombrement des traditions romaines*, and was first published in Sedan in 1631. It is divided into two parts, the first defending the supreme authority of Scripture against unwritten traditions, 'un menu fatras d'inventions humaines inventées pour le gain, et des artifices malicieux pour déprimer le peuple au dessous des Ecclésiastiques, et le retenir en ignorance' (p. 19). The second part is exclusively aggressive, beneath the superficial objectivity of an enumeration—superficial because the distinction between quotation (from a variety of sources of unequal authority) and comment/ interpretation remains in many cases ambiguous. The overall context, as well as the attitude to such matters as papal authority and eucharistic doctrine, is clearly quite distinct from that of the *Provinciales*, as is Du Moulin's emphasis on the sole authority of Scripture, against Pascal's appeal to the early Fathers, Popes, and Councils alongside it. But the underlying accusation that ancient and authentic material has been superseded by erroneous inventions is nevertheless a common one.

The first point to strike the reader in search of similarities is no doubt also the one which most accounts for the comparison being made in the first place: hostility to the Society of Jesus. Indeed, the work is also situated in the context of a polemical exchange, and a certain amount of attention in the first part is devoted to an attack on the work of a 'misérable jésuite', Alexandre Regourd (1585–1635), the *Démonstrations catholiques ou l'art de réunir les prétendus réformés…à la créance, et à la communion de l'Eglise Romaine. Avec les Impostures des Ministres singulièrement de Pierre Du Moulin et Jean Mestrezat* (Paris, 1630). Alongside various accusations is found the 'audace du Jésuite Regourd à dénigrer l'Ecriture' (p. 69). And Jesuit polemical tactics are also deplored in openly derogatory terms: 'Quelques menus brouillons de Jésuites, se sentant faibles à la rencontre, … se sont avisés d'une chicanerie importune, qui tend à accrocher la dispute dès l'entrée, et empêcher que jamais on ne vienne à l'examen de la doctrine. Leur usage est d'interroger toujours, au lieu d'argumenter' (p. 269).

It is more particularly in the second part however that we recognize familiar material, and some similarity of presentation; and where, among traditions condemned, we find most notably for our purposes the tolerance (or indeed encouragement) of moral and penitential laxity. Brief quotations to that effect are presented and identified, with none of the sustained satirical elaboration of Pascal (although there is an occasional sarcastic rejoinder), but in the same spirit. Jesuits are far from the only authorities cited, but of course in a Protestant work their standing alongside papal and conciliar statements in a general condemnation is unsurprising. The following offer striking parallels:

Celui qui tue quelqu'un par appétit de vengeance ne pèche point, quand cet appétit est si ardent qu'il n'est pas en sa puissance de le réprimer. *Tolet. de instruct. Sacerd. lib. 3. cap. 1. §5.* (p. 409)[2]

Un homme qui paillarde étant ivre, ne pèche point. (p. 410)

Un homme qui a ravi ou soustrait le bien d'autrui n'est pas obligé à le restituer, quand il ne le peut faire qu'avec son déshonneur. Car l'honneur vaut mieux que l'argent. (p. 417)

Celui n'est pas menteur qui supplée en son esprit quelque addition mentale sans laquelle il mentirait. (p. 420)

La loi de Dieu ne nous oblige point à charité. Et on peut accomplir la loi de Dieu sans charité. (p. 426)

Le jeûne n'est point violé pour boire du vin, ni pour manger quelque chose après avoir bu, de peur que le breuvage ne nuise à l'estomac. (p. 428)

Un homme qui a reçu dix sous pour chanter une messe, peut trouver un autre en sa place qui la chante pour cinq, et retenir pour soi les autres cinq. (p. 468)

Pour être absous de l'excommunication, il n'est pas nécessaire que le pécheur ait aucune contrition, ou veuille être absous. Car même on le peut absoudre malgré lui. (p. 502)

Un second confesseur, quoi qu'inférieur, peut pour cause raisonnable exempter un pécheur des pénitences imposées par un autre confesseur en les changeant en d'autres, combien que ce second confesseur ne sache pas quels sont les péchés pour lesquels ces pénitences lui ont été enjointes. (pp. 505–6)

On the other hand disobedience to traditions which are shown to be unfounded in Scripture carries a heavy penalty, thus: 'C'est un péché mortel de chanter messe sans chandelle : et pour cela un prêtre doit être déposé. Combien qu'il n'apparaisse pas que Jésus-Christ en ait eu lorsqu'il célébra le Saint Sacrement avec ses disciples' (p. 432). A further notable similarity then occurs in the

---

[2] I have not continued to give the exact identification of remaining passages; but each is followed by an equally precise reference.

attack on the teachings of the Church on grace. The three following maxims alleged to be traditions are thus implicitly condemned:

Dieu ne nous commande rien qui ne soit possible à notre franc arbitre. Dont s'ensuit que les païens peuvent accomplir la loi de Dieu. (p. 436)

Dieu donne à tous hommes une grâce suffisante, même à ceux qui n'ont jamais ouï parler de Jésus-Christ. (p. 436)

Il y a deux sortes de grâce de Dieu: l'une qui donne le pouvoir, mais ne donne pas le faire, qui est la grâce suffisante; l'autre qui donne le pouvoir et le faire, qui est la grâce efficacieuse. Dont s'ensuit que la grâce suffisante n'est pas suffisante, puis qu'elle n'a pas assez d'efficace, et que la grâce de pouvoir sans la grâce de faire ne suffit pas. (pp. 436–7)

Not only the tenor here, but also the use of play on words, are very close to those found in the first and second *LP*s. And finally we also notice familiar observations on the self-destructive power of untruth: 'C'est le propos du mensonge de dire et se dédire, et s'envelopper soi-même de contradiction' (p. 150).

A good deal of coincidental material is in evidence, therefore, and there is an indisputable temperamental affinity between the two works in the areas I have designated. At the same time, our partial view has substantially obscured the far more wide-ranging attack on major sacramental questions in the second part, and the stress on the primacy of scriptural authority in the first, which combine to give the work *in toto* an entirely distinct polemical status from Pascal's letters. Whatever the nature of the Jesuit accusations against Pascal, a consideration of an overtly Protestant argument serves rather to show those areas in which Pascal either remains silent or else vigorously asserts his orthodoxy. Nevertheless, such a comparison remains the most obvious and the most damaging accusation.

By far the most entertaining attack on Port-Royal's alleged heresy is the *Lettre d'un Provincial au Secrétaire du Port-Royal* (dealing with the first six letters),[3] a spoof sequel to the reply to the second *LP* included in the series, which heaps up 'incriminating'

---

[3] *Lettre d'un Provincial au secrétaire du Port-Royal.* See Appendix I. iii.

evidence under the guise of thanking the writer of the *LPs* for saving the day when things were getting very difficult for the Jansenists: 'Vous nous avez fourni dans vos Lettres des moyens aisés et agréables pour éluder tous leurs efforts [= their adversaries], tournant le sérieux en ridicule, et nous apprenant à substituer la raillerie où la raison et la justice nous ont manqué' (p. 1). The reason for the apostles not having adopted a similar style is explained: 'Ce secret n'était pas encore reconnu en ce temps-là; la divine Providence attendait le siècle des Jansénistes pour révéler au monde cette nouvelle manière de défendre la foi, en riant; et de satisfaire par des réponses facétieuses à ceux qui la combattent, quand on ne sait plus que leur dire' (p. 2). The burden of the letter is however to suggest that Charenton (with its Protestant *temple*), England, Switzerland, and Holland are all on the Jansenists' side (information gleaned from another 'correspondent'): 'On nous écrivait que dans Paris il arrive assez souvent que les dames Calvinistes se conjouissent dans la conversation avec les dames Jansénistes, sur la conformité de leur foi à l'égard des questions du temps' (p. 3). Here, as far as England, Switzerland, and Holland are concerned, the writer expresses, with heavy irony, a confidence born of support: 'Courage donc, Monsieur. Si Rome nous persécute, l'Angleterre nous soutiendra' (p. 5) (after quoting the approval of the *London Gazette* (3 January 1656) for Jansenius, 'though a Popish bishop' (p. 4)). And of Switzerland, having learnt of the support of one Henri Ottius, 'prédicant et professeur à Zurich', he exclaims 'que nous importe-[t-]il que le livre de la Grâce Victorieuse[4] ait été condamné à Rome, puisque nous voyons qu'il a été approuvé à Zurich' (p. 6). The letter is dated 'De Neuv' Eglise, ce 25 Avril 1656'!

The doctrinal arguments for the heretical position of Port-Royal, besides the original ones emanating from the *Cinq Propositions*, concern penitential and (later) eucharistic practice and belief. Morel, in particular, accuses Port-Royal of making the Christian life impossible for all but the most perfect. He suggests that what

---

[4] Noël de La Lane, *De la Grâce victorieuse de Jésus-Christ, ou Molina et ses disciples convaincus de l'erreur des pélagiens ou des semi-pélagiens* (Paris, 1651).

he calls Pascal's maxim, 'Je ne me contente pas du probable, je veux le sûr', is potentially at risk of preventing many people from going to confession and communion by virtue of 'le spécieux titre de sûreté' (p. 51). This is then turned against 'le Secrétaire du Port-Royal' with the injunction to leave the community and follow the teachings of the Church if it is 'sûreté' that is most important to him (p. 53). The first specific attack on Jansenist eucharistic doctrine is in fact addressed not to Pascal but to Arnauld (the *Port-Royal et Genève d'intelligence contre le Saint-Sacrement de l'Autel* by the Jesuit Père Bernard Meynier (May 1656)), and it will not be until the later parts of the counter-polemic (and the sixteenth *LP*) that it emerges as a major theme within the series. When it does, however, the polemicist's defence of the eucharistic sacrament is particularly fervent, and explicitly anti-Calvinist (xvi. 303ff.). In addition Port-Royal is accused of attacks on Marian devotion, also a feature characteristic of Calvinistic attitudes. Morel again deals at some length with the arguments of the eighth and ninth *LPs* (pp. 40–4), defending Jesuit attitudes, and concluding: 'Vous avez... autant de siècles que le christianisme en compte depuis sa naissance, qui condamnent ou votre erreur ou votre dégoût, et qui justifient pleinement les pieuses industries de notre dévotion' (p. 43). Pascal's critical attention to certain Marian devotions does indeed seem to go against a stream in popular Catholic teaching which, while not denying the primary need to love God, would endorse the practice of simple and apparently harmless devotional exercises —and thereby again both to suggest a particularly austere spirituality and, from another angle, to align Port-Royal superficially with certain Protestant attitudes.[5]

[5] D. Maingueneau, in his *Sémantique de la polémique* (Lausanne, 1983), devotes an entire section to 'la figure mariale'. He emphasizes how 'dans l'Eglise post-tridentine le culte de la Vierge et des saints constitue l'un des lieux névralgiques où la Contre-Réforme marque son altérité par rapport aux théologiens protestants. Dans la mesure où la stratégie constante des jésuites va être d'essayer de tirer le discours janséniste vers le protestantisme, on conçoit que la controverse sur le culte marial soit un des révélateurs privilégiés de la tension différenciatrice entre les deux discours' (p. 113). Furthermore, the production of Marian devotional literature 'culmine vers 1630, associée en particulier au triomphe de la Compagnie de Jésus, dans les rangs desquels se rencontrent la majorité des zélateurs de la Vierge' (p. 114).

The first part of the second *Réponse* of the *RLP* concludes with the *XIXe Imposture*; and the second part of the second *Réponse* ('contenant la réponse au reste des *Lettres Provinciales*') begins with the reply to the eleventh letter. Before dealing with the later counter-polemic, therefore, I shall first turn to the other major contextual aspect of this study, the relationship between the case put forward by Pascal in the *LPs* and the fragments of the *Pensées* (those apparently designed to contribute both to an apologetic and a polemical project); and then turn to the later *LPs* themselves.

Provinciales *and* Pensées

(1) Ideology and Pragmatism

THE need in an eventual apologetic project to correct mis-apprehension is one that is saliently and forcefully expressed in the *Pensées*; here, as in the *LPs*, the terms in which the argument is to be conducted have to be established, and the level and material appropriate to the enquiry articulated against erroneously held (pre)conceptions. The *Pensées* contain, in this context, three major fragments, in which the apologist is given vigorous and direct statements of opposition to voices hostile to Christianity; these hostile voices are not however blamed primarily for impiety but for ignorance, as the incipits display: 'Qu'ils apprennent au moins quelle est la religion qu'ils combattent avant que de la combattre' (L 427); 'Ils blasphèment ce qu'ils ignorent' (L 449); 'J'admire avec quelle hardiesse ces personnes entreprennent de parler de Dieu' (L 781). Pascal seems here to be writing with full awareness of the capacity for spiritual blunting that the nominal Christianity of his age and state provides; and of what he would see as the coexisting tendency to mistake for Christianity what are in fact the tenets of deism. The resultant confusion is once again between nature and grace, and the errors of the deists are shown as being cognate with those of the Jesuits. In order for this confusion to be dispelled, the putative reader is provided with a definition of Christianity argued in terms of a contrast with the erroneous views of such figures (often simply and unspecifically designated in the fragments as 'ils') who have misapprehended its nature, doctrine, and claims to adherence. Furthermore Pascal's objections to deism in the *Pensées* are argued on parallel grounds to his attacks on the Jesuits in the *LPs*—ideological and pragmatic—although the degree of emphasis accorded to each is dictated by the different aims of the respective works, and indeed genres.

The apologist of the *Pensées* is concerned to incite those who are 'malheureux et raisonnables' (L 160) to ask questions about their condition, and to arrive at Christian answers to those questions; and the terms in which the *problématique* is erected will substantially describe, indeed prescribe, the kind of solution which may be satisfactorily proposed—man must concede the terms of a self-perception which, rightly interpreted, affords both a coincidence with and a need for Christian doctrine. Towards this end, the whole patterning of the apologetic project of the *Pensées* is conceived in terms of a series of dualities: in man's nature, most fundamentally (*misère: grandeur*); in its ensuing historical explanation (first nature: second nature); and in the desiderata of a religion (explanation: solution). This duality is carried into the opposition to deism (ideology = it isn't true: pragmatism = it doesn't work). The deistic position to which it is contrasted is monadic, proposing a harmony between man, God, and nature, which cancels out the need for one of each of these terms (*misère*, second nature, solution, pragmatism). It is thus unable to provide (or perhaps, more accurately, disabled from providing) the kind of complementary pattern that the apologist has rendered axiomatic by his establishment of a dual view of human nature: 'Il faut nécessairement que la véritable religion nous enseigne et qu'il y a quelque grand principe de grandeur en l'homme et qu'il y a un grand principe de misère. Il faut encore qu'elle nous rende raison de ces étonnantes contrariétés' (L 149). There is thus a disparity between an implicitly christianizable (and increasingly explicitly Christian) view of man and a deistic view of God. Since therefore in the terms of any religious enquiry, and *a fortiori* that of Pascal's seeker, the case for coherence rests on the view of man and the view of God being entirely interdependent, once a disharmony is conceded between the apologist's dualistic paradigm and deism's monadic world-view, the deistic arguments are deemed inadequate; and yet the uninformed observers, mistaking them for Christianity, rather hold Christianity to be false because they are unable to reconcile it with their deistic expectations of a perpetual revelation:

Ils s'imaginent qu'elle [= la religion chrétienne] consiste simplement en l'adoration d'un Dieu considéré comme grand et puissant et éternel...

Et de là ils concluent que cette religion n'est pas véritable, parce qu'ils ne voient pas que toutes choses concourent à l'établissement de ce point, que Dieu ne se manifeste pas aux hommes avec toute l'évidence qu'il pourrait faire. (L 449)

Deistic proofs are not however condemned with the same degree of ruthlessness as Jesuit practices. Man's awareness of his 'disproportion' (L 199) is unlikely to coexist with the cryptically resumed cosmological argument that 'le ciel et les oiseaux prouvent Dieu', as can be seen from the brief (presumably) apologist–seeker dialogue (L 3), or from the longer 'Préface de la seconde partie' (L 781), supported by the fragment: 'C'est une chose admirable que jamais auteur canonique ne s'est servi de la nature pour prouver Dieu' (L 463). Certainly the apologist disclaims it as a specifically Christian view. But there are carefully qualified exceptions in the cases of those apparently endowed with this conviction as a result of their Christian belief: 'encore que cela est vrai en un sens pour quelques âmes à qui Dieu donna cette lumière' (L 3, cf. L 934). Such figures find comfort, and not bewilderment and fear, in their perception of anthropocentrism, and presumably, in so far as they are Christians, must do so in order for the creation myth to stand. Likewise the 'preuves de Dieu métaphysiques', as challenged in, for example: 'Le Dieu des chrétiens ne consiste pas en un Dieu simplement auteur des vérités géométriques et de l'ordre des éléments' (L 449), are not considered rationally absurd so much as categorically inapposite; the ideological objection to them (in a deleted fragment) is that they are wrong-headed and irrelevant rather than offensive: 'Cela est inutile et incertain et pénible. Et quand cela serait vrai, nous n'estimons pas que toute la philosophie vaille une heure de peine' (L 84). Although they pursue a particular argument or solve a particular problem satisfactorily, they do so within a self-contained system, and thus function only in accordance with the 'esprit géométrique', the linear application of the middle order: 'Cet ordre, le plus parfait entre les hommes, consiste non pas à tout définir ou à tout démontrer, ni aussi à ne rien définir ou à ne rien démontrer, mais à se tenir dans ce milieu' (*De l'Esprit Géométrique*, in *OC* 350). The enclosed perfection of such proofs does not thereby impinge on man's soul any more than on his senses. They are only, albeit perfectly, satisfying to the 'milieu' that is his intellect.

But the deeper dissatisfaction that the apologist expresses with such methods is of course pragmatic; they don't work in what Cruickshank describes as Pascal's 'soteriological apologia', which 'claims not only to explain man by means of Christian teaching, but to give him the possibility of total salvation'.[1] Or in Pascal's words:

Il faut que la religion qui instruit de [nos] devoirs nous instruise aussi de [nos] impuissances et qu'elle nous apprenne aussi les remèdes. (L 205, cf. L 216)

Que peut-on donc avoir, que de l'estime pour une religion qui connaît si bien les défauts de l'homme, et que du désir pour la vérité d'une religion qui y promet des remèdes si souhaitables. (L 595)

The practical inadequacy of deistic proofs pertains on two over-lapping levels, the apprehensive and the experiential. The objection on the apprehensive level stems from man's incapacity to retain the proofs in their totality, in the absence of a mechanism for their retention at the level of the automaton such as is provided by Christianity (L 821). 'Les preuves de Dieu méta-physiques sont si éloignées du raisonnement des hommes et si impliquées, qu'elles frappent peu et quand cela servirait à quelques-uns, cela ne servirait que pendant l'instant qu'ils voient cette démonstration, mais une heure après ils craignent de s'être trompés' (L 190). However this objection on the relatively neut-ral psychological/physiological level is reinforced by the ex-periential objection, taking as its starting-point the dual nature of man, namely that deism is inefficacious in providing a *remède* (because of course it sees no need for one). Even if man is per-suaded intellectually by deistic arguments, the apologist asserts, 'cette connaissance, sans Jésus-Christ, est inutile et stérile... Je ne le trouverais pas beaucoup avancé pour son salut' (L 449). The terms of the dualistic paradigm prevail finally in the re-jection of a monadic deism in the name of salvation; at the same time, by using deism and its exponents as a demonstration of an unworkable system, the apologist has thrown into higher and

[1] J. Cruickshank, *Pascal: Pensées* (London, 1983), 44.

clearer relief the uniqueness of Christianity and the types of claim it may make.

If we now turn to the *LPs*, we find that the Christian model which corresponds to the dualism in human nature, as manifested in the incarnation, is cross: resurrection. The cross reflects man's *misère*; the resurrection restores his *grandeur*. And the Jesuits, in the phrase of the 'ami janséniste', 'suppriment le scandale de la Croix' (v. 76). They are thereby shown, in the polemical context, to promote a denial of the fundamental paradigm of Pascal's apologetic data, a denial which, I would suggest, points in turn to the interplay of polemics and apologetics.

The passage at the beginning of the fifth letter in which the accusation occurs indeed suggests the more general correlation between the contemporary dispute to which it superficially attends and the teachings of the universal Church, centring as it does on a contrast between the apparent flexibility of Jesuit teaching and the immutable truth of Christian doctrine: 'Ils en ont pour toutes sortes de personnes et répondent si bien selon ce qu'on leur demande, que, quand ils se trouvent en des pays où un Dieu crucifié passe pour folie, ils suppriment le scandale de la Croix, et ne prêchent que Jésus-Christ glorieux, et non pas Jésus-Christ souffrant' (v. 76). The immediate context is the *Querelle des Rites*;[2] the broader implications are manifest: the 'pays où un Dieu crucifié passe pour folie' is as easily contemporary France as Cochin-China:

---

[2] This refers to the long-running controversy surrounding the toleration by Jesuit missionaries in the Far East of local practices alongside Christian ones (principally concerning the names accorded to God, and the rites for the dead). It continued in various forms from 1635 until well into the 18th cent., but had its starting-point in the attempts made by the Italian Jesuit Matteo Ricci in the early years of the 17th cent. to syncretize Christianity and confucianism, attempts which were criticized and denounced to Rome by later missionaries. The question was enjoying some actuality in the 1650s, and in 1656 (23 Mar.) a decree from the Holy Office signed by Alexander VII showed considerable tolerance towards accommodation. There seems to have been little polemical attention specifically devoted to it until later in the 17th cent. Clearly however its overtones of a lack of Christian rigour with the association with the Society of Jesus makes it an easy target, and a telling analogy, for Pascal. At the same time the status of the crucifixion does not in other respects seem to loom very large as a point at issue.

La vérité est si obscurcie en ce temps et le mensonge si établi qu'à moins que d'aimer la vérité on ne saurait la connaître. (L 739) Ce n'est point ici le pays de la vérité; elle erre inconnue parmi les hommes. Dieu l'a couverte d'un voile qui la laisse méconnaître à ceux qui n'entendent pas sa voix'. (L 840)

More metaphorically, and less topographically, this 'pays' represents the areas of secular or indeed erroneous religious thought which deny or suppress the role of the crucifixion in Christian teaching because they deny or suppress the areas of human experience to which it corresponds: pain, suffering, sin, death —*misère* in other words. As Miel remarks: 'Pascal never tires of pointing out that the Jesuits have . . . weakened the priesthood, and the sacraments, and even rendered the Redemption unnecessary'.[3] Indeed this whole passage can be taken as an allegorical prelude to and preparation for the letters on Jesuit practices, continuing as it does: 'Ils ont permis aux Chrétiens l'idolâtrie même, par cette subtile invention, de leur faire cacher sous leurs habits une image de Jésus-Christ, à laquelle ils leur enseignent de rapporter mentalement les adorations publiques qu'ils rendent à l'idole' (v. 77). The sense is clear, then, in which the Jesuits correspond within the Church to the same kind of misapprehension, for which those outside the Church who pursue a monadic line of enquiry (and/or reach a monadic conclusion) are responsible. They are guilty of the same error as the mistaken seekers of the *Pensées*, but *en connaissance de cause*; to paraphrase the opening of L 449, 'ils blasphèment ce qu'ils connaissent', and do so not just in the name but, according to the 'ami janséniste', in the promotion of a debased variant of Christianity. They will thus be challenged by Montalte in the same terms as their deistic counterparts of the *Pensées*: ideology, and pragmatism.

The truth with which their teaching is contrasted is vigorously and repetitively asserted throughout the *LPs*, but particularly in the later letters; indeed the sarcasm with which the deistic fallacies are dismissed in the *Pensées* is mild alongside the intensity with which the primacy of Christian truth is defended in the *LPs*. The search for and possession of metaphysical truth (two ideas always

---

[3] *Pascal and Theology*, p. 146.

intimately linked in the *Pensées*) are combined in fragment L 599: 'Rien ne donne l'assurance que la vérité; rien ne donne le repos que la recherche sincère de la vérité.' This truth, expressed by a Christian as the theology of the revelation, 'les vérités que l'esprit de Dieu a révélées' (xi. 195)—in other words doctrine— manifests itself in man's attitude towards the here and now (ethics) and the beyond/hereafter (spirituality). A part of this cohesive interdependence is expressed in fragment L 189: 'Hors de là [a knowledge of God through Christ] et sans l'Ecriture, sans le péché originel, sans médiateur nécessaire, promis et arrivé, on ne peut prouver absolument Dieu, ni enseigner ni bonne doctrine, ni bonne morale. Mais par J.-C. et en J.-C. on prouve Dieu et on enseigne la morale et la doctrine.' This truth is transmitted by tradition, endorsed by authority, and admitted by faith.

Furthermore it is immutable, and attributed with possessing weight, power, and strength, as we see, now in the polemical context, in the triumphal conclusion to the twelfth letter:

Qu'on ne prétende pas de là néanmoins que les choses soient égales : car il y a cette extrême différence, que la violence n'a qu'un cours borné par l'ordre de Dieu, qui en conduit les effets à la gloire de la vérité qu'elle attaque : au lieu que la vérité subsiste éternellement, et triomphe enfin de ses ennemis, parce qu'elle est éternelle et puissante comme Dieu même. (xii. 234–5; cf. L 85, xvi. 324, L 974)

This conviction is then expressed as a threat in such fragments as: 'Vous sentirez la force de la vérité et vous lui cèderez' (L 960). Elsewhere however it is suggested that some balance with charity is required in the cause of truth: 'Qu'on les [= presumably Jesuits] a traités aussi humainement qu'il était possible de le faire pour se tenir dans le milieu entre l'amour de la vérité et le devoir de la charité' (L 949). But the need is equally reiterated for war to be preferred to a 'false peace' (L 924, L 974, *Ecrits des Curés*, ii), and, in this last piece, silence is equated with just such an unavailable option: 'Il est donc indubitable que les personnes qui prennent toujours ce prétexte de charité et de paix pour empêcher de crier contre ceux qui détruisent la vérité, témoignent qu'ils ne sont amis que d'une fausse paix, et qu'ils sont véritablement ennemis, et de la véritable paix, et de la vérité' (Cognet, p. 426). The polemicist also provides a vigorous allegory in the eleventh letter in defence of speaking out on moral issues: 'Si ces personnes étaient en danger d'être assassinées... au lieu de se détourner de leur chemin pour l'éviter, s'amuseraient-elles à se plaindre du peu de charité qu'on aurait eu de découvrir le dessein criminel de ces assassins?' Therefore, he goes on: 'D'où vient donc qu'ils trouvent qu'on manque de charité quand on découvre les maximes nuisibles à la religion, et qu'ils croient au contraire qu'on manquerait de charité, si on ne leur découvrait pas les choses nuisibles à leur santé et à leur vie?' (xi. 202–3). And again in the first *Ecrit des Curés*, concerning the maxim from the *Apologie pour les Casuistes*: 'Que c'est à la raison naturelle à discerner quand il est permis ou défendu de tuer son prochain', we find: 'Si nous nous taisions après cela, nous serions indignes de notre ministère... Dieu nous punirait justement d'un silence si criminel... Nous sommes donc dans une obligation indispensable de parler en cette rencontre' (Cognet, pp. 413–14).

Among the counter-polemicists too, we find expressed the need to speak out against error. Morel, for example, concedes: 'Certes je tairais volontiers tout cela', but goes on 'mais la vérité est préférable à la complaisance' (p. 6). He too introduces an altruistic motive, quoting Augustine: 'Un mot d'avertissement corrige ce que le silence ou la flatterie corrompt, et il vaut mieux essayer de guérir un malade que de lui cacher son mal' (p. 7); and writes later again that if the Society and other writers did not respond to the *LPs*, 'leur silence serait plutôt un effet de lâcheté que de modestie' (p. 8). Certain voices on both sides, notably Angélique Arnauld, did advocate silence in the face of provocation but, as is manifest, they did not prevail.

The truth then has to be defended for its own sake. In the notes for the nineteenth letter (and in the *Pensées*), we find the statement: 'On attaque la plus grande des vertus chrétiennes qui est l'amour de la vérité' (xix. 383, and cf. L 979). But what underlies this ideological forcefulness is again the pragmatic argument; and the burden of the refutation in the *LPs* is identical to that in the *Pensées*: the Society of Jesus, by its suppression of the 'scandale de la Croix' and all that follows from it (which is illustrated in moral terms in the debate on the 'morale relâchée'), does not just offend the sacred truth; it also, it is asserted—in, paradoxically, the very

act of proselytizing—makes the claims of Christianity inefficacious and so, ultimately, unbelievable.

The relationship between cause and effect would of course
differ in the views of the two sides. The Jesuits would emphasize
the role of practical necessity both in doctrinal accommodation in
missionary activity and in moral casuistry in the resolution of
dilemmas encountered within the direction of conscience. The
ideal remains, but the reality involves compromise. Pascal on the
other hand would attribute, via the voice of the 'ami janséniste', a
motive of gaining the maximum number of believers as much to
the adoption of a 'morale relâchée' as to that of ritual concessions.
He thus suggests that it is by a liberalization/deformation of
Christian teaching that the Society gains (and seeks to gain)
adherents. But equally he implies that its use of accommodation
in the process constitutes a form of self-subversion.

It could furthermore be argued that Pascal seems perpetually
anxious, even in a polemical context, to view Christian faith with
the detached perspective of the seeker of the *Pensées*, as well as
from the viewpoint of the believer. His polemic in the first ten
letters contains a strong apologetic undercurrent, since for him,
as the dualistic paradigm is confronted with Jesuit monadism, the
Christian equation is rendered false. And a fragment of the
Pensées, germane to both projects, reinforces this point: 'Ainsi
notre religion est divine dans l'Evangile, les apôtres et la tradition, mais elle est ridicule dans ceux qui la traitent mal' (L 287).
Thus although the place of the Society within the nominal Christian framework apparently necessitates the polemical medium
and the concomitant development in ideological emphasis of the
LPs, its relationship to orthodox doctrine places it in every other
respect alongside the secular philosophies, 'autres religions', deistic misconceptions, and so pragmatic arguments of the *Pensées*.[4]

---

[4] It is paradoxical to note that these are exactly the terms, in the context of the
Jesuit attack on the eucharistic orthodoxy of Port-Royal in the 16th *LP*, in which
Port-Royal is challenged. Quoting the *Port-Royal et Genève d'intelligence contre le
très-saint sacrement de l'autel*, the polemicist notes that Port-Royal is deemed to
constitute 'une cabale secrète… *pour ruiner le mystère de l'Incarnation, faire passer
l'Evangile pour une histoire apocryphe, exterminer la religion chrétienne, et élever le
Déisme sur les ruines du Christianisme*' (xvi. 320). Shortly afterwards the Port-
Royal *Chapelet du Saint-Sacrement* is described as 'une instruction *de Déisme*' (xvi.
321).

The implications of the Jesuit imbalance are explored in different ways in the letters preceding and following the eleventh; this crucial and pivotal letter contains however, in its response to the accusation of 'raillerie des choses saintes' (to which we shall return), the underlying justification of the series leading up to it. What it also contains within this context is a passage whose parallelism with a major if brief fragment of the *Penseés* is salient:

Car, mes Pères, puisque vous m'obligez d'entrer en ce discours, je vous prie de considérer que, comme les vérités chrétiennes sont dignes d'amour et de respect, les erreurs qui leur sont contraires sont dignes de mépris et de haine, parce qu'il y a deux choses dans les vérités de notre religion: une beauté divine qui les rend aimables, et une sainte majesté qui les rend vénérables; et qu'il y a aussi deux choses dans les erreurs: l'impiété qui les rend horribles, et l'impertinence qui les rend ridicules. (xi. 195)

Les hommes ont mépris pour la religion. Ils en ont haine et peur qu'elle soit vraie. Pour guérir cela il faut commencer par montrer que la religion n'est point contraire à la raison. Vénérable, en donner respect. La rendre ensuite aimable, faire souhaiter aux bons qu'elle fût vraie et puis montrer qu'elle est vraie. Vénérable parce qu'elle a bien connu l'homme. Aimable parce qu'elle promet le vrai bien. (L 12)

In both texts 'la religion'/'les vérités chrétiennes' are 'aimable(s)' and 'vénérable(s)'. The emphasis in the *LPs* text is however much more on the value of the 'vérités chrétiennes' *per se*: they are 'dignes d'amour et de respect' because they are endowed with a 'beauté divine' and a 'sainte majesté', qualities of an object worthy of being cherished for itself. This is the, albeit polemical, discourse of one believer to another, whatever his aberrations, expressed so that the previously latent and now sharpened Christian conscience of the 'ami provincial', and the actual Christian conscience of the committed reader should be touched; on this level, the ideological, indeed quasi-aesthetic, celebration of truth has no need for the pragmatic justification which is underlined in the apologetic fragment. The 'bons' who are to be brought to belief in the *Pensées* do, on the other hand, need to be convinced of the claims of the 'vérités chrétiennes'; and so the nebulous terms of 'beauté divine' and 'sainte majesté' are replaced by explanations: 'parce qu'elle a bien connu l'homme' and 'parce qu'elle promet le vrai bien'. But even if the definitions provided because required by the apology are left out of the *LPs*, they none the less underpin the justifications of 'raillerie': the Jesuits' error is thus (to synthesize the two passages and paraphrase Pascal) worthy of 'haine', 'parce qu'elle a mal connu l'homme', and of 'mépris', 'parce qu'elle ne promet pas le vrai bien'. Furthermore, if hatred is the believer's response to the Society's ideological inadequacy, laughter, born of 'mépris', is, in one manifestation at least, the expression of the pragmatic dissatisfaction of the critical observer. Even if the *LPs* are not primarily devoted to the persuasion of the non-believer, therefore, they are still shown to be very much concerned by their format—and by the tenor of the 'Réponse du provincial' which follows the second letter—to elicit the support of the fair-minded but initially disinterested on-looker, closely related to the seeker of the *Penseés*, and personified at the outset in the 'ami provincial'.

It is therefore clear that Pascal sees questions of morality as entirely germane to the plausibility of the *grandes lignes* of belief; they are for him a part of the 'doctrine de la foi'. Thus in the last paragraph of the first *Ecrit des Curés*, we find: 'Comme il y a des hérésies dans la foi, il y a aussi des hérésies dans les mœurs... et qui sont d'autant plus dangereuses, qu'elles sont conformes aux passions de la nature, et à ce malheureux fond de consupiscence dont les plus saints ne sont pas exempts' (Cognet, p. 417). The Jesuits however do not present them in this light, rather consider-ing them as part of the 'doctrine de l'Ecole', matters with which those within the Church, and more particularly the higher clergy, are concerned. Their detail does not concern the faithful, and even less does it concern the seeker or the catechumen. It is furthermore Pascal's insistence that the erroneous moral teaching of a part of the Church can negate its fundamental truths that he opposes to the Jesuit accusation that erroneous doctrinal teaching can have the same effect. It is this simple point that endows the *LPs* with a capacity to disconcert any reader, whatever his beliefs. And the same kind of basic appeal informs the *Pensées*. Any intelligent reader will have some curiosity about the 'doc-trine de la foi'; not even all Christians will know or will want to know much about the 'doctrine de l'Ecole'. In this way, by presenting in both works his arguments as and in terms of simple essentials, Pascal reduces his adversaries, Jesuits or deists, to the status of 'esprits géométriques', allowing the idealized readers to associate with the 'esprits de finesse', and thereby provoking an immediate, intuitive, and favourable response in them. The 'ami provincial' is also an 'esprit fin'.

To take this one stage further, it could be argued, first, that the capacity of Christianity to satisfy these two imperatives ('connaître l'homme'/'promettre le vrai bien') is the most fundamental of all obligations uniting the two works and is indeed a restatement of the broadest *question de droit*; and secondly, and relatedly, that the successful outcome of the polemical debate to which the *LPs* are devoted impinges directly and fundamentally on the issues raised in the apologetic project contained in the *Pensées*.

It may then seem worth asking why the polemical dispute is only conducted outside the apology; after all, many untruths or partial truths are combated within it, and indeed put to great persuasive use. The apologist uses the correction of misapprehension astutely, and the cogency of his opposition to those who seek truth in deism and elsewhere contributes substantially to the positive arguments advanced for the credibility of Christianity; he bounces these exuberantly off the refutation of the monadic system of enquiry, in order to demonstrate its inapposite application to a dualistic dilemma. (And the efficacy of this kind of persuasion is presumably one of the ideas of which Pascal is trying to convince Saci in the *Entretien avec Monsieur de Saci*).

Partly the autonomous status of the *LPs* from the *Pensées* (always admitting the notes on the Jesuits to be found therein, but equally noting the lack of any sustained, let alone independent section devoted to the problem) must stem from the urgency because actuality of the debate. It is a question to which Pascal is drawn because it is current; its combating is a direct response to events rather than a rhetorical device of hyperbolic juxtaposition.

Partly it is again a question of the interplay of ideology and pragmatism. It is generically characteristic that in the projected apology pragmatic arguments will outweigh ideological objections, since even the seeker may not initially be held to cherish the

Christian doctrines for themselves; in the polemical context the reverse will be the case, since the framework of the argument and expectations of the adversary are Christian, however much its presentation is also designed to appeal to the common sense of the uncommitted reader. The 'ami provincial' is progressively assumed to engage his Christian conscience and the committed reader has already taken sides; the hypothetical interlocutor(s)[5] of the apology is/are asked initially only to engage his/their intelligence and will and, even if his/their development may in some ways be seen to parallel that of the 'ami provincial', no element of curiosity towards theological issues can initially be assumed. In this way the various idealized readers of both works specify the generic differences, and propose the ideal responses of the empirical readers.

But most of all it is because the existence of the Jesuit threat challenges from within the plausibility of Pascal's apology because it makes parallel claims, as Pascal presents it, with reference to the same system of belief, disguised in a more superficially attractive way: the Jesuits 'couvrent leur prudence humaine et politique du prétexte d'une prudence divine et chrétienne' (v. 78), and thus make possible the effortless movement between worldly practice and nominal Christian belief. As Davidson puts it: 'the effect is to allow the Christian to continue as he is with the added security of a quiet conscience'.[6] Thus, in the ninth letter, the use of easy devotions is described as 'plus propre à entretenir les pécheurs dans leurs désordres, par la fausse paix que cette confiance téméraire apporte, qu'à les en retirer par une véritable conversion que la grâce seule peut produire' (ix. 156). And a similar sentiment is found in the context of the Port-Royal miracles: 'Ceux qui en faisant profession de le [J.-C.] suivre pour ses miracles ne le suivent en effet que parce qu'il les console et les rassasie des biens du monde, ils déshonorent ses miracles quand ils sont contraires à leurs commodités' (L 855). The Jesuits therefore fulfil a different function from, for example, the Jews

---

[5] See Parish, 'Mais qui parle?', *passim*.
[6] *Audience, Words and Art*, p. 128. P. Wolfe, in 'Langage et vérité dans les *Provinciales* XI à XVI', remarks: 'Les Jésuites écrivent donc une anti-Bible à l'usage des âmes ignorantes' (p. 79).

(in 'Raisons pourquoi figures'), who pointed to the truth by their own error, because of their chronological relationship to the establishment of orthodoxy: 'Ceux qui ont rejeté et crucifié Jésus-Christ qui leur a été en scandale sont ceux qui portent les livres qui témoignent de lui et qui disent qu'il sera rejeté et en scandale, de sorte qu'ils ont marqué que c'était lui en le refusant' (L 502).

Pascal indeed enumerates in a further fragment of the *Pensées* a hierarchy of 'enemies of the Church', wherein each of the three categories is qualitatively distinct from the other two, and invites (because characteristically gives) a different kind of attack: 'L'Eglise a trois sortes d'ennemis : les Juifs qui n'ont jamais été de son corps, les hérétiques qui s'en sont retirés, et les mauvais chrétiens qui la déchirent au-dedans. Ces trois sortes de différents adversaires la combattent d'ordinaire diversement' (L 858). We notice too in this context that Pascal's hostility towards those with whom he takes issue becomes progressively stronger across his *œuvre* as they approximate more closely to what he sees as the truth: pagans and Muhammadans are let off relatively lightly, with just a few apologetic commonplaces; Jews treated much more carefully and substantially; deists, Calvinists (in the *Ecrits sur la Grâce*), and secular philosophers (notably pyrrhonists and stoics in the *Entretien avec Monsieur de Saci*) dismissed more systematically again; and the 'mauvais chrétiens' of this frag-ment, identified specifically in the *LPs* as the Jesuits, with the most attention and ferocity of all. If however the paradoxically juxtaposed need to refute and capacity for demonstration are exploited most systematically in views whose relative lack of proximity to the truth permits them to carry this dual function, the Jesuits, *par contre*, are debarred from fulfilling such a partly illustrative role. Whereas they may throw incidental light on the truth by standing in contradistinction to it, the brunt of Pascal's task in the *LPs* is, in Robert Nelson's term, adversarial.[7]

The appeal of the Jesuits is thus represented as constituting a kind of counter-apology (all the more so as they too are in the

---

[7] Nelson, *Pascal, Adversary and Advocate*, argues that Pascal alternates between these two tendencies.

business of proselytizing), whose dismissal must be effected alongside, rather than within, the 'true' apology. Christian polemics (fighting within the Christian understanding and terms as to the interpretation and enactment of doctrine) and Christian apologetics (which may employ the terms of other beliefs, but essentially in the service of a unified reading of Christianity) do not therefore easily coexist in the same work, even if the apologist may at some stage have to involve the putative believer in polemical issues. For the time being, then, polemics stands as the counterpart to apologetics, with all the qualities of independence and interdependence that that status implies. Both works seek essentially to persuade, and the polemical evidence relates to the apologetic statement; yet its very proximity to the aims of the project debars it from contributing internally to its argument.

It may still be tempting to argue from this that Pascal's Christianity, even in its polemical manifestations, is substantially addressed to those outside the Church, and therefore in need of attending to the kinds of question understood by 'doctrine de la foi'; whereas the Jesuits attend to those within, and whose concerns are dealt with in the 'doctrine de l'Ecole'. It may indeed be temperamentally characteristic of Pascal that he never seems fully to view Christianity from the inside, but always retains an awareness of its claims as they are manifesting themselves by its adherents to the eyes of the unbeliever. Some of the reasons for this must lie in the characteristics of Christianity as he presents them.

8

Provinciales *and* Pensées

(II) Simplicity and Complexity

THE apologist of the *Pensées* is at great pains to insist that Christianity is not a natural, unlearnt, even less instinctive belief. The difficulties presented by the Christian revelation emanate both from its situation in history and its relative paucity yet clarity of evidence, and are such as to make its detail and interpretation both problematic and of supreme importance. The related questions of the coherence, paradox, and specificity of Christianity therefore exact a significant amount of attention in the fragments; and the tension between them may be expressed in terms of Christianity's coexisting simplicity and complexity.

In one sense, as I have been stressing, Christianity is bound to be depicted as simple, and the fundamental equation on which Pascal's argument rests reflects the simplicity; the source of error lies not in any point of detail, but in a gross ignorance of half of human nature; this characterizes heresy—which comes from the Greek word for 'choosing':

D'ordinaire il arrive que ne pouvant concevoir le rapport de deux vérités opposées, et croyant que l'aveu de l'une enferme l'exclusion de l'autre, ils [= les hérétiques] s'attachent à l'une, ils excluent l'autre. (L 733)

Les deux raisons contraires. Il faut commencer par là sans cela on n'entend rien, et tout est hérétique. Et même à la fin de chaque vérité il faut ajouter qu'on se souvient de la vérité opposée. (L 576)[1]

So, positively, the capacity of Christianity to offer two utterly essential truths which correspond to the *contrariété* in man's nature is starkly and emphatically stated: 'la foi chrétienne ne va presque qu'à établir ces deux choses: la corruption de la nature et la

[1] Cf. 'l'esprit de finesse', where 'l'omission d'un principe mène à l'erreur' (L 512).

rédemption de Jésus-Christ' (L 427). After the struggles of the
seeker to come to terms with the human condition, this solution
will have an apparent, and real, simplicity. Man will have toiled
with his 'excellence' ignoring his 'corruption', or with his 'in-
firmité' ignoring his 'dignité', before understanding that 'la seule
religion chrétienne a pu guérir ces deux vices, non pas en chassant
l'un par l'autre par la sagesse de la terre, mais en chassant l'un et
l'autre par la simplicité de l'Evangile' (L 208). The complication
arising from asking the wrong questions of the evidence will be
transformed into simplicity when the right questions are asked
and the right answers found; a deliberately emphasized difficulty
becomes a feature of the simple solution when examined in the
correct perspective. Furthermore, since doctrine leads to ethics,
the concomitant moral imperatives will be equally simple: thus
Pascal, in the second *Ecrit des Curés de Paris*, is able to conclude:
'Nous présenterons toujours un même visage à tous leurs visages
différents, et nous n'opposerons à la duplicité des enfants du siècle
que la simplicité des enfants de l'Evangile' (Cognet, p. 429). In
the *LPs* too, therefore, evangelic simplicity cuts through the
tortuous casuistry of the Jesuits (as it is presented by Pascal) in the
letters following the eleventh, just as it breaks down the hyperbolically established *contrariétés* of the human condition in the
Pensées. Pascal's use of *dispositio* in both cases endows the Gospel
with a liberative and simple quality which is *mis en valeur* by its
relationship to a rhetorically established complexity.

This kind of presentation proposes the way in which Christianity could be described as simple; and against this simplicity the
Jesuits, who have followed one form of 'la sagesse de la terre',
propose the complexity of casuistry, making for the emphasis on
detail, definition, qualification, accuracy, context, and so on, in
the counter-polemic. It is, in the polemical domain, the complexity which arises from the attempt to reconcile the Jesuit creed, as it
is enacted, with the exigencies of (nominal) Christianity.

At the same time, as I suggested, Christianity in the *Pensées* is
presented as being neither a natural, obvious religion, nor a vague
religion, for related reasons dependent on its historically revealed
nature. A number of people may find themselves innately Christian, if God has inclined their hearts (L 110: 'ceux à qui Dieu a

donné la religion par sentiment de cœur'), but the majority will not; and it is to this majority that Pascal and the Jesuits are addressing themselves in different ways. It will, for Pascal, have to contend in its acquisition of belief with two major difficulties: with paradox, and with specificity.

The central feature of paradox is, of course, the theory of the hidden God: the statement always implicit (and sometimes explicit) in the whole of the apologetic exercise is that the major impediment to belief lies in the absence of any perpetual revelation. The response of the apologist is to make out of God's concealment, and in the light of the historical revelation, an argument for the truth of Christianity. The unbeliever must be persuaded that the ensuing divine obscurity becomes a distinctive characteristic of the Christian God, and therefore a further pointer to his unique aptitude for (Christian) man, reflecting at once his aspirations and his unworthiness: 'S'il paraît une fois, il est toujours; et ainsi on n'en peut conclure, sinon qu'il y a un Dieu, et que les hommes en sont indignes' (L 448). Secondly, if the fundamental tenets of Christianity are simple in their major experiential claims to validity, if they provide an adequate if improbable answer and remedy, they are nevertheless only demonstrably true, in the sense that they are not an invented story, within this specific historical framework. The incarnate revelation of the Christian God took place in history, and it is to this fact, with all the weight of time which preceded and has followed it, that Christianity must look for its verification. There is then for Pascal a vigorous obligation binding Christianity to the detail of its historical events; and so it is clear that in this respect too it will depend on evidence outside the domain of 'raison'/'lumière naturelle', and in this respect too will fail to be simple, as is witnessed by the fund of biblical justification amassed under such headings as 'Figures', 'Prophètes', 'Preuves de J. -C.' and so on in the apologetic fragments.

In these two respects, paradox and specificity, Pascal's Jesuits address themselves to the majority by now replacing complexity with simplicity: by their monadic if unacknowledged appeal to the sufficiency of human nature, implying the potential means for man directly to know God, and denying thereby the theology of the Fall and the Redemption; and by their readiness to espouse novelty, and what is seen as a cavalier attitude towards scriptural (and patristic) authority, in its service. Indeed this attempt at universal appeal by a deformation of authority ('Ils en ont pour toutes sortes de personnes' (v. 76)) is almost a parody of the Church's universality of appeal (L 895: 'La religion est proportionnée à toutes sortes d'esprits').

The Christian revelation is depicted in one vital fragment of the *Pensées*, clearly originally intended to be part of the anti-Jesuit case, as a kind of releasing encumbrance, different from both expectations and parallels, and presented in such a way as to make it remarkably germane to both the apologetic and the polemical project:

Toutes les religions et les sectes du monde ont eu la raison naturelle pour guide; les seuls chrétiens ont été astreints à prendre leurs règles hors d'eux-mêmes, et à s'informer de celles que Jésus-Christ a laissées aux anciens pour nous et retransmises aux fidèles. Cette contrainte lasse ces bons Pères. Ils veulent avoir comme les autres peuples la liberté de suivre leurs imaginations. C'est en vain que nous leur crions comme les prophètes disaient autrefois aux Juifs; allez au milieu de l'église, in-formez-vous des voies que les anciens lui ont laissées et suivez ces sentiers. Ils ont répondu comme les Juifs : nous n'y marcherons point mais nous suivrons les pensées de notre cœur. Et ils ont dit : nous serons comme les autres peuples. (L 769)

The arguments advanced here are developed in the satirical letters with the same relationship to ideology and pragmatism as those concerning Christianity's applicability to the human condition. Christianity, as opposed to geometric deism, is tied to its ex-periential dualism as is, or should be, evidenced by its ethics and spirituality. But it is also tied to the particularity of an historical event, on whose veracity it depends in order to be believable (as opposed to a fairy story), a dimension which is actualized through antiquity and orthodoxy. A fairy story is no more salvific than geometry; and the complexity of veracity-through-historicity must coexist with the simplicity of veracity-through-coherence.

The evidence of this historical truth in the Scriptures is, in the early years of Christendom, erected into a theology, a means of articulating the revealed God: the Word is made flesh, and then the flesh is made the words by which the Church carries on the work of the incarnation. The need for this scriptural evidence to be interpreted correctly for the truth of the revelation to be understood is paramount; the revelation is contained in history, and recorded once and for all in Scripture, in the Fathers, Popes, and Councils of the early Church (although the status of the early Christian centuries as against the later developments is, of course, one of the questions at issue). This corpus of orthodoxy stands immutable, not only because of its holiness in the eyes of the Christian (ideology), but also because it uniquely makes sense of the events which it also records (pragmatism). Heresy is objectionable to the Christian because it is incoherent, a point of view implied, needless to say, by both polemics. Time and again, therefore, the writings of the Church Fathers are quoted by Pascal against those of the Jesuits. Already in the third letter: 'Ce qui est catholique dans les Pères devient hérétique dans M. Arnauld;... ce qui était hérétique dans les semi-Pélagiens devient orthodoxe dans les écrits des Jésuites' (iii. 51). Then in the fifth: 'Je croyais ne devoir prendre pour règle que l'Ecriture et la tradition de l'Eglise, mais non pas vos casuistes. O bon Dieu! s'écria le Père. Vous me faites souvenir de ces Jansénistes!' (v. 84), where, shortly afterwards, we find the exchange: 'Je ne sais comment vous pouvez faire, quand les Pères de l'Eglise sont contraires aux sentiments de quelqu'un de vos casuistes... Les Pères étaient bons pour la morale de leur temps; mais ils sont trop éloignés pour celle du nôtre' (v. 90), establishing a tension, expressed above all in terms of the central and conclusive questions of penitential practice in the tenth letter. Then, later again in the fifth letter, Montalte introduces the trio that will be the standard point of oppositional reference in the debate between the 'anciens pères' and the 'nouveaux casuistes': 'l'Ecriture Sainte, les Papes et les Conciles, que vous ne pouvez démentir, et qui sont tous dans la voie unique de l'Evangile' (v. 94) (and compare the fifth *Ecrit des curés de Paris*: 'Comme [notre religion] est toute divine, c'est en Dieu seul qu'elle s'appuie et n'a de doctrine que celle qu'elle a reçue de lui, par le canal de la tradition' (Cognet, p. 435)).

On the other hand, in Pascal/Montalte's accusation, the Jesuits create a chronological *décalage* between morality and doctrine: the idea that an ancient doctrinal orthodoxy may claim to be retained alongside modern ethical practice is an incoherence; and again the implication must be that an abandonment of the morality of the 'anciens pères' betokens an abandonment of their theology, and that an abandonment of their theology is in turn a challenge to the historicity of Christianity. The Jesuit morality is thus, by being a fairy story couched in the terms of Christianity, implicitly accused of reducing the Christian revelation to the status of an unbelievable historical invention. History stands in opposition to nature in the conflict of theologies, since the rejection of the old is the rejection of an historical religion; and the correlation between new morality and nature reasserts, now in different terms again, a monadic view (present only) against a dualism (past: present). Pascal's Christianity functions by the perpetual enactment in the present of a set of beliefs and practices which are rooted in a specific past. The separation between an ethical present and a doctrinal past therefore destroys the constricting yet uniquely validating historical grounding, as natural morality (or immorality) again signifies *de facto* deism.

Reinforcing the historical complexity of Christianity is the related idea of *perpétuité*. All man's natural feelings will be hostile to Christianity, and yet it has endured: 'La seule religion contre la nature, contre le sens commun, contre nos plaisirs est la seule qui ait toujours été' (L 284). Against this, 'ils [the Jesuits] ne peuvent avoir la perpétuité et ils cherchent l'universalité et pour cela il font toute l'Eglise corrompue afin qu'ils soient saints' (L 707), since 'ils détruisent la perpétuité par la probabilité' (L 894). In this context the whole theme of hostility to theological (and by extension moral) innovation takes on far more than simply the value of conservatism. It derives from the conviction that the very survival of the Church serves, following on from the antiquity of the Jewish people and faith, as in itself a guarantee of the truth of the Christian religion. The whole Jewish story is a prefiguration of the truth of the Messiah, and the antiquity of the Jews is a feature of their positive attractiveness to the seeker of the *Pensées*: 'Un peuple particulier séparé de tous les autres peuples de la terre, le plus ancien de tous et dont les histoires précèdent de plusieurs siècles les plus anciens que nous ayons... La rencontre de ce peuple m'étonne, et me semble digne de l'attention' (L 454). Following the incarnation, the duration of the Church is also a sign of its authority: 'Cette église qui adore celui qui a toujours été a subsisté sans interruption et ce qui est admirable, incomparable et tout à fait divin, est que cette religion qui a toujours duré a toujours été combattue' (L 281). This central conviction of the Church's survival against all odds serves as a cumulative proof of its claims; and in another fragment it is pointed out that: 'Si l'ancienne Eglise était dans l'erreur, l'Eglise est tombée. Quand elle y serait aujourd'hui ce n'est pas de même car elle a toujours la maxime supérieure de la tradition de la créance de l'ancienne Eglise. Et ainsi cette soumission et cette conformité à l'ancienne Eglise prévaut et corrige tout' (L 285). The teaching of the early church that has been transmitted as orthodoxy has to be relied upon, and error assessed against it and eradicated if necessary, since 'l'histoire de l'Eglise doit être proprement appelée l'histoire de la vérité' (L 776). As Miel remarks, 'the appeal is to orthodoxy, to the weight and sanctity of the Gospels and the tradition. The question is a theological one and Pascal is outraged not at the heartlessness, but at the heresy of the Jesuits'.[2] Elsewhere in the *Pensées* (as in the *Ecrits sur la Grâce*), the Church is shown to be threatened by conflicting error: 'L'Eglise a toujours été combattue par des erreurs contraires. Mais peut-être jamais en même temps comme à présent, et si elle en souffre plus à cause de la multiplicité d'erreurs, elle en reçoit cet avantage qu'ils [*sic*] se détruisent' (L 733, cf. L 791; L 567). More explicitly, in the fifth *Ecrit des Curés*, the writer deplores the fact that Protestants will take the teachings of the Society of Jesus as representative of the whole Church, and thus as a vindication of their position, 'comme s'ils [Jesuits] avaient pour objet de fournir aux Calvinistes tout le secours qu'ils peuvent souhaiter' (Cognet, p. 433).

In this context, therefore, the Jesuits' error lies in their attitude towards kinds of information; they are committing an epistemological mistake by selecting, emending, and at worst suppressing, information that it is their duty simply to transmit, and

---

[2] *Pascal and Theology*, p. 129.

replacing it with novelty. Since, however, the corpus of Christian doctrine is not susceptible to recurrent empirical analysis—a conviction which informs the whole attack on moral innovativeness—the Society is deemed, in failing to respect the principle of *perpétuité*, to threaten the very grounds for survival of the Church.

Hostility to novelty, understood here as doctrinal heresy, is of course also encountered in the counter-polemic: in the introduction to the first *Impostures*, the writer claims to defend 'la morale des Jésuites' and also 'celle de tous les docteurs Catholiques, que l'hérésie naissante du Port-Royal tâche de décrier sous le nom de ces religieux' (*RLP* 1); he will therefore 'se venger des Jésuites, qui ont témoigné leur zèle contre ces nouveautés dangereuses' (*RLP* 2). The *XXIIᵉ Avertissement* then contains the warning: 'Apprenez de St. Thomas, que la simplicité de ceux qui suivent les opinions téméraires et dangereuses de leur Maître ne les excuse nullement; parce que lorsqu'il s'agit de la foi, il ne faut pas adhérer légèrement aux nouveautés périlleuses' (*RLP* 113). And Morel writes: 'Voulant détruire la foi de nos aïeux, pour élever sur ses ruines des nouveautés horribles, elle [votre malice] attaque obstinément tout ce qui peut arrêter ce furieux dessein' (p. 24). Finally Pirot, in the *Apologie pour les Casuistes*, makes the scathing attack:

Toute leur doctrine consiste à dire qu'ils suivent l'antiquité, la tradition et les Pères. Toutes les preuves de cette antiquité, qu'ils prétendent suivre, se réduisent à quelques canons abrogés, à quelques textes des Pères mal expliqués, ou à quelques opinions des Pères qui ont été solidement réfutées par d'autres Pères de l'Eglise. (p. 126)

Each polemic thus takes from the vast amount of historical evidence the kind of material which supports its argument. Furthermore, each proposes that failure to understand either the claims, the historical detail *per se*, or the perpetuity of Christianity, that is the continuing respect for and implementation of the revelation, will constitute heresy. And in turn, as each side seems tacitly to acknowledge, heresy will lead to disbelief.

'La vraie nature de l'homme, son vrai bien et la vraie vertu et la
vraie religion sont choses dont la connaissance est inséparable'
(L 393). The coherence of the letters, at the deepest level, and
their relationship with the *Pensées*, depends on such a view of the
comprehensiveness of Christianity. Pascal brings together in his
apology evidence for Christianity's applicability, efficacity, authority, and coherence; if it is to be worthy of respect it must be
because it can claim all these things, not because of its suitability
to man's superficial needs, but to his ultimate desire for happiness
as the 'souverain bien'. The coexistence of these truths defines
Christianity, and any exclusion of a constituent part defines error:
'Il y a donc un grand nombre de vérités, et de foi et de morale qui
semblent répugnantes et qui subsistent toutes dans un ordre
admirable. La source de toutes les hérésies est l'exclusion de
quelques-unes de ces vérités' (L 733). The Jesuit departure from
this coherence is thus portrayed by Pascal as a loss of efficacity in
terms of the claims made for Christianity. The fact that the
Christian truths may seem 'répugnantes', presumably to the
unconverted observer, furthermore makes their survival and
credibility particularly tenuous. Christianity's strangeness contributes to its vulnerability, and the process of disintegration
is therefore one to which human nature readily assents. The
fictional Jesuits of the *LPs* give hyperbolic expression to that
readiness.

Furthermore if, as I have suggested and as the satirical *LPs*
show, ethical questions, deformed for polemical purposes,
are best argued on their own ground and in their own terms,
they nevertheless impinge fundamentally on the serious
issues of doctrine, a point which the impassioned speech
of the 'ami janséniste' in the fifth letter makes clear. Or
as one fragment succinctly puts it: 'Jugez de leur foi par leur
morale' (L 985). Truth for Pascal is manifested in man's
attitude towards the contingent and the transcendent, and
departure from sound moral and spiritual practices constitutes therefore for him a theological, that is doctrinal,
aberration. As Miel again observes, 'Pascal became interested
in the casuistry and moral laxity of the Jesuits only when he
saw them as moral heresies emanating from false theological

doctrine'.³ And certain fragments again underline this coherence: 'Toute religion est fausse qui dans sa foi n'adore pas un
Dieu comme principe de toutes choses et qui dans sa morale
n'aime pas un seul Dieu comme objet de toutes choses' (L 833).
Pascal therefore points in the two central series of letters (v–x and
xii–xvi), and above all in the eleventh letter, to certain inextricably linked areas of Christian concern by demonstrating that the
denial of man's sinfulness and of the need to love God—negations
which imbue the satirical letters—cannot coexist with sound
theology: 'Je vous dis que vous anéantissez la morale chrétienne
en la séparant de l'amour de Dieu, dont vous dispensez les
hommes' (xvii. 331). Certain unflattering parallels are also drawn
with other groups: in a fragment of the *Pensées* (in the 'Papiers
classés' under 'Perpétuité') we find: 'Les chrétiens grossiers
croient que le Messie les a dispensés d'aimer Dieu' (L 286, and cf.
L 287), a remark which occurs in the discussion of '2 sortes
d'hommes en chaque religion' (Judaism and Christianity). And
in the same context the following statement is also made: 'La
religion des juifs... consistait... seulement en l'amour de Dieu...
Les Juifs, manque de cet amour, seraient réprouvés pour leurs
crimes et les païens élus en leur place' (L 453), thereby establishing
an implicit hierarchy in which the Jesuits now run the risk of
being placed below the pagans.

All Christian behaviour, indeed all behaviour, constitutes for
Pascal some kind of comment on the Christian God, a statement
that must indicate the reasons for the *Pensées* and the *Provinciales*
being both related and yet, in one sense, diametrically opposed:
whereas in the former, natural behaviour points to the Christian
God, in the latter, Christian behaviour points back to pagan man.

In the Pascalian apologetic schema even ignorance and indifference are endowed with significance:

Reconnaissez donc la vérité de la religion dans l'obscurité même de la
religion, dans le peu de lumière que nous en avons, dans l'indifférence
que nous avons de la connaître. (L 439)

Non seulement le zèle de ceux qui le cherchent prouve Dieu, mais
l'aveuglement de ceux qui ne le cherchent pas. (L 163)

³ Ibid. 125.

Again, in the opposition to the hyperbolically apathetic voice of fragment L 427:

En vérité, il est glorieux à la religion d'avoir pour ennemis des hommes si déraisonnables; et leur opposition lui est si peu dangereuse, qu'elle sert au contraire à l'établissement de ses vérités;

and, making the same point:

Je leur demanderais s'il n'est pas vrai qu'ils vérifient par eux-mêmes ce fondement de la foi qu'ils combattent, qui est que la nature des hommes est dans la corruption. (L 432 (29))

Thus even the most fundamental barriers and objections to man's belief are charged with meaning, and the ultimate paradox is hinted at, whereby the first impediment to the attainment of the end point becomes, transformed by the perspective of that truth, the first pointer to it. Even the need to shake men out of apathy tells them, in Pascal's view, something about the Christian God; by as basic a perception as the awareness of that apathy, a statement has been made which, rightly understood, indicates and illustrates the Christian solution.

It is this very fact that Pascal's God-view and man-view are so inextricable which necessarily implies that any tacit or implicit assumptions about human nature which emerge from Jesuit practices carry with them a tacit or implicit comment on their theology. The Jesuits, by their moral and spiritual aberrations, are portrayed as enacting a false doctrine: 'la licence qu'on a prise d'ébranler les règles les plus saintes de la conduite chrétienne se porte jusqu'au renversement entier de la loi de Dieu' (x. 191); so, comparing Jesuits with Jansenists in the sixteenth letter: 'Leurs [= Jansenists'] discours sont aussi catholiques que les vôtres; mais leur conduite confirme leur foi, et la vôtre la dément' (xvi. 318). But the implications go further than this, since if an appeal to the dictates of human nature is made within a Christian context, the signs become reversed. The Jesuit evidence, by taking Christianity as its starting-point, leads believers to an erroneous view of the Christian God and thus of man; their practices betoken so radical an imbalance as to render the revelation incompatible with man's self-understanding since, starting now from a Christian standpoint, they promote a theology which fails to account for the human condition. The same terms of reference (*misère*: *grandeur*) which bring the seeker of the *Pensées* to recognize the truth of Christianity thus equally underpin the rejection of Jesuit morality.

This removal of Christianity's appeal to coherence has also negated the meaning of any claim made in its name; and further-more necessitated, because emanated from, the introduction of an alternative monadic deification of human nature to explain man's condition. The Jesuit actions have taken meaninglessness, unimportant in the purely semantic *questions de fait*, through the medium of behaviour into theology, and then back to man's self-perception. Their 'idolâtrie du signifiant' ('verbal' = 'prochain', 'suffisant')' has become an 'idolâtrie du signifiant' ('humain'); man has necessarily become his own yardstick of behaviour and belief as the system by which he behaves and believes has lost its transcendent referent. This reversal is clearly spelt out in the twelfth letter (on simony): 'Vous avez suivi votre méthode ordinaire, qui est d'accorder aux hommes ce qu'ils désirent, et donner à Dieu des paroles et des apparences' (xii. 224). Or in the thirteenth, more succinctly: 'Vous êtes hardis contre Dieu, et timides envers les hommes' (xiii. 250). Or again in the first *Ecrit des Curés de Paris* (the first part of which serves as a résumé of the major accusations of the *LPs*): 'Ces nouveaux théologiens, au lieu d'accommoder la vie des hommes aux préceptes de Jésus-Christ, ont entrepris d'accommoder les préceptes et les règles de Jésus-Christ aux intérêts, aux passions et aux plaisirs des hommes' (Cognet, p. 406). The language of Jesuit behaviour is thus portrayed as distorting in a far more important way than the language of Sorbonne pedantry the signified real-ities behind it. As Christians have ceased to be sacramental of Christ, since the grey area of morality has become so dark as to reconceal the hidden God, so at the same time the theology as enacted has disabled Christianity from claiming coherence or allegiance because of the incomplete view of man which it is seen to promote. If what the Jesuits preach and practice is true, the *Provinciales* suggest, then Christianity is unbelievable, failing as it does to account for God or for man. The case of the 'libertins qui ne cherchent qu'à douter de la religion' is evoked in the fourth letter, and their objection could be extended to all parts of the Jesuit position: 'Ils diront que si vous n'êtes pas véritables en un article, vous êtes suspects en tous: et ainsi vous les obligerez à conclure ou que la religion est fausse, ou du moins que vous en êtes mal instruits' (iv. 61).

We thus begin to see too how the attack on Jesuit behaviour can be described in linguistic terms. But this accusation of meaninglessness is of course also reflected in the terminology and usage of the Society: the unreality of its God, endowed only with 'paroles et apparences', is betrayed by the insubstantial nature of its theological discourse, and , in particular, its dogmatic assertions. It is in this light that its accusations of heresy are dismissed as unbelievable: 'Qui le croira, mes Pères? Le croyez-vous vous-mêmes?' (xvi. 320). Whereas the Académie Française can protect the words that are threatened with meaninglessness, though, it falls to Pascal to protect the meaning of the prevenient reality, both for its own intrinsic value, and for the sake of its credibility. He will thus embark on his second attack on meaninglessness, not however now in order to proceed through it to a more important question, but in order to reassert the means for Christianity to signify to its adherents, actual and potential. The way in which this specifically linguistic attack is developed will be explored in the next chapter.

9

The Terms of Confrontation

THE move towards confrontation in the first ten letters becomes increasingly more explicit as the series progresses, and is given its final fictional expression at the end of the Montalte–Jesuit dialogues. Then, in the eleventh letter, the theoretical underpinning of the series so far is established; and thereafter, in the letters following the eleventh, *cas-limite* examples of moral and spiritual perversion are placed in stark opposition to the immutably Christian viewpoint which challenges them with its contrasting absolutism. The polemicist now counters one extreme with another, yet his position, by virtue of its inspirational and scriptural endorsement, is made to seem particularly unvulnerable to counter-argument of a detailed, specifying kind.

This polarization is already prepared for in a sequence of juxtapositions, beginning in fact with the play on 'prochain' in the first letter. The first five letters then function on a loose rhythm of confrontation and development, with each encounter sharpened by the information provided directly or indirectly in the interim. After the middle of the fifth letter, one single confrontation then carries the burden of evidence with it, as each elucidation provided intensifies the disaccord between Montalte and his Jesuit. The shifts of direction (in the opening of letter iv, and half-way through letter v) serve temporarily to release the tension created by the increasingly strained self-control exercised by Montalte (in addition to the function of ironizing the preceding material)—as do such exclamations as 'Heureux les peuples qui l'ignorent [= prochain]! Heureux ceux qui ont précédé sa naissance!' (i. 19), with their biblical resonance. But after each break the pitch is heightened, leading in the series of satirical letters, and after the outburst of the 'ami janséniste' in the fifth, to the final build-up of tension, with the more and more informed and partisan first person enquiring of and responding to a single informant. This is made explicit, and thus further intensified, in the eighth letter:

Je suis obligé à me contraindre; car il ne les [discours] continuerait pas, s'il s'apercevait que j'en fusse si choqué ... Il est bien pénible de voir renverser toute la morale chrétienne par des égarements si étranges, sans oser y contredire ouvertement. Mais, après avoir tant enduré pour votre satisfaction, je pense qu'à la fin j'éclaterai pour la mienne, quand il n'aura plus rien à me dire. Cependant je me retiendrai autant qu'il me sera possible. (viii. 134; see also Duchêne, *IL* 188–91)

Montalte's mobility of the earlier letters decreases, and then ceases altogether, accompanying a development in the symbolic status of the Jesuit position. And the variety of fictional voices which began the whole series, each contributing a particular dimension to the picture, also recedes, as the principal burden of the satire is revealed, and the fictional emphasis falls more narrowly on the Montalte–Jesuit encounter (illustrative material now being provided by quotation). The degree of enlightenment thereby achieved thus enables the generic shift (as Duchêne has shown it to be)[1] from the tenth to the eleventh letter to take place smoothly, and in such a way as to satisfy the reader's expectations.

We already find in the tenth letter a *cas-limite* situated alongside an evangelic injunction (with only the expression of disgust of Montalte in between) foreshadowing the tone of the later pieces:

On peut rechercher une occasion [de péché] directement et par elle-même, primo et per se, *pour le bien temporel ou spirituel de soi ou du prochain.* . . .

Quel rapport y a-t-il, mon Père, de cette doctrine à celle de l'Evangile, qui oblige *à s'arracher les yeux, et à retrancher les choses les plus nécessaires quand elles nuisent au salut?* (x. 181–2)

This in turn prepares for the letter's concluding peroration, describing the antithetical terms in which the remainder of the series will function (and anticipating its use of sarcasm):

---

[1] 'La lettre familière cède le pas à la lettre ouverte. On a changé de genre littéraire' (*IL* 205).

Ainsi on rend dignes de jouir de Dieu dans l'éternité ceux qui n'ont jamais aimé Dieu en toute leur vie! Voilà le mystère d'iniquité accompli. Ouvrez enfin les yeux, mon Père; et si vous n'avez point été touché par les autres égarements de vos casuistes, que ces derniers vous en retirent par leurs excès. Je le souhaite de tout mon cœur pour vous et pour tous vos Pères, et je prie Dieu . . . qu'il remplisse de son amour ceux qui osent en dispenser les hommes.

Après quelques discours de cette sorte, je quittai le Père, et je ne vois guère d'apparence d'y retourner. (x. 191–2)

Montalte has fallen out with his 'ami jésuite'. Or, as Marc Fumaroli remarks: 'Au fur et à mesure qu'on avance vers la onzième *Provinciale* [le personnage de Montalte] a de plus en plus de mal à retenir l'indignation qu'il éprouve, et le masque glisse un peu. Il y a . . . un effet de progression'.[2] Thus the tension achieved in the later parts of the dialogue requires and makes convincing the outburst which the eleventh letter provides; and the extremism of the cases with which these letters conclude makes necessary their countering with the tone of moral absolutism which informs the letters following the eleventh, where the same kind of juxtaposition is developed in an explicitly combative context. We may now turn to the terminology in which this confrontation is expressed and indeed justified. Our enquiry will begin with a further reference to the *Pensées*.

Changes of Language

The rehabilitated *question de droit* which unites polemic and apologetic—(why) is Christianity 'aimable' and 'vénérable'—is argued out initially in the equally rehabilitated, but still satirical *questions de fait* of the first of the two central series of letters (v–x). Pascal has thereby effected a preliminary change of language and arena, via a transitional stage of meaninglessness ('prochain' etc.). The terms of the original debate have been provisionally dismissed: but the ensuing debate still employs a fictional and frivolous medium, albeit in the service of a different enquiry. A second change of perspective has eventually to be brought about

---

[2] In *débat* following Morel, 'Pascal et la doctrine du rire grave', in *Méthodes chez Pascal*, p. 222.

in the *LPs*, therefore, in order to introduce true Christian values. For this to happen, the shift that has been made implicitly from doctrine to ethics will now be supported by an explicit linguistic development; and this will in turn share much with the emptying out of one set of terms in favour of another which accompanies the conversion of the unbeliever of the *Pensées*.

The unbeliever must be brought to see his ideal of fulfilment as illusory; the 'puissances trompeuses', led by the imagination, create an inauthentic state of happiness which the apologist must annihilate before indicating its permanent replacement: '[L'imagination] remplit ses hôtes d'une satisfaction bien autrement pleine et entière que la raison ... Elle ne peut rendre sages les fous mais elle les rend heureux, à l'envi de la raison qui ne peut rendre ses amis que misérables' (L 44). As the terms of man's view of himself become those of the apologist, the apparatus of 'divertissement'/imagination-engendered happiness is removed; the trough of despair born of man's awareness of his 'misère' is experienced, and the 'grandeur' of thought completes the picture. This creation of a certain view of man is the prelude to his release (and that is how it is arranged rhetorically) because of the construction of an arena of debate whereof the parameters have been so defined as to prevent all (acknowledged) alternative issues. Given the dilemma proposed by the apologist and con-ceded by the seeker, and given the range of alternative solutions presented and rejected, Christianity will be accepted as the uniquely satisfying explanation and solution. Pascal's view of man is like a matrix, waiting to be filled by Pascal's view of God.

What has to happen to the perspectives of the man who undergoes this transition is furthermore fundamental. The effect of Christianity is to bring about a 'renversement' in the way in which he sees life, death, self, and so on, a change which will impinge on his whole conduct: 'Changeons la règle que nous avons prise jusqu'ici pour juger de ce qui est bon. Nous en avions pour règle notre volonté; prenons maintenant la volonté de Dieu : tout ce qu'il veut nous est bon et juste, tout ce qu'il ne veut pas (mauvais et injuste)' (L 948). This change of perspective is expressed paradigmatically in two further fragments from the *Pensées*, which will in turn serve to illustrate my arguments in the two parts of this chapter. The first proposes that: 'Le péché originel est folie devant les hommes, mais on le donne pour tel. . . Mais cette folie est plus sage que toute la sagesse des hommes' (L 695, cf. L 291). And its obverse, which reverberates throughout the 'Raison des Effets' section of the 'Papiers Classés' (and related fragments) is expressed by the paradox: 'Les choses du monde les plus déraisonnables deviennent les plus raisonnables à cause du dérèglement des hommes' (L 977). We shall begin, in the light of the first of these fragments, by considering what I shall call converted meanings.

Pascal is concerned in both the *LPs* and the *Pensées* to introduce or rehabilitate the perspective of eternity. Christian meanings operate *sub specie aeternitatis* or, perhaps more correctly, *quasi oculo Dei*, as we see in another context—the *Oraison Funèbre* of Henriette d'Angleterre—where Bossuet, having reduced his subject to a 'je ne sais quoi, qui n'a plus de nom dans aucune langue', invites his hearers: 'Changeons maintenant de langage', and re-examines events in the Christian perspective. Throughout the *Pensées* too we are aware of an ambivalence of referent in the use of certain words, most particularly in the discussion of man's state before and after conversion. The ambiguity is already present in the bipartite division of the project's elaboration:

(1.) Partie.   Misère de l'homme sans Dieu.
(2.) Partie.   Félicité de l'homme avec Dieu. (L 6)

Here the 'misère' in question is not, presumably, only coextensive with an awareness of 'unhappiness', but rather includes an acknowledgment of all that provisional happiness provided by 'divertissement'; equally, it is contrasted with a 'félicité' which transcends, and perhaps contradicts, human models. We find on occasion a distinction made by the use of 'véritable'/'vrai' between true happiness, justice, and so on, and their illusory counterparts, thus: 'Il y a eu autrefois dans l'homme un véritable bonheur' (L 148), that is the 'bonheur de [sa] première nature', contrasted with the 'misères de [son] aveuglement' (L 149). Or again, 'notre vraie félicité est d'être en lui [God]' (L 149). In the seventeenth *LP*, too, Pascal writes to Annat: 'Votre bonheur est digne de compassion, et ne peut être envié que par ceux qui ignorent quel est le véritable bonheur' (xvii. 353). In other fragments what is clearly true happiness has, however, simply to be understood as such:

Le bonheur n'est en effet que dans le repos et non pas dans le tumulte. (L 136)

Si l'homme n'est fait pour Dieu pourquoi n'est-il heureux qu'en Dieu. (L 399)

Le bonheur n'est ni hors de nous ni dans nous; il est en Dieu et hors et dans nous. (L 407)

En lui est toute notre vertu et toute notre félicité. (L 416)

And in L 148, for example, we find one noun qualified, and the other not: 'Que l'homme sans la foi ne peut connaître le vrai bien, ni la justice'. The same principle applies to false happiness:

Les hommes…se sont avisés, pour se rendre heureux, de n'y point penser. (L 133)

Toute la félicité des hommes consiste dans cette estime. (L 411)

Ceux qui…ne pensent à se rendre heureux que dans cet instant seulement. (L 428)

Cette félicité languissante ne le [roi] soutiendra point. (L 136)

This pattern could also be transferred to verb-governed examples: 'La seule chose qui nous console de nos misères est le divertissement…le divertissement nous amuse' (L 414)). It would no doubt be tempting to attribute to each of the terms, 'bonheur' and 'félicité', a stable meaning; but clearly, from the above examples, incorrect, since both words are used in both senses. Furthermore, the same ambiguity may exist in references to false, that is transitory, unhappiness: 'l'homme est si malheureux qu'il s'ennuierait même sans aucune cause d'ennui' (L 136).

But if the difference between false and true unhappiness is one of perception, since both describe and emanate from the same condition (true unhappiness is the mental state which takes account of the 'misère', and seeks to transcend it rather than relapsing into 'divertissement'), it is the recognition of the falsity of worldly happiness that will lead man to aspire to, and potentially achieve, its true counterpart. The complexity of this process in relation to the human condition, and in terms of 'bassesse' and 'grandeur', is demonstrated in a fragment on 'les philosophes':

Les philosophes ne prescrivaient point des sentiments proportionnés aux deux états. . .

Il faut des mouvements de bassesse, non de nature, mais de pénitence non pour y demeurer mais pour aller à la grandeur. Il faut des mouvements de grandeur, non de mérite mais de grâce et après avoir passé par la bassesse. (L 398)

Such an ambivalence of attitude towards a single state or action is also of course reflected in the idea of direction of intention or motive—the former in terms of the Jesuit confessional practice, and the latter in terms of Pascal's own distinction between types of action in the fourteenth letter, to which we shall return. And the matter is further complicated by the existence of an element of the legitimate prelapsarian 'grandeur' in such aspirations or actions. The desire for 'estime' is base in itself, but points to the remnant of a complementary, but noble desire: 'La plus grande bassesse de l'homme est la recherche de la gloire, mais c'est cela même qui est la plus grande marque de son excellence; car, quelque possession qu'il ait sur la terre, quelque santé et commodité essentielle qu'il ait, il n'est pas satisfait, s'il n'est dans l'estime des hommes' (L 470).

All such terms are therefore capable of being situated in a semantic area which implicitly overturns the natural/'diverti' concepts of 'malheur' and 'bonheur'. Man aspires to 'bonheur' and may believe he possesses it, in his own terms. But when he truly does possess it (in God's terms), it is entirely different from what he imagined it would be, and the achievement of the 'félicité avec Dieu' must emanate from the adoption of the anti-natural strictures of Pascal's Christianity, among which most notably the counsel of self-hatred. As Molinier, in his 1891 edition of the *LPs*, writes of the Christian dilemma: 'Plus qu'aucune autre, la religion chrétienne dérive d'une réaction contre la nature'.[3] If furthermore the status of the terms in some of the fragments we have examined is relatively clear, that of some others used in the process of persuasion is more uncertain. What, for example, is

[3] *Lettres Provinciales*, ed. A. Molinier, 2 vols. (Paris, 1891), i, Introduction, p. cxli.

the apologist telling his interlocutor when he writes: 'Nul n'est heureux comme un vrai chrétien, ni raisonnable, ni vertueux, ni aimable' (L 357)? Or in 'Il n'y a que la religion chrétienne qui rende l'homme aimable et heureux tout ensemble' (L 426)? 'Raisonnable' and 'vertueux' both carry quite clear meanings (from this point of view at least) within the *Pensées*. But 'aimable' and especially 'heureux' are, as we have seen, capable of interpretation both on the immanent and transcendent levels. Would the unbeliever recognize himself after conversion as 'heureux' in the sense in which he now understands the term?

The 'pari' illustrates this difference as well as any fragment, in the use of such apparently objective, but in fact highly ambivalent terms as the 'tout'/'rien' of: 'Si vous gagnez vous gagnez tout, et si vous perdez vous ne perdez rien'; or in: 'Il y a une éternité de vie de bonheur... il y a ici une infinité de vie infiniment heureuse à gagner' (L 418).

Elsewhere the apologist seems to be emphasizing that the terminology he uses is that of unconverted men; this is most striking in a fragment dealing with original sin, in which expressions of strangeness and even offence abound: 'Cet écoulement ne nous paraît pas seulement impossible. Il nous semble même très injuste... Certainement rien ne nous heurte plus rudement que cette doctrine' (L 131). The semantic marker in this fragment is however provided by the epithet in the associated rhetorical question: 'car qu'y a(-t-)il de plus contraire aux règles de notre misérable justice?' Or again we find: 'Le christianisme est étrange; il ordonne à l'homme de reconnaître qu'il est vil et même abominable, et lui ordonne de vouloir être semblable à Dieu' (L 351). (It would seem from one fragment (in which the interplay of voices is however very unclear) that the innate Christian is also particularly aware of the strangeness of his belief: 'On a beau dire : il faut avouer que la religion chrétienne a quelque chose d'étonnant. C'est parce que vous y êtes né dira(-t-)on' (L 817); but perhaps 'étonnant' has a more colloquial meaning here.)

We may then ask disingenuously how this strange religion, 'contre la nature, contre le sens commun, contre nos plaisirs' (L 284) can accord with the hyperbolic description of the true Christian as 'raisonnable, heureux, aimable'? The answer must lie in the tacit addition of 'notre/nos misérable(s)' to 'nature', 'sens commun', and 'plaisirs'; yet not to 'raisonnable', 'heureux', 'aimable'. There is thus an overlap, not always identified by lexical differentiation; it is furthermore an overlap within which the transcendentally signified term may imply exactly the opposite of the immanently signified one. This kind of distinction again comes to the surface in the 'pari', where the assurance: 'Vous serez fidèle, honnête, humble, reconnaissant, bienfaisant, ami sincère, véritable' is followed by the concession: 'A la vérité vous ne serez point dans les plaisirs empestés, dans la gloire, dans les délices, mais n'en aurez-vous point d'autres?... Vous connaîtrez à la fin que vous avez parié pour une chose certaine' (L 418). In the *LPs*, too, the same point is made; and a quotation from St Augustine in the twelfth letter provides a cryptic illustration: 'Nous avons beaucoup de superflu... si nous ne gardons que le nécessaire' (xii. 223).

A perspective will eventually prevail, the perspective of grace, which ensures this transition/translation, once the immanent has been displaced and the transcendent introduced. And the achievement of this perspective is the end point of both works; they start from a multiplicity of viewpoints (disinterested/hostile/'mauvais chrétien', etc.), but they posit a single terminus. The view of the believer that emerges from the apology as adumbrated in the *Pensées* will place him in the same tradition as that of the polemicist of the *LPs*. As Baudin observes (with no doubt somewhat too lurid a view of the Pascalian addressee): 'Pascal est le convertisseur-né de tous ceux qui crient vers Dieu du fond d'un épicurisme déçu... Ce sont peut-être là ses plus authentiques disciples, et qui le suivent le plus volontiers — jusqu'au jansénisme exclusivement'.[4] This is the perspective too which prevails in the words of the 'ami janséniste': 'Pour dégager l'âme de l'amour du monde, pour la retirer de ce qu'elle a de plus cher, pour la faire mourir à soi-même, pour la porter et l'attacher uniquement et invariablement à Dieu, ce n'est l'ouvrage que d'une main toute puissante' (v. 79); or of the evolving Montalte, who deems that Jesuit 'dévotion aisée' is more likely to: 'entretenir les pécheurs

---

[4] *Etudes historiques et critiques*, II. ii. 369.

dans leurs désordres, par la fausse paix que cette confiance
téméraire apporte, qu'à les en retirer par une véritable conversion
que la grâce seule peut produire' (ix. 156). It must furthermore be
assumed to be the terminal position of the 'ami provincial'.

The deepest tone of consolation in the *Pensées* (whatever the
status of the fragment in the apologetic project) occurs significantly in the *Mystère de Jésus*, juxtaposed with the most fervent
expression of identification with the suffering Christ, again
relating to that 'véritable conversion de cœur, qui fait autant
aimer Dieu qu'on a aimé les créatures' (x. 182), whereby 'le cœur
de pierre et de glace... soit sincèrement changé en un cœur de
chair et d'amour' (xvi. 318). The practice of self-hatred can thus
itself be 'renversé' in the process of movement 'du pour au
contre', so that, in the light of Christianity, self-love can coexist
with it: 'Il faudrait que la véritable religion... portât à l'estime et
au mépris de soi' (L 450); but it is only through the knowledge of
Christ that such a perspective is achieved.

The question of Jesuit 'renversement' in the *LPs* is understood
within this whole context of changing perspectives: it is a knowing rejection of the counsel of self-hatred, a re-espousing of
nature, couched in the terminology of Christianity. The Society's
adoption of nature is thus a deliberate reversal of Christian terms,
as the 'ami janséniste' implies: 'Comme leur morale est toute
païenne, la nature suffit pour l'observer' (v. 78, cf. L 601), or as
'admitted' by the fictional Jesuit in the line: 'les hommes sont
aujourd'hui tellement corrompus, que, ne pouvant les faire venir
à nous, il faut bien que nous allions à eux' (vi. 103). Later again
Montalte too exclaims: 'Il est bien pénible de voir renverser toute
la morale chrétienne par des égarements si étranges' (viii. 134);
thereafter, at the end of the ninth letter, the Jesuit asks: 'N'est-ce
pas là un merveilleux changement?' (ix. 170); and the polemicist
charges Vasquez in the pre-1659 editions with 'un si visible
renversement de l'Evangile' (xii. (221)).[5] Finally an equation is

---

[5] The phrase in the earlier edns. reads: '[Vasquez] n'est pas digne de ce
reproche, après avoir établi, comme il a fait, par un si visible renversement de
l'Evangile, que les riches...'. In the 1659 edn. it reads simply '[Vasquez] n'est
pas digne de ce reproche, après avoir établi, comme je l'ai fait voir, que les
riches...'.

made between novelty and 'renversement' in the eleventh letter: 'Quelle nouvelle charité qui s'offense de voir confondre des erreurs manifestes et qui ne s'offense point de voir renverser la morale par ces erreurs' (xi. 202). As such, the Jesuit position is a post-Christian rather than a non-Christian state, and its culmination is translatable into the terms of eternity as the 'misère de l'homme avec Dieu'. It progresses from, rather than taking no account of, the Christian order, and can therefore be expressed in terms of a development, as Montalte exclaims at the end of the seventh letter: 'Il vaudrait autant avoir affaire à des gens qui n'ont point de religion, qu'à ceux qui en sont instruits jusqu'à cette direction' (vii. 131), a view of the Society which also emerges in a fragment of the *Pensées*: 'Si c'est un aveuglement surnaturel de vivre sans chercher ce qu'on est, c'en est un terrible de vivre mal en croyant Dieu' (L 623).

Again we see a complementary relationship between the two works: the context of the *Pensées*, that of the world, contains an appeal for 'renversement', and a promise of that 'félicité' that is the outcome, indeed the translated equivalent, of self-hatred; the *LPs* take the context of the Church, and thus appeal against the opposing 'renversement', because it will create that transitory 'bonheur' whose ultimate falsity will, in the perspective of eternity, be demonstrated. And it goes without saying that Pascal is also accused in similar terms: in the twelfth *Réponse*: 'Vous confondez toutes choses par un renversement prodigieux de la théologie' (*RLP* 219); or in Pirot, where we find: 'Qui eût cru que dans Paris les choses fussent tellement renversées que des esprits à qui un marchand ne voudrait pas confier le jugement d'un procès de dix pistoles, s'érigeassent en juges des théologiens dans les matières les plus difficiles' (p. 181).

This endless changing of perspectives is of course most vigorously turned round on the Jesuits in the defensive thrust of the eleventh letter, to which we shall attend in the next section of this chapter; and the ultimate vindication of the Christian order comes in the apocalyptic pronouncements which are to be found in the conclusion to the twelfth: 'La violence n'a qu'un cours borné par l'ordre de Dieu, qui en conduit les effets à la gloire de la vérité qu'elle attaque : au lieu que la vérité subsiste éternellement, et triomphe enfin de ses ennemis, parce qu'elle est éternelle et puissante comme Dieu même' (xii. 234–5)—of which Sellier remarks: 'La péroraison de la douzième *Provinciale* offre un exemple saisissant de ces amples scènes d'affrontement auxquelles Pascal trouve des délices insurpassables' (*IL* 343).

The complementary expression of this semantic opposition —what I shall call inverted meanings—is made explicit in the distinction between two languages made in the fourteenth and fifteenth letters (but is illustrated in passing elsewhere in the series).[6] The context is the choice proposed to the Jesuits between their identification with and opposition to the Gospel. This choice is articulated in a variety of terms, leading to the linguistic/ topographical metaphor: 'Voyez donc maintenant, mes Pères, duquel de ces deux royaumes vous êtes. Vous avez ouï le langage de la ville de paix, qui s'appelle le Jérusalem mystique, et vous avez ouï le langage de la ville de trouble, que l'Ecriture appelle *la spirituelle Sodome* : lequel de ces deux langages entendez-vous? lequel parlez-vous?' There follows a quote from the Jesuit authorities ('Ecoutons donc le langage de votre Ecole') and then the question: 'Est-ce là le langage de Jésus-Christ?' (xiv. 272). The semantic principles of their language are then gradually exposed, and, in the next letter, its characteristics are demonstrated. The polemicist uses the anecdote of a certain M. Puys, who, having been accused of immorality, impiety, and heresy by the Jesuits, publicly declared his affection for the Society and, 'par ces seules paroles… revint de son apostasie, de ses scandales et de son excommunication, sans rétraction et sans absolution' (xv. 284). From this he concludes: 'C'est donc une même chose dans votre langage d'attaquer votre Société et d'être hérétique?… Il est bon, mes Pères, qu'on entende cet étrange langage, selon lequel il est sans doute que je suis un grand hérétique' (xv. 285).

Three major points emerge from this passage. First of all, it is a language which functions entirely subjectively, and accusations made through its medium are shown to be false, because the

---

[6] Wolfe remarks: 'Les *Provinciales* XI à XVI seront donc avant tout une comparaison de deux langages : le langage de la charité, tenu par Pascal, et le langage de l'imposture, tenu par la Société' ('Langage et vérité dans les *Provinciales* XI à XVI', p. 80).

words in which they are expressed do not signify according to either natural or transcendent usage. The accusation of heresy is as empty as the orthodoxy of lip-service which is demanded since here, as at the beginning of the work, words are shown to have a purely political significance. Jesuit semantic principles give the Society the freedom to change language in a variety of ways to this end: in the *LPs*, 'en disant d'une même maxime qu'elle est dans vos livres et qu'elle n'y est pas; qu'elle est bonne et qu'elle est mauvaise' (xv. 288), illustrating the assertion in the *Pensées*: 'Gens sans paroles, sans foi, sans honneur, sans vérité, doubles de cœur, doubles de langue et semblables... à cet animal amphibie de la fable' (L 909); in the pedantic heresy-spotting in the sixteenth letter (xvi. 310 ff.); or in the accusation in the second *Ecrit des Curés*: 'ils ont bien changé de langage à notre égard' (Cognet, p. 419). In the end it is again truth itself that is threatened. As the Jesuit exclaims ironically in the eighth letter: 'Vraiment vous êtes admirable! Il semble, de la façon que vous parlez, que la vérité dépende de notre volonté' (viii. 148), an irony that is then made explicit in the twelfth, where the variability of the Society in terms of its own doctrines is exposed: 'Ainsi vous les [maximes jésuites] reconnaissez ou les renoncez, non pas selon la vérité qui ne change jamais, mais selon les divers changements des temps' (xii. 220–1). Of course, the one change they have not effected is the radical and only acceptable one which is that of perspective, 'de sorte que le changement de leur style n'est pas l'effet de la conversion de leur cœur, mais une adresse de leur politique, qui leur fait prendre tant de différentes formes en demeurant toujours les mêmes' (*Second Ecrit des Curés*, Cognet, p. 420).

Most important of all in the polemical context, their ambiguity born of subjectivity is extended by the Jesuits to their (hostile) interpretation of the writings of others: 'Et qui ne ferez-vous point passer pour Calviniste quand il vous plaira, si on vous laisse la licence de corrompre les expressions les plus canoniques et les plus saintes par les malicieuses subtilités de vos nouvelles équivoques?' (xvi. 304). Or more intensely still, 'ils rendront hérétique tout ce qu'ils voudront, et même l'Ecriture sainte' (xvi. 311), thereby working the linguistic deformation round to an implicit defence of Port-Royal's orthodoxy. A summary of the topsy-

turvy results of these procedures is then found in a fragment of
the *Pensées*: 'Des pécheurs purifiés sans pénitence, des justes
sanctifiés sans charité, tous les chrétiens sans la grâce de Jésus-
Christ, Dieu sans pouvoir sur la volonté des hommes, une
prédestination sans mystère, une rédemption sans certitude' (L
864). In such a passage a whole series of Christian tenets is
qualified by a clause which negates them and thus reduces them,
by this semantic conceit, to the meaninglessness that Jesuit
Christianity epitomizes for Pascal.

Secondly, and relatedly, it is described as an 'étrange langage',
but with the use of 'étrange' directly opposed to the sense in
which 'le christianisme est étrange'. Christianity is strange in the
eyes of the world; the Jesuits' language is strange in the eyes of the
believer. But the Society has again proceeded so far into a
perverse use of language, of the kind seen as early as the first letter,
that the strangeness has become perceptible to the eyes of common sense. Their subjective attribution of meaning has made
clear a disparity between signifier and signified lying behind the
apparent restoration of 'natural', that is received/immanent
meaning. In this way, the language of Christianity is being forced
back into the secular domain so violently that it is disabled from
serving in this, its common-sense context. The model I have used
in terms of the appeal to nature's recognition of the distortion that
offends Christian truth may thus also be seen to function linguistically (see Fig. 2). Therefore the Jesuit attacks on Jansenist
eucharistic orthodoxy, made by the application of a pedantic use
of literalism, meet in the fifteenth and sixteenth letters the same
objections of common sense as did their counter-natural moral
teaching. In answer to the second of the proofs of heresy,
emanating from the equation 'opposition to Jesuits = heresy', the
polemicist writes: 'Si vous n'avez point de sens commun, je ne
puis pas vous en donner. Tous ceux qui en ont se moqueront
assez de vous' (xvi. 313). The strange language of the Society of
Jesus will be greeted with ridicule as its semantic principles are
identified.

Thirdly, we note that this language, in order to be understood
or rather dismantled, needs an interpreter and thus, as Descotes
remarks, 'la présence de Montalte se justifie, entre les Jésuites et le

truth (ultimate meaning)

|

Christian ('renversé') converted meanings

|

common sense/natural usage

|

Jesuit ('renversé') inverted/private meanings

|

meaninglessness

FIG. 2

public, par la nécessité de cette "traduction"'.[7] To demonstrate this apparent linguistic barrier, Montalte and his Jesuit interlocutor spend long periods in a kind of contrived *dialogue de sourds*: 'Vous voyez par là que vous ne savez pas seulement ce que les termes signifient, et cependant vous parlez comme un docteur. J'avoue, lui dis-je, que cela m'est nouveau' (vii. 122). The *dialogue de sourds* is then later identified as such by the outburst of the thirteenth letter; incomprehension is here retrospectively shown to be short-lived, as enlightenment is expressed in its place: 'On l'entend, mes Pères, ce langage de votre école. Et c'est une chose étonnante que vous ayez le front de le parler si haut' (xiii. 252). Perhaps by applying the code of fragment L 557—'Les langues sont des chiffres où, non les lettres sont changées en lettres, mais les mots en mots. De sorte qu'une langue inconnue est déchiffrable'—the language of the Society of Jesus has been understood. It can now be translated, and the move from the satirical to the confrontational register in the letters following the eleventh corresponds to that translation. As Montalte has become the polemicist, he has learnt a new language.

The letters thus function on three overlapping linguistic levels —the converted, the common-sense, and the inverted. The polemical force of the later part of the series largely arises from

[7] 'Fonction argumentative', p. 61.

the shared offence/surprise encountered by the speakers of the
first two at the exposed terminology of the third.

Associated with these linguistic questions are the identification
of multiplicity (betokening error) against the unity characteristic
of truth; and the attendant charge of populism which recurs
throughout the letters. Of the former, Reisler writes of 'a basic
dichotomy of unity and multiplicity, with the former represent-
ing truth and the latter falsehood';[8] and Davidson's description of
Pascal's wish for 'univocity, singleness of meaning for each
term'[9] may also be transferred into this context. On the latter, the
Society is attacked on the grounds that it employs 'les adoucisse-
ments de la Confession... pour attirer tout le monde et ne rebuter
personne' (x. 171). The attack is not therefore based on the
attempt to bring Christianity to a greater number of people, but
on the charge of adapting it by means of ambiguity in order to do
so. In this way, 'vous retenez dans l'Eglise les plus débordés et
ceux qui la déshonorent si fort que les synagogues des Juifs et
sectes des philosophes les auraient exclus comme indignes et les
auraient abhorrés comme impies' (L 923). By a flexible and
subjective understanding of Christian terms, an accommodation
is made possible even with those who live most at odds with
them. What however in Jesuit terms is accommodation with
converted meanings, only arguable within a spectrum, is for
Pascal an introduction of inverted meanings, argued at the limits
of that spectrum or beyond. And it is in order to show this, as we
have seen, that Pascal uses extreme examples, judged by a
relativizing ethic.

The case made by him stems largely, here again, from the
absolute because inspirational view which he holds of efficacious
belief: 'La religion chrétienne qui seule a la raison n'admet point
pour ses vrais enfants ceux qui croient sans inspiration' (L 808).
And the same kind of radical alteration of perspective which
characterizes the Pascalian conversion also imbues the polemical
effort. Because of its intensity and absolutism it exists outside
category and case, the very essence of the Jesuit moral system.

---

[8] 'Persuasion through Antithesis', p. 174.
[9] *Audience, Words, and Art*, p. 120.

The details of the particular occupations and circumstances of individuals which succeed each other already in the fifth and sixth letters therefore represent for Pascal both an irrelevance and an incoherence—they are terms which are untranslatable into the transcendent perspective. Furthermore, any authentic unity is threatened as the Jesuits make the fundamentally simple truth universal only by means of endless qualification; as different authorities are again quoted as suiting different individuals (including, notably, those who seek a stricter code of practice) in the thirteenth letter, the polemicist exclaims: 'C'est donc cette variété qui vous confond davantage. L'uniformité serait plus supportable' (xiii. 253). And fragment L 729 comments succinctly on the outcome: 'Leur grand nombre loin de marquer leur perfection marque le contraire', perhaps pointing thereby to the two views of the Church (inclusive and exclusive) which lie beneath the opposing positions.

Turning to Pirot, we find the complementary paradigm in the *Apologie pour les Casuistes*, in which he uses everyday examples, judged by an absolutizing ethic, thereby demonstrating the inapplicability of (converted) unity of meaning to the ambiguous circumstances of common moral dilemmas. The sheer number of examples which Pirot gives, quite apart from its persuasive factor, serves to demonstrate the unrealistic implications of an absolutist standpoint, and the breadth and complexity with which a pragmatic ethical system is bound to contend (even if he takes exemplification to the opposite extreme). He insists on the freedom to hold divergent views, disagreeing himself on occasion with a reported doctrine, or pointing out that a particular subject (for instance scandal) gives rise to a variety of opinions: 'Si...ceux qui entre les Jansénistes sont théologiens avaient étudié au fond ces questions, ils auraient jugé que de toutes les matières de la morale chrétienne il n'y en a pas de plus difficile que celle du scandale' (p. 150). But if Pirot's appeal depends on the complementary disparity to that on which the polemicist bases his argument, it is in both cases by a lack of terminological appropriateness that common sense is offended.

Finally, for Pascal, the failure of true universality in Christianity will betoken its error, a prediction attributed by the polemicist, in the explanation of his opposition to multiplicity, to 'vos propres Généraux': 'Le dérèglement de votre doctrine dans la morale pourrait être funeste non seulement à votre Société, mais encore à l'Eglise universelle' (xiii. 253). Thus what is true for case ethics is again reflected in doctrine: if Christianity has to absorb and explain dualistically, its means of salvation, the Church, must reflect the triune nature of the Godhead, whose trinity expresses numerical unity rather than numerical plurality. Human nature is dualistic, and human dilemmas are multifarious, in distinction to God; but Christianity works for the reachievement of unity in its saints (the erection of a corresponding supernatural dualism to that in man deriving from the heresy of Manichaeism). The existence of ambiguity, reflecting such a dualism in Jesuit moral teaching, is thus roundly condemned at the end of the thirteenth letter: the Jesuits have sought to 'offrir deux chemins aux hommes, en détruisant la simplicité de l'Esprit de Dieu, qui maudit ceux qui sont doubles de cœur, et qui se préparent deux voies' (xiii. 254).[10] A fragment from the *Pensées* adds with aphoristic equilibrium: 'La multitude qui ne se réduit pas à l'unité est confusion. L'unité qui ne dépend pas de la multitude est tyrannie' (L 604). And the achievement of such unity will be reflected in the universal and unambiguous adoption of converted meanings.

Having introduced the circumstances for the second change of language, the polemicist is now arguing within the terms of his choice: the first shift, from doctrinal *fait* to moral *droit*, has been followed by a development of the inverted semantic principles of the Society of Jesus (in both their moral and doctrinal dimensions), to the point at which, reduced in the ways we have seen to meaninglessness, they are confronted by their converted correlative, the perspective of eternity and grace.

---

[10] In his article (cit. n. 5), Wolfe studies the metaphor of 'le chemin' in the *L Ps*. He remarks in particular with reference to this quotation: 'Le voyage est multiple... Multiforme, ce voyage se dénonce par là-même comme désastreux, car il s'oppose à l'intemporalité et à l'incorruptibilité de Dieu et du texte divin, dont les commandements sont invariables' (p. 84).

'Raillerie' and 'Fureur': The Eleventh Letter

Returning to the eleventh letter, it is first worth looking at the attacks on 'raillerie', 'cet ornement de comédie et de roman' (*RLP* 2), which occur at all stages of the counter-polemic. They are both frequent and repetitive, playing on the idea that heresy gives rise to frivolity in serious matters, and that the author would do better to limit himself to the domain to which he is accustomed (usually considered to be the novel) rather than attempting more serious genres. The *Première Réponse* of the *RLP* attacks his tendency to 'rendre les Jésuites ridicules... par des façons de répondre qu'il leur attribue, niaises, et badines, qui font le plus beau de ses dialogues puériles' (*RLP* xiv), and talks of his 'style railleur et bouffon, indigne... d'un chrétien' (*RLP* xvi), concluding 'aussi est-ce une espèce de blasphème, que de traiter les choses saintes en raillerie' (*RLP* xvii). Appeals to discipleship of St Augustine are dismissed on the grounds that St Augustine abstained in his writings from frivolity; demons, on the other hand, adopt 'raillerie' 'pour inciter la populace à un ris dissolu, l'ennemi de la dévotion, et la ruine de la religion' (*RLP* xvii) (it is later claimed that the whole work is aimed to 'faire rire des athées et des libertins' (*RLP* 20)) and the *Première Réponse* ends with the exhortation, based on *Proverbs*: 'Chassez et éloignez de vous le moqueur et le bouffon, il ne mérite que le mépris, et de sa personne, et de son ouvrage' (*RLP* xviii). Then, in the *VIIIe Avertissement*, the writer objects: 'Il est honteux que vous n'ayez point d'autres écrivains à opposer aux théologiens, qu'un faiseur de lettres' (*RLP* 39). More specifically, he pours scorn in the *VIIe Imposture* on the use of a list of foreign names to cause laughter: 'Pensez-vous qu'un homme sage se paie de vos fades railleries, qui ne sont bonnes qu'à étonner quelque faible cerveau, et à tromper quelque étourdi?' (*RLP* 34), but concludes the final *Avertissement* of the first series with a similar list, now of heretics, enclosed within the question 'si tous les gens que vous voyez ici. . . étaient véritablement chrétiens?' (*RLP* 89–90). It must however be acknowledged that certain of the counter-polemicists, and especially Morel, seem also to believe that a list is an argument (e.g. *Réponse générale*, p. 13).

The tone of the replies, it is stressed, will (and indeed largely does) display a higher degree of seriousness: 'Je vous laisse ces railleries: il faut être plus retenu que vous n'êtes en des disputes sérieuses' (*VIIIe Avertissement, RLP* 41). And Morel also promises: 'Je n'apporterai rien que de sérieux... Si vous savez surprendre le monde, je sais l'instruire, et le détromper si vous l'avez charmé' (p. 3). He later describes Pascal as having 'hérité du génie de Lucien, de l'humeur de l'hérésiarque Arius, et de l'esprit de Rabelais et [de] Du Moulin'. He goes on: 'Les railleurs pèchent toujours doublement quand ils raillent, parce qu'ils font en se moquant ce qui devrait les faire pleurer, et désobligent cruellement autrui, parce qu'en lui [*sic*] faisant du mal, ils veulent qu'il rie' (p. 38).

It is perhaps also worth quoting the *Réponse et remerciement* which, presumably ironically, nevertheless describes the qualities of the letters particularly well:

Monsieur Arnauld dans ses longues lettres ne fait qu'ennuyer ses lecteurs; et toutes ces broderies des marges commencent à n'être plus à la mode. Vous avez plus heureusement rencontré que tous les autres, et par un merveilleux artifice, vous joignez ensemble le sérieux et le facétieux; de telle sorte qu'en lisant vos Lettres, on trouve en même temps de quoi se divertir, et se rendre savant. (p. 1)

Accompanying such remarks is the familiar attack on ignorance, taking up, without acknowledging its part of irony, the claims of a lack of theological knowledge. Thus in the *Préface* to the *Deuxième Réponse*, rather petulantly: 'Il joint à cette grossière ignorance tant d'impostures, tant d'impiétés, tant de contradictions et d'erreurs, qu'il est tout à fait insupportable' (*RLP* xlvii).

It goes without saying that the love of 'raillerie' is also associated with heresy. Marandé, quoting the Spanish bishop Lucas de Tuy in his *Au Lecteur*, writes that heretics 'par des jeux sacrilèges ... tournent en raillerie et en dérision les choses saintes... afin que par ce moyen ils puissent fasciner les yeux et l'esprit des fidèles'. They fail however to see 'ce que la Sainte Ecriture remarque sur ce sujet, quand elle dit que le fou ou l'insensé commet les crimes les plus énormes par manière de raillerie' (p. v). He then describes the whole series in a long and entertaining analogy with 'quelques femmes qui se perdent dans le grand monde', who, after a period of immorality, 'se piquent de chasteté et d'honneur beaucoup plus que ne font les femmes les plus chastes et les plus vertueuses' (p. vi). But then 'l'effronterie succède à la pudeur affectée' and 'elles se portent à la dernière infamie, et arrivent enfin à une telle impudence, qu'elles tirent leur gloire de la matière de leur honte et de leur propre confusion' (p. vii). It is therefore his duty 'd'empêcher que la fourbe ou la ruse de l'hérésie nouvelle, déguisée et travestie maintenant en raillerie sous ces Lettres bouffonnes, ne séduise les simples' (p. viii). Again the behaviour is characterized as typical of 'des hérétiques anciens et modernes, qui pour énerver les censures qui les ont foudroyé [*sic*], ont fait un jeu et une raillerie de leur propre condamnation' (p. iii).

Finally in the last stages of the dispute Pirot still objects sarcastically: 'il eût été bien plus séant à un Janséniste, qui fait le pénitent et le réformé, d'écrire d'un style grave et sérieux' (p. 121), and, dealing with the subject of 'raillerie' in the last *Réponse* of the *Apologie pour les Casuistes*, concludes: 'depuis que l'Evangile a voulu introduire dans le monde la sainteté des mœurs, le diable a persécuté par des railleries ceux qui se consacraient à ce saint emploi' (p. 173).

It is in this context too that the eleventh letter, more than any other, serves to bring out the tacitly understood terms of the dispute, by describing and defending the 'forme' as well as the 'fond' of the series as a whole. In order to achieve this, it must first justify the adoption of the terms of 'raillerie' in the preceding letters, and it does so by bringing into the open the patristic (and scriptural) justification for satire, notably in the points taken from St Augustine: 'Les sages rient des insensés, parce qu'ils sont sages, non pas de leur propre sagesse, mais de cette sagesse divine qui rira de la mort des méchants' (xi. 197), and from Tertullian: 'Ce que j'ai fait n'est qu'un jeu avant un véritable combat' (xi. 199). Superficially, then, the desire for seriousness in religious debate is common to both parties: the polemicist goes on to assert that: 'l'esprit de piété porte toujours à parler avec vérité et sincérité; au lieu que l'envie et la haine emploient le mensonge et la calomnie' (xi. 203); and, directly mirroring the Jesuit position: 'l'esprit de bouffonnerie, d'impiété et d'hérésie, se rit de ce qu'il y a de plus sacré' (xi. 205). But Pascal has 'tourné les choses saintes en raillerie' only if the Jesuit morality is a 'chose sainte'. Since rather it is itself, he believes, a turning round of what is holy, it is its own register of 'raillerie' that he has employed in its examination. It is here that we can take up our second fragment L 977—'les choses du monde les plus déraisonnables deviennent les plus raisonnables à cause du dérèglement des hommes'—to make the point. The polemicist claims to have achieved an identity of perspective with his adversaries in that he has in one respect stripped their terms of the Christian denotation of which he considers them unworthy, and thus enabled himself to attend to them legitimately, not just by secular, but by comic means: 'en me moquant de votre morale, j'ai été aussi éloigné de me moquer des choses saintes, que la doctrine de vos casuistes est éloignée de la doctrine sainte de l'Evangile' (xi. 195). It is the 'dérèglement' of the Jesuits that has endowed with legitimacy a procedure which in Christian terms would otherwise be considered 'déraisonnable'; and which has also unleashed the comic appeal to the uncommitted reader. (In fact, although Pascal again places the blame on his adversaires for dictating the terms of the debate—quoting Tertullian, 'S'il se trouve des endroits où l'on soit excité à rire, c'est parce que les sujets mêmes y portaient' (xi. 199)—and although the terms may indeed be theirs, the treatment is of course firmly his. As Duchêne points out: 'Les *Provinciales* donnent une idée fort inexacte du ton et du contenu des livres qui y sont cités et commentés. C'est l'auteur qui, par la façon dont il les fait connaître, transforme des traités savants et construits en ouvrages grotesques et comiques' (*IL* 221–2)).

Taking Pascal's defence at face value, however, we find that nature is represented as responding by laughter to what is anti-natural, at the opposite extreme from Christian anti-nature. But orthodoxy is once again appealed to alongside nature, and the committed reader alongside the uncommitted, since Christianity, anti-nature at the other extreme, can therefore *à plus forte raison* find itself able, even obliged, to ridicule its diametrical opposition. Satire answers parody; precisely because 'l'esprit de bouffonnerie, d'impiété et d'hérésie, se rit de ce qu'il y a de plus sacré' (xi. 205), therefore 'les saints ont... pour l'erreur ces deux sentiments de haine et de mépris, et leur zèle s'emploie également à repousser avec force la malice des impies, et à confondre avec risée leur égarement et leur folie' (xi. 195). Nature will induce the uncommitted reader to laugh, therefore, but grace will oblige the committed reader to the same response. The nonsense terminology of inverted meanings, like all jibberish, elicits laughter in the speakers of both immanently and transcendentally rooted languages, as the appeal to the world and the Gospel yet again come together in Pascal's scheme.

The aspects of the eleventh letter dealing with comedy are examined in considerable detail by Duchêne,[11] both in their own right and in relationship to Arnauld's views on the matter as revealed in the *Lettre à une personne de condition* (1655). Duchêne remarks that Pascal, going further than Arnauld, 'soutient que la raillerie est toujours licite contre l'erreur, exclue d'avance et par définition du domaine de la religion' (*IL* 215). He goes on: 'la question de savoir si l'on peut employer le rire dans la controverse religieuse se transforme avec les *Provinciales* en affirmation que l'on peut, et même que l'on doit, utiliser la moquerie contre l'erreur' (*IL* 215). Duchêne also develops the corrective idea of laughter (*IL* 218), and finally, referring to the polemicist's demonstration of how laughter is awoken by the view of a disproportion '[Lorsqu]' on entend ces décisions et autres semblables, il est impossible que cette surprise ne fasse rire, parce que rien n'y porte davantage qu'une disproportion surprenante entre ce qu'on attend et ce qu'on voit' (xi. 200), he comments: 'De nouveau Pascal définit ici le mécanisme du rire, mais cette fois du point de vue de son fonctionnement par rapport au lecteur. Le rire résulte d'une attente déçue, d'un décalage entre ce qu'on croyait et ce qui se passe effectivement' (*IL* 219).[12]

If, for the polemicist, 'cette pratique est juste,...elle est

---

[11] In his chapter 'Rire avec Pascal', in *IL* 209–33.

[12] Cf. H. Bergson, *Le Rire*: 'Une situation est toujours comique quand elle appartient en même temps à deux séries d'événements absolument indépendantes, et qu'elle peut s'interpréter à la fois dans deux sens tout différents' (*Œuvres* (Paris, 1959), 433). It goes without saying that other Bergsonian models, notably those of the mechanical response ('le diable à ressort') and of the cumulative development ('la boule de neige') could easily be applied to the comic elements of the 'père Jésuite' series.

commune aux Pères de l'Eglise, et... elle est autorisée par l'Ecriture, par l'exemple des plus grands saints, et par celui de Dieu même' (xi. 195–6), the kind of laughter he provokes is, in the specific reply to the eleventh letter, compared unfavourably with the 'ris de courroux et d'indignation' of the saints and Fathers (*RLP* 193). Rather, 'vos Lettres... sont pleines de faux textes, de fausses citations, et de faux reproches, accompagnés d'une perpétuelle bouffonnerie, sans qu'on y puisse remarquer un seul raisonnement, ni une seule pensée digne d'un théologien' (*RLP* 194). The polemicist is asked: 'Pourquoi employer l'Ecriture pour nous dire qu'il y a des moqueries charitables, puisque les vôtres sont envenimées de haine?' (*RLP* 195); Bede, the Council of Toledo, St Bernard, and St John Chrysostom are quoted against 'moqueurs'; the polemicist's injunction that 'il est nécessaire *pour le juste emploi de la raillerie, qu'elle soit fondée sur la vérité et non sur le mensonge*' is juxtaposed with the evidence of falsification from the *Impostures* (*RLP* 198); and in a final attack on inapposite frivolity, the question is put: 'S'il faut que la raillerie soit noble, modeste, honnête et discrète afin qu'elle fasse un bon effet, qu'y a-t-il de plus bas que ce hoho! de comédie, que vous faites éclater si souvent dans vos Lettres?' (*RLP* 199–200).

Each stage of the letters, as we have seen, throws into relief the ironic status of the preceding one (this is as true of the transition between iii and iv as of that between x and xi); but in so doing negates the possibility for its continuation. The theoretical attention given to 'raillerie' in the eleventh letter thus signals and dictates the disappearance of that perspective in those that follow (although there is a brief sardonic resurgence in the postscript to the fourteenth), a point which also receives a good deal of attention in a recent critical discussion,[13] where a similar view is expressed in the article of Jacques Morel: 'La onzième *Lettre* a pour objet la justification de la manière enjouée qui vient d'être abandonnée et, du même mouvement, celle de la manière grave définitivement adoptée.' And at the end of his paper, Morel proposes: 'Au moment où se clôt la onzième *Lettre*... Pascal n'a

---

[13] J. Morel, 'Pascal et la doctrine du rire grave' in *Méthodes chez Pascal*, pp. 216, 219.

plus de choix qu'entre le silence, l'humour tragique ou l'explosion de l'invective... Il ne lui reste plus que l'invective.' The eleventh letter then moves, with the play of 'renversement' and counter-'renversement' in the background, from a justification of the polemicist's 'raillerie des choses [understood] impies' to an attack on Jesuit 'raillerie des choses [truly] saintes' (even if it must seem to us particularly puritanical of Pascal to object to the poem and the metaphor which he uses in the eleventh letter to demonstrate Jesuit impiety), since it is they who are deemed to 'railler et parler indignement des choses les plus sacrées' (xi. 212). It is thus incumbent upon, and rhetorically fitting for, their adversary to move into a soberer register. The polemicist has thus moved from the defence of his own 'raillerie' to the attack on the opposing one, and this in turn drives him onto the serious territory previously occupied by the Jesuits. The 'temps de rire' of the concluding scriptural reference is over; the 'temps de pleurer' has begun (xi. 214).

It goes without saying that this change of tone attracted no more approval from the counter-polemicists: 'il devient furieux, quand il veut être sérieux' is the judgement on the fifteenth *LP* (just as he became 'bouffon' when he meant to be 'plaisant') (*Préface* to *Deuxième Réponse* in *RLP* xlvii); in the *Réponse à la 14ᵉ Lettre* too, we find:

Vous allez toujours aux extrémités; et après avoir fait si longtemps le railleur, tout à coup vous voulez faire le docteur... On voit bien que vous n'êtes pas dans votre élément quand vous êtes sur le sérieux : vous paraissez trop chagrin et rêveur : tous vos songes sont fâcheux, comme ceux d'un malade, et vos rêveries ne sont que de meurtres, que d'homicides, et de sang. (*RLP* 265–6)[14]

And the seventeenth *Réponse* likewise concludes (rather paradoxically, given the persistent attack on 'raillerie'), 'dès que l'esprit de bouffonnerie le quitte il ne fait rien qui vaille dans ses Lettres, et se rend ennuyeux et méprisable à ceux qui les lisent' (*RLP* 428). Pirot, comparing the treatment of the obligation of rich people to give of their 'superflu' in letters vi and xii, remarks:

---

[14] Maingueneau comments in *Sémantique de la polémique*: 'Ainsi l'auteur. . . se voit-il assigner la place du fou mélancolique' (p. 61).

'En la sixième, il paraît comme un singe enjoué, et dans la douzième on dirait qu'il est métamorphosé en ours' (p. 53).

Montalte, having become, if not Pascal, then an anonymous adversary of the Society of Jesus, now embarks on what is really a reworking of some of the previous material, albeit now in the framework of an open polemical debate (the eleventh letter ends with the writer's reception of the *Première Réponse* of April 1656). The eleventh letter thus stands pivotally between the fictional/satirical/ironic and the factual/direct/literal treatment of related themes. The letters following it still continue to function in the domain of *cas-limites* and generalizations (Molinier in his edition[15] remarks that Pascal's reply to Nouet's detail 's'est borné aux points les plus importants'), but instead of simply developing those preceding it, they rather mirror them in a different, more disputational register. Various important issues that had been initiated in the preceding series are thus taken up in letters xi to xiv—the need to love God, simony, the behaviour of religious, and the obligation to hear mass—and, in detail, the eleventh letter takes points from letters vi, vii, ix, and x, the twelfth from vi and viii, the thirteenth from vii, the fourteenth from vii, and the fifteenth from v and x.[16] (Cognet further notes that in certain of these cases the later quotations by Pascal are more accurate than the earlier ones.)[17] The polemicist also becomes more limited by the features of the debate as it has now evolved, but at the same time retains a degree of flexibility, as is manifest at the beginning of the fourteenth *LP*: 'Comme je trouve bien plus important de donner au monde de l'horreur de vos opinions sur ce sujet [= l'homicide] que de justifier la fidélité de mes citations, je serai obligé d'employer la plus grande partie de cette lettre à la réfutation de vos maximes' (xiv. 255). It is indeed true that this letter (and the later *LPs* in general) still gives an impression of a sweep of illustrated argument, against a good deal of the counter-polemic, which reads more as quotation, illustration, and example, with commentary. This must also be because of the

---

[15] *Lettres Provinciales*, i, Introduction, p. xxxi.
[16] See Cognet's notes *passim*.
[17] e.g. Cognet, p. 225 n. 1; p. 226 n. 1.

independent nature of the writer, who conveys a concomitant freedom of treatment of material against the corporate responsibility he attributes to his adversaries. Furthermore in letters xii–xiv, as we shall see in Chapter 11, the emphasis remains on the issues that Montalte had initiated, that is the 'morale des casuistes', thereby countering the Jesuit defence, but not yet attending to the Jesuit attack.

The eleventh letter functions therefore as a hinge, with a fixed ideological and theoretical axis, joining the two central parts of the series, but also indicating the palindromic construction of the work as a whole, which will finally come to the surface in the last two complete pieces. It is, as we saw in the last chapter, the letter which most directly ties together the *Provinciales* and the *Pensées*;

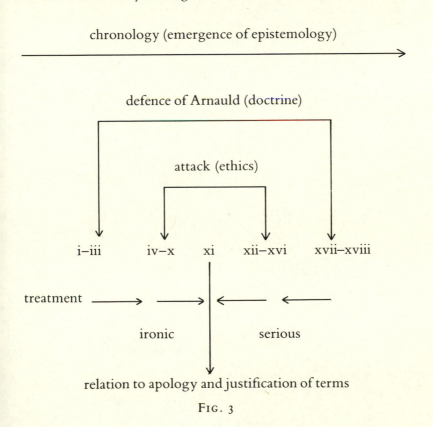

FIG. 3

and at the same time, and enhanced by this status, it is the letter which addresses itself most explicitly to the terms of the polemical enterprise. At the centre of the complete (if not completed) series, this crucial piece thus demonstrates both the fundamental implications and the theoretical justification of the *LPs* debate by relating it to the kind of discussion of essentials which the *Pensées* propose. As Fig. 3 shows, the linear/horizontal reading which stretches out before and after the eleventh letter is therefore grounded by this reference in a system of belief and a mode of argument; and this grounding, this vertical emphasis, acts both progressively and retrospectively upon the horizontal one.

10

Persona and Motive

WE might now return to the figure of Montalte, with an over-
view of the whole series, in order to clarify the question of his
status. A good deal of critical attention has recently been given to
the fictional elaboration of the *LPs*, and Louis de Montalte must
figure centrally in such a debate (even if the name is only
specifically introduced in 1657).[1] The work as a whole proceeds
from a fictional to an actual epistolary exchange, as we have seen:
the Montalte persona definitively sheds his disguise of ingenuousness (and thus his *raison d'être*) at the beginning of the
eleventh letter, to be supplanted by the anonymous but direct and
implicated epistoler (the polemicist), addressing the Society
('Mes Révérends Pères'), which is then specified further when a
single addressee, Père Annat, is named in the seventeenth letter.
For this, and other reasons which I shall develop, I would refer to
the 'je' of the last two letters as Pascal. All these terms, however,
call for some justification.

For the reasons of the satirical interest which his persona
engenders, it has seemed to me helpful to identify a distinct
Montalte role in the letters up to and including the tenth, and thus
to refer to their fictional writer/protagonist as Montalte. Even
if the polemicist/Pascal is more and more visible behind the
Montalte persona, we lose a good deal of the primary ironic and
comic potential of the game if we do not concede thus far the
Montalte fiction. We also lose the potential for interplay between
the different personae of the first ten letters, most notably
between Montalte and the second 'père jésuite'. If we then turn to
the opening of the eighth letter, we find that the fictional status of

---

[1] The name initially occurs in the title of the first (in-4°) collected series of 18
letters: *Les Provinciales ou les lettres écrites par Louis de Montalte à un provincial de ses
amis et aux RR. PP. Jésuites sur le sujet de la morale et de la politique de ces Pères* (1657).

Montalte seems indeed to draw attention to its autonomy, in the discussion on its identity. Montalte here concludes, after discussing various theories: 'Tous ces faux soupçons me font connaître que je n'ai pas mal réussi dans le dessein que j'ai eu de n'être connu que de vous [l'ami provincial], et du bon Père qui souffre toujours mes visites' (viii. 133–4). By this definition of his role, he incorporates himself on an equal footing into the fictional trio which prevails for the duration of the later satirical letters; all three contributors exact the same suspension of disbelief in the game that is being played. Of course the *arrière-pensée* that allows us to identify it as such informs our whole reading, but at the expense of the entire fictional superstructure, not just that of Montalte. The Montalte persona here is only as real or as unreal as the Jesuit interlocutor. We might also notice the remark of Ferreyrolles,[2] suggesting perhaps too that the identity of Montalte derives retroactively from other fictional identities in the work: 'Il fallait que le "bon Père" n'eût pas devant lui un adversaire déclaré, un janséniste, un Pascal, mais un simple honnête homme en quête d'éclaircissements'.

At the same time, what I earlier referred to as the polemicist-'je' which gradually and ironically emerges out of the Montalte-'je' (although still for the time being without destroying the persona) could perhaps better be described as establishing a pseudonymous development within the persona. It is making exactly the same kinds of point that will be made by the polemicist in the post-xi series, but in a different framework, and without the loss of fictional status. The persona of Montalte thus progressively gives way to the pseudonym of Montalte (a specifically nominal fiction) as we move towards the definitive change in register; and an ironic awareness of the point of view towards which the Montalte persona is moving accompanies this progression.

In some parts of the counter-polemic, attention is indeed primarily drawn to the pseudonymous status of the writer of the letters: in the *Première Réponse* of the *RLP*, the possibility of his having the function of a mouthpiece is suggested: 'Personne ne peut nier que l'auteur des Lettres qui courent aujourd'hui, et qui

---

[2] *Blaise Pascal: Les Provinciales*, p. 46.

font tant de bruit dans le monde, ne soit un Janséniste; si toutefois c'est un seul homme, et non plutôt tout le parti' (*RLP* iii). And later in the same *recueil*, in the preface to the *Deuxième Réponse* (evidently added when the *RLPs* were published as a series), a further remark points to the implications of the pseudonym: 'Le nom de Montalte, sous lequel paraissent aujourd'hui les *Lettres Provinciales*, que les nouveaux hérétiques ont publiées depuis deux ans contre les Jésuites, n'est qu'un faux nom, qui vous donne à connaître, mon cher lecteur, que l'auteur qui l'a pris n'est qu'un faussaire' (*RLP* xxxix). Such remarks apparently go no further than recognizing that a 'real' person has disguised his name (and no more than that) beneath a pseudonym. A fuller fictional identity, now acknowledging a disguised persona, is however suggested in the first *Lettre à une personne de condition*, by the reference to 'le *personnage* [my italics] qu'il fait le mieux, qui est celui de plaisant et de railleur' (*RLP* lxii). And a similar sort of usage is found in Nicole's *Avertissement*:

[The author of the first four letters] y *représente* [my italics] une personne peu instruite de ces différends, comme le sont ordinairement les gens du monde dans l'état desquels il se met et se fait éclaircir de ces questions insensiblement par ces docteurs qu'il consulte, en leur proposant ses doutes et recevant leurs réponses, avec tant de clarté et de naïveté que les moins intelligents entendirent ce qui semblait n'être réservé qu'aux plus habiles.

Dans les six Lettres suivantes [i.e. v–x] il explique toute la morale des Jésuites, par le récit de quelques entretiens entre lui et l'un de leurs casuistes, où il *représente encore* une personne du monde qui se fait instruire et qui, apprenant des maximes tout à fait étranges, s'en étonne et... les écoute avec toute la modération qu'on peut garder. (Cognet, p. 471)

Persona and pseudonym are both abandoned—albeit not quite simultaneously—in the eleventh letter. The first person which begins the eleventh letter briefly retains an implicitly pseudonymous status by the mention of '[les lettres] que j'ai écrites à un de mes amis' (xi. 193). However, and although apparently maintaining the fiction, this is in reality the last flash of a now fully self-conscious irony, an irony which is then negated by the rapidly introduced discussion of the tone of that very fiction, by the change of epistolary 'destinataire(s)' from an imaginary friend to a real enemy, by the attendant shift of register, and by the appearance of the word 'auteur' in the title. The letters preceding the eleventh are written 'à un Provincial par un de ses amis'; those following 'par l'auteur des Lettres au Provincial aux Révérends Pères Jésuites' (and then finally 'au Révérend Père Annat, Jésuite'). The 'je' of the eleventh letter, by virtue of its participation in a commentary on the Montalte letters, differentiates itself thereby in persona, but also I would suggest in name, from the preceding first person. My reading here differs from that of Duchêne, who suggests that 'ces titres... se bornent à indiquer les changements de destinataires et à marquer fortement, fondée sur l'unité de "l'auteur des Lettres au Provincial", une continuité que souligne, malgré d'évidentes ruptures, une numérotation suivie' (*IL* 10). For Duchêne this identification underlines a continuity; for me it denotes a break.[3] The attention drawn to the 'auteur' of the letters preceding the eleventh gives to those letters, or reinforces retrospectively, the status of a fiction, which is thereby removed from those that follow it. It effects the identification of the first person of the previous letters as fictional (the product of an 'auteur') and that of the following ones as the product of, *but also identical with* the same writer (the polemicist) who thus takes over from the Montalte persona (whose evolution has, as we have seen, prepared for such a transfer). There has been a brief overlapping function fulfilled by the pseudonymous 'je', surviving for the duration of the reference to the 'ami provincial' —the Montalte pseudonym has served to ease the transition between the Montalte persona and the polemicist—but the change of register and 'destinataire(s)' have disallowed this residual fiction from continuing. At the same time, the 'auteur'

[3] I do note that in the title of the 1657 edn. (see n. 1) the pseudonym of Montalte is explicitly carried through the whole series with no distinction made between the earlier and later letters. The primary function of the title when the work appeared was that of disguise, however, and a more elaborate examination of the role of persona and pseudonym in the light of a modern critical reading would not therefore seem to me to be disallowed by it. There seems too to be some slight inconsistency in Duchêne's reading, since he later writes of the generic break between letters x and xi: 'C'est seulement par commodité et à des fins publicitaires qu'il a, malgré cette rupture, employé une numérotation continue' (*IL* 206).

remains unidentified, and is writing public letters rather than, as will be the case in letters xvii and xviii, engaging in a published personal correspondence.

The question of what to call the 'je' has also arisen in recent critical debate. Descotes,[4] while recommending caution in the use of 'Montalte', proposes its utility 'pour désigner commodément la personne qui dit "Je" dans le texte, et qui est distincte de Pascal lui-même', and refers therefore to the epistoler as Montalte throughout. On the other hand, Duchêne deliberately refrains from using the name Montalte for 'le personnage fictif d'épistolier et d'enquêteur mis en scène dans les *Provinciales*', on the grounds that it is 'lui donner trop de réalité et risquer d'oublier qu'à chaque page de l'œuvre, comme l'a dit Valéry pour les *Pensées*, "on voit trop la main de Pascal"' (*IL* 12 n. 1). I rather believe, as I have suggested, that we miss a lot of the ironic development engendered by the persona if we immediately accord to the earlier letters the full degree of hindsight provided by the resolution to the series. Pascal does more than simply '[créer] un personnage qui lui est imposé par les circonstances' (*IL* 13). Descotes for his part does concede that once the way has been made clear for the real Jesuits to replace fictional Jesuits in a confrontation with Montalte, 'on assiste alors à un changement de structure du spectacle. Désormais, le Montalte des dialogues s'efface, et le Montalte narrateur parle en son nom propre, directement à ses ennemis. . . Du fait que Pascal est parvenu à faire parler les véritables Jésuites. . . la scène s'est élargie aux dimensions de la réalité'.[5] It is in order to underline this distinction that I have used the title 'Montalte' only for Descotes's 'Montalte des dialogues', and preferred 'the polemicist' for the later 'Montalte narrateur'. I have also, I hope, clarified the overlap.

One last point could perhaps be introduced about the last two letters, whose enhanced contextual quality provides their 'dimensions de la réalité'. They are only half a correspondence, and the other half is now provided by a single named respondent. This personal element in their composition is what has encouraged me

[4] 'Fonction argumentative', p. 64, n. 4.
[5] Ibid. 57–8.

finally to give the name Pascal to their first person. In further support however, I would draw attention to similarities in tone, and indeed in the principles being established, between a remark addressed to Annat and the conclusion to the letter of 29 October 1647 to the Père Noël. This early piece, on the vacuum, concludes:

Je trouve que votre lettre n'est pas moins une marque de la faiblesse de l'opinion que vous défendez, que de la vigueur de votre esprit.

Et certainement l'adresse avec laquelle vous avez défendu l'impossibilité du vide dans le peu de force qui lui reste, fait aisément juger qu'avec un pareil effort, vous auriez invinciblement établi le sentiment contraire dans les avantages que les expériences lui donnent. (*OC* 204)

The following remark is addressed, more succinctly, to Annat: 'Je m'assure que, si vous en étiez mieux informé, vous auriez du regret de ne vous être pas instruit avec un esprit de paix d'une doctrine si pure et si chrétienne, que la passion vous fait combattre sans la connaître' (xvii. 358). The writer of the *Provinciales*, and the Pascal identified in an earlier correspondence, have now become identical.[6]

The polemicist of the later letters is now an isolated figure. There is no more possibility of a 'nous'. He has lost the epistolary support, however functional it had become, of the 'ami provincial', as well as the social connections, and in particular the 'ami janséniste', of the first series. This isolation is used to good effect however, as the single adversary takes on the whole Society. He thus adopts the persuasive position of the solitary voice of truth against the massed forces of error, a characteristically poignant and evangelic (and reformist) stance, and one which parallels the solitary figure of Arnauld pitted against the numerical weight of his adversaries in the first letters ('tant de docteurs si acharnés sur un seul' (iii. 44)). The polemicist now takes over the role of the defender of grace as enunciated by the 'ami janséniste' in the second letter, and in the tradition that is evoked by him: 'Elle [la grâce] ne manquera jamais de défenseurs... Elle demande des

---

[6] As Ferreyrolles also remarks: 'Cette première polémique de Pascal avec un jésuite... nous retient par la similitude des reproches alors adressés au P. Noël et de ceux qui viseront en 1656–1657 les casuistes de la Compagnie' (*Blaise Pascal: Les Provinciales*, pp. 85–6).

cœurs purs et dégagés, et elle-même les purifie et les dégage des intérêts du monde, incompatibles avec les vérités de l'Evangile' (ii. 34).

The emotive potential of such a voice is exploited in, for example, the opening of the twelfth letter:

En vérité, mes Pères, vous en êtes plus suspects [d'impostures] que moi; car il n'est pas vraisemblable qu'étant seul comme je suis, sans force et sans aucun appui humain contre un si grand corps, et n'étant soutenu que par la vérité et la sincérité, je me sois exposé à tout perdre, en m'exposant à être convaincu d'imposture. (xii. 216)

The writer of the *Réponse à la douzième Lettre Provinciale* remarks perceptively: 'Je crois fermement que vous voulez faire pitié aux gens' (*RLP* 208). This would also seem to be the desired effect of certain passages of the sixteenth, as well as the opening of the unfinished nineteenth *LP*. Again at the beginning of the seventeenth letter, the autonomy and individuality of the writer are heavily stressed in distinction to the corporate responsibility of the Society of Jesus: 'personne ne répond de mes Lettres que moi, et... je ne réponds de rien que de mes Lettres' (xvii. 333). And finally, in two fragments of the *Pensées*, Pascal takes up the defence again:

La folle idée que vous avez de l'importance de votre compagnie vous a fait établir ces horribles voies... Vous blâmez en moi comme horribles les moindres impostures que vous excusez en vous, parce que vous me regardez comme un particulier et vous comme *Imago*. (L 904)

Plus ils marquent de faiblesse en ma personne plus ils autorisent ma cause. (L 960)

As Derôme remarks in the Introduction to his edition of the *LPs*[7] (reflecting the tone of the letters if not the historical reality): 'Pascal...est le type de l'esprit particulier, tandis que la Compagnie de Jésus est le type de l'esprit de corps, de l'absence d'opinion personnelle'.

There is some discussion of this 'solitude' in the *Réponses*. In the *XXIIᵉ Avertissement*, attention is drawn to polemicist's 'amour de

---

[7] *Lettres écrites à un Provincial*, ed. L. Derôme (Paris, 1885–6), i, Introduction, pp. clxxxvii–clxxxviii.

la singularité' which has separated him from 'les opinions communes, que les docteurs Catholiques approuvent, et la conduite ordinaire de l'Eglise' (*RLP* 115), and in the reply to the thirteenth letter, we find: 'Si tous ceux qui les enseignent [= opinions probables] sont avec eux [= Jésuites], et si vous les enveloppez dans le même relâchement, vous prenez tous les docteurs Catholiques à parti, et vous demeurez véritablement *tout seul sans force, sans appui*, et sans autre défense que celle des disciples de Luther et de Calvin' (*RLP* 261).

The polemicist's isolation thus further serves to exemplify opposition to the Jesuits' alleged adaptability, by endowing the first person with an authority consonant with a simple and unqualified exposition of the truth; but at the same time the anonymity of the writer and the corporate nature of the addressees still allow the attack to appear impersonal. By the time the last two letters are reached a simple bipartite correspondence has taken over, and a much more enclosed form is reached; the individual writer has identified himself in all but name (and the addressee is specified), as he returns to the resolution of the particular quarrel that is still in play.

The insistence becomes strong in the later letters too on the sense of obligation felt by the polemicist to engage in the debate/pursue the debate/carry it on in particular terms, contributing as well to the persistent emphasis on the responsibility of the Jesuits for the terms, and indeed existence, of the dispute overall. In the eleventh letter the obligation topos is applied to various subjects: 'Car, mes Pères, puisque vous m'obligez d'entrer en ce discours' (xi. 195); 'vous m'engagez à vous dire ce que je devrais apprendre de vous' (xi. 203). This is continued more and more threateningly in the twelfth: 'Vous m'avez obligé par là de changer mon dessein' (xii. 216); 'vous me traitez comme un imposteur insigne, et ainsi vous me forcez à repartir' (xii. 216); and 'souvenez-vous au moins que c'est vous qui m'engagez d'entrer dans cet éclaircissement, et voyons qui se défendra le mieux' (xii. 217). Again in the fifteenth: 'Je me sens obligé… de découvrir un mystère de votre conduite' (xv. 275), or the seventeenth, where he describes himself as 'bien résolu de les pousser [= vos maximes] autant que je croirai que Dieu m'y engagera' (xvii. 331). Finally, in the

second *Ecrit des Curés*, we find the writer justifying the continuation of the dispute: 'C'est ce qui nous oblige à nous élever de
nouveau contre cette nouvelle hardiesse' (Cognet, p. 419); and
later:

C'est donc une vérité capitale de notre religion, qu'il y a des temps où il
faut troubler cette possession de l'erreur que les méchants appellent
paix... Or, s'il y en eut jamais une occasion et une nécessité indispensable, examinons si ce n'est pas aujourd'hui qu'elle presse et qu'elle
contraint d'agir. (Cognet, p. 427)

The expressed wish is however not just self-defence but also
correction: 'Je voudrais bien, mes Pères, que ce que je vous dis
servît non seulement à me justifier, ce serait peu, mais encore à
vous faire sentir et abhorrer ce qu'il y a de corrompu dans les
maximes de vos casuistes' (xii. 224). And in the sixth *Ecrit des
Curés* the desire is restated with hindsight: 'un de nos principaux
souhaits a été que les Jésuites mêmes renonçassent à leurs erreurs'
(Cognet, pp. 444–5). However the very perspective that the
Society adopts is shown to be the impediment to the recognition
of its error through self-knowledge, and so the altruistic motive
goes unrecognized since 'il faudrait que vous fussiez bien revenus
de vos égarements pour le reconnaître' (xv. 285) (just as man has
to be freed from his imagination to recognize his true *misère*). The
motivation is furthermore identified as 'charité' on the authority
of St Augustine—both for laughter (xi. 200–1, and p. 201 n. 1)
and indeed more strenuous correction (xi. 206). (Duchêne in this
context quotes one of Arnauld's descriptions of the mockery of
the Fathers as 'charitables et judicieuses railleries' (*IL* 212)). This
then is 'ancienne charité', contrasted with the 'nouvelle charité',
'qui s'offense de voir confondre des erreurs manifestes et qui ne
s'offense point de voir renverser la morale par ces erreurs' (xi.
202).

The eleventh letter elaborates to this end a countering scheme
of direction, or rather discernment, of intention to that which has
been satirized in the attack on the Society. Pascal would not then
deny the validity of such an exercise, but would challenge its
abuse, in the cause of indiscriminate exculpations (thus 'Œuvres
extérieures... La manière étant [*sic*] ainsi aussi importante que la
chose, et peut-être plus, puisque Dieu peut du mal tirer du bien, et

que sans Dieu on tire le mal du bien' (L 928)). The criterion for judgement in such questions must however be the divine and nót the human perspective if the context is to dictate the quality of the action, as we have seen in the case of laughter. Thus, in the ninth letter, devotions to the Virgin are 'd'un grand mérite, quand elles partent d'un mouvement de foi et de charité' (ix. 156), a point which finds its extreme illustration in the fourteenth letter in the example of the killing of criminals undertaken in the name of divine justice: 'Ces meurtres, qui seraient des attentats puiss-ables sans son ordre, deviennent des punitions louables par son ordre, hors duquel il n'y a rien que d'injuste' (xiv. 256). Thus, as Jacques Plainemaison writes: 'Bien loin de nier que ce soit l'inten-tion, c'est-à-dire la référence à Dieu, qui fonde la valeur morale des actes humains, Pascal pense que c'est elle seule qui qualifie moralement nos actes'.[8] It is the reference to God that authenti-cates the moral evaluation; the Jesuit direction of the *LPs* pro-poses rather a submission of God's law to men. The polemicist then enumerates the 'marques [que] les Pères de l'Eglise nous ont données pour juger si les répréhensions partent d'un esprit de piété et de charité, ou d'un esprit d'impiété et de haine' (xi. 203), again contrasted by their simplicity (particularly in the résumé which defines the 'esprit de charité' (xi. 205–6)) with the elab-orate qualifications of the preceding letters. And the intention behind the whole exercise is identified as 'l'esprit de charité, [qui] porte à avoir dans le cœur le désir du salut de ceux contre qui on parle, et à adresser ses prières à Dieu en même temps qu'on adresse ses reproches aux hommes' (xi. 206).

The same features are also present in the counter-polemic. In the first *Réponse*, the Jesuit presents the Society as having finally felt obliged to reply: 'puisque leur patience à souffrir, et leur modestie à se taire, est une partie du scandale qu'apporte leur accusation, il faut donner aux lecteurs de ces infâmes Lettres du contre-venin' (*RLP* v). And in the *Avertissement* to the first *Imposture* an altruistic motive is again suggested: 'Il faut que je rende le bien pour le mal, et la vérité pour le mensonge' (*RLP* 8).

---

[8] J. Plainemaison, 'La 'Méthode géométrique' contre la 'doctrine des équi-voques' dans les *Provinciales*', in *Méthodes chez Pascal*, p. 229.

Morel too attributes to the Jesuits an entirely altruistic spirit: they will thank Pascal if he has done good by his writing, 'et il est également certain... qu'ils ne vous rendront jamais le réciproque, si vous leur avez fait du mal' (p. 2); and Pirot quite simply turns Pascal's criteria for legitimate correction back against the Jansenist party in the last part of the *Apologie pour les Casuistes* (pp. 178–91). In the *IXe Avertissement* a protective tone towards the gullible readers (albeit more aggressive towards the writer) is evident in: 'Il est sans doute qu'étant comme vous êtes hérétiques déclarés, et Calvinistes couverts, non seulement vous êtes en état de damnation, mais vous servez encore de piège aux âmes faibles' (*RLP* 46). But Pirot is again more conciliatory when he writes: 'Je prie Dieu... tous les jours qu'il use de patience envers vous, et qu'il ne coupe pas ce figuier infructueux : mais qu'il vous donne des grâces pour faire pénitence, afin que nous puissions tous mourir en paix dans le sein de l'Eglise Romaine' (p. 78). And Morel concludes his piece, guided he insists by 'la charité chrétienne', with a long and flattering appeal to Pascal to use his gifts to better purpose: 'Pourquoi donc usez-vous de la part que vous y avez [= des dons du Ciel], comme si vous cherchiez de vous en faire priver, au lieu d'en user si bien, que vous la voyez tous les jours croître?' (p. 60). He wishes for him what with hindsight must seem powerfully ironic: 'qu'après une sincère et constante réconciliation avec les Jésuites, vous tourniez votre plume contre les restes de l'hérésie, les langues impies et libertines, et les autre corruptions du siècle' (p. 61), before concluding: 'Si vous me faites justice, vous avouerez que je suis le meilleur de vos amis, puisque je travaille à vous rendre ami de Dieu; et encore le plus utile de vos serviteurs, puisque je négocie votre salut, qui est la plus grande et la plus importante de vos affaires' (p. 64).

The new company enjoyed by the first person in the later letters has now become that of the definers and defenders of Christian tradition: 'les saints ont... pour l'erreur ces deux sentiments de haine et de mépris'; 'cette pratique est juste... elle est commune aux Pères de l'Eglise, et... autorisée par l'Ecriture, par l'exemple des plus grands saints, et par celui de Dieu même' (xi. 195–6), an assertion rapidly endorsed by quotation and illustration, in an enumeration of authorities, 'examples sacrés'

(contrasting with that provided by the 'père Jésuite'), of which
the polemicist can assert: 'Je n'ai donc pas cru faillir en les suivant'
(xi. 199). Indeed in one passage the writer seems to give himself a
quasi-allegorical status, concluding: 'C'est une étrange et longue
guerre que celle où la violence essaye d'opprimer la vérité'(xii.
234). The *Réponse* to the fourteenth *LP* takes up the challenge,
and after enumerating (at length) saints, cardinals, Civil and
Canon Law as the company of the Society of Jesus (*RLP* 286–92)
cites briskly as the polemicist's companions 'Calvin, Luther,
Mélancthon et Du Moulin' (*RLP* 292).

The difficult question of links with Port-Royal is inevitably
raised in these letters, too. The polemicist finally dissociates
himself from any allegiance (as from ordination): he denies the
association in the sixteenth letter ('encore que je n'aie jamais eu
d'établissement avec eux' (xvi. 301)), and reiterates it in the
following one, again emphasizing his independence: 'Je suis
seul... Je ne suis point de Port-Royal' (xvii. 329), and yet again in
the same letter: 'Je ne vous crains ni pour moi, ni pour aucun
autre, n'étant attaché ni à quelque communauté, ni à quelque
particulier que ce soit' (xvii. 330). (Fragment L 955 also states:
'Vous dites que je suis janséniste, que le P[ort]-R[oyal] soutient
les 5 p(ropositions), et qu'ainsi je les soutiens. 3 mensonges'.)

This obviously calls for some elucidation. There is a major
contribution by Duchêne (in *IL*), who summarizes the problem
thus (with reference to the claim: 'Je ne suis point de Port-Royal'),
and which I will quote *in extenso*:

Si l'on admet que les *Provinciales* sont un roman épistolaire où il y a un
personnage qui dit 'je' et qui évolue de l'indifférence à la conversion et se
trouve finalement du côté des jansénistes contre les jésuites parce qu'il a,
après enquête, au bout de dix-sept ou dix-huit lettres, constaté que la
vérité est de ce côté-là, cette affirmation n'a aucun caractère scandaleux.
Si on met au contraire l'accent sur le fait que l'instance qui dit 'je' est un
personnage fictif dans les dix premières lettres, et qu'à partir de la
onzième, elle correspond à un personnage qui assume les lettres pré-
cédentes, de telle sorte qu'on ne peut plus guère distinguer le personnage
mis en scène à la première personne et la personne même de Pascal, alors,
à ce moment-là, dire 'Je ne suis pas de Port-Royal', ça devient une
magnifique équivoque, d'autant plus scandaleuse que les *Provinciales* ont
dénoncé les équivoques. Car il est bien vrai que Pascal n'est pas *stricto*

sensu de Port-Royal, mais il est bien vrai aussi qu'il est 'le secrétaire de Port-Royal'. (*IL* 363–4)

Since I have argued for a tripartite identification (Montalte–polemicist–Pascal), whereby I would propose that the 'je' from the eleventh to the sixteenth letter does take a different status from that preceding, but would also argue that it is distinguishable from that following (in letters xvii and xviii), I believe it necessary to investigate the 'équivoque' further.

More quotation from the *IL* 'débat' may serve as a starting-point. Mesnard later (rightly) contests the title 'Secrétaire de Port-Royal' (*IL* 370), on the grounds that it was used predominently hostilely by Pascal's adversaries. Descotes replies to Duchêne that 'Pascal ne fausse pas. Quand il dit : "Je ne suis pas de Port-Royal", ça veut dire: "Je ne suis pas un de ces messieurs de Port-Royal qui y sont à demeure"' (*IL* 364), quoting Nicole in support. Sellier also proposes that 'il n'y a aucune équivoque dans ce texte' (*IL* 364); and finally Mesnard again suggests that: 'Pascal... a beaucoup tenu à son indépendance vis-à-vis de Port-Royal' (*IL* 371).

There is then a question of affiliation and a question of persona. At one level, even if we accord to the 'je' in question the status of Pascal, what it says is literally, or in Duchêne's words *stricto sensu*, true. I would still however argue, as does Duchêne, that some degree of 'équivoque' prevails if, as also in the case of my proposed differentiation of status, one deprives the 'je' of the middle series of the fictional status of Montalte (even if not calling him Pascal), and attributes to him rather an intermediate functional or exemplary quality. In my view he does as such still lean on an 'équivoque', and does so in order, paradoxically, to rid himself of identification with a corporate allegiance, which would potentially be reflected on him by virtue of the corporate nature of his adversaries. In a dialogue, however adversarial, there emerges a sense of equivalence of participation unless a statement is made to the contrary: thus the Jesuits are taken to assume a partisan adversary, working within a larger group, once the conflict has been brought out into the open, away from fictional exchanges. So the polemical insistence on independence from Port-Royal is in other words a device to protect the isolation of the 'je', with all its flexibility and emotive potential, in a context whose nature increasingly suggests that a corporate statement might be the most appropriate response. The first ten letters have a clearly fictional (and clearly independent) Montalte-'je' as their major first-person utterance: 'vous êtes libre et particulier' (ii. 31); the last two, by virtue of the purely individual nature of the exchange, reflect the single 'destinataire' in a single first-person epistoler (even though the Jesuit reply to the sixteenth *LP* is still addressed to 'Messieurs de Port-Royal'). But because of the status of the middle series, it comes closest of all to proposing a corporate identity (Port-Royal), with a spokesman ('le secrétaire' as the Jesuits would suggest) occupying the first-person discourse. Given the polemical value of the isolated first person in this context, therefore, such a corporate allegiance has to be strenuously denied. The statements so doing are truthful; the reason for making them, yet again, is tactical.

The tone of authenticity that these denials give to the encomiastic assessment of Port-Royal which follows the passage in the sixteenth letter is important, even if disingenuous: 'Je sais, mes Pères, le mérite de ces pieux solitaires qui s'y [= à Port-Royal] étaient retirés, et combien l'Eglise est redevable à leurs ouvrages si édifiants et si solides...' (xvi. 301). (It is thereby also given to understand that, just as the Jesuits claim not to be alone in holding the opinions they hold, nor is Port-Royal alone in opposing them.) Morel, on the other hand, plays on the role of Port-Royal in an attempt to appeal to the polemicist against his alleged masters, whom he accuses of exploiting him: 'Jugez je vous prie, mais sans passion, où l'animosité de ceux que vous servez s'emporte' (p. 10).

In the seventeenth letter there occurs too a fervent first-person affirmation of Catholic orthodoxy and, on a tone of outright rejoicing, of entire independence (again in distinction to Jesuit corporateness but now supported by the individuated epistolary dialogue). The characteristics of epistoler and Society as they emerge throughout these later letters are therefore diametrically and paradoxically opposed: he is alone, but supported in his isolation by the historical teaching and authority of the Church and its traditions (and thus representative of much more than adherence to Port-Royal); the Jesuits are united in a body which supports its members, but which has *per se* no authority independent of the Church. Or, worse and unsaid, they epitomize a far more widespread corruption within contemporary orthodoxy: 'Dieu n'a pas voulu absoudre sans l'Eglise. Comme elle a part à l'offense il veut qu'elle ait part au pardon. Il l'associe à ce pouvoir... mais si elle absout ou si elle lie sans Dieu, ce n'est plus l'Eglise... mais un corps révolté' (L 706).

11

Letters XII–XVI

THE polemicist is at pains in these later letters to remind the Jesuits of the real context of the debate in so far as it concerns them, in other words to draw attention to its polemical, intra-Christian nature. This emphasis is accompanied by three features. First of all a readjustment of the idealized readership has taken place, primarily because of the direct exchange of which the later letters represent only one part (even more the case in the last two letters): there is now a new category of specified non-fictional reader, replacing the fictional and (initially) uncommitted recipient constituted by the 'ami provincial'; and there is an explicitly committed polemicist, expressing the position of Jansenist orthodoxy. Secondly it is because the use of satire based on the pretence of *naïveté* has disappeared, to be replaced by a more serious register. Thirdly it is because of a move onto the defensive and into points of detail; it is not a willing move, but the nature of the refutations the polemicist has met obliges him to examine some, at least, of the specific accusations of inaccuracy. Such *questions de fait* do not however make very interesting reading in the long term, and it is perhaps notable that the illustrations he uses (for example, in the thirteenth *LP*, the 'soufflet de Compiègne', or, in the fifteenth, the story of M. Puys) have still a certain actuality and 'pittoresque'. As the polemicist undertakes, 'j'essaierai de vous ennuyer le moins qu'il se peut en ce genre d'écrire' (xii. 217).

The Jesuits are now confronted directly with the terms of a Christian challenge, and their nominal allegiance allows the polemicist to ask of them 'qu'ils considèrent donc devant Dieu combien la morale que vos casuistes répandent de toutes parts est honteuse et pernicieuse à l'Eglise' (xi. 203), preluding the more detailed examination of the moral *questions de fait* which occupy letters xii–xiv. The polemical context, now made explicit, brings about the polemicist's insistence on the, for him, only possible perspective, and it is increasingly 'devant Dieu' that the arguments are conducted; the framework within which the 'renversements' and counter-'renversements' interacted is now defined by the debate's conclusive rehabilitation (and thus point of reference for all else) that is provided by the vision of truth triumphant.

The appeal to a common-sense reaction does not however disappear in these letters, even if their ultimate direction is pulling away from it, since error continues to offend at that level. The guiding perspective is now explicitly intra-Christian, but those readers invited to consider and eventually condemn still remain more wide-ranging. As Duchêne remarks: 'En s'adressant aux Jésuites, c'est toujours le public qui l'intéresse'.[1] The empirical readership may thus still be assumed to include both fervent believers and disinterested but fair-minded observers, but they are now reduced to the status of onlookers, by virtue of the loss of their fictional point of reference. What however remain are the statements of coincidence between the Christian imperative and the common-sense dictum, and at the beginning of the fourteenth letter (on homicide) the polemicist can still evoke 'les principes les plus simples de la religion et du sens commun' (xiv. 256). But even this appeal to common sense (or the lack of it) is now also directed straight at the Jesuits. In the sixteenth letter they are told: 'Si vous n'avez point de sens commun, je ne puis pas vous en donner. Tous ceux qui en ont se moqueront assez de vous' (xvi. 313), thereby also incorporating the justification of 'raillerie' in natural terms.

It is particularly in the area where civil and religious legislation are closely connected that this appeal has its greatest resonance. (This conjunction is also exploited by Pirot in the *Apologie pour les Casuistes*, where he fears that the implementation of a 'morale' based on the *Cinq Propositions* would lead to chaos—'[si] Jésus-Christ n'est pas mort pour tous, voilà le vice sur le trône, et la vertu aux fers' (p. 6)—and would promote disorder in the state. And he cites in support of this Saint-Cyran's alleged opinion that

---

[1] In *débat* following D. Jaymes, 'La Méthode d'ironie dans les *Provinciales*', p. 211.

the 'justes' need not have any concern for 'les lois extérieures' (p. 7)). This kind of appeal is in turn given a characteristically hyperbolic form in the *LPs* by the inclusion, among those who subscribe to certain laws, of 'les païens': 'le relâchement de vos opinions est contraire à la sévérité des lois civiles, et même païennes. Que sera-ce donc si on les compare avec les lois ecclésiastiques, qui doivent être incomparablement plus saintes?' (xiv. 265). In the same letter, Jesuit Christianity has been placed below the practices of idolaters and infidels: 'Les Chrétiens font-ils plus d'état des biens de la terre, ou font-ils moins d'état de la vie des hommes que n'en ont fait les idolâtres et les infidèles?' (xiv. 260). And in the second *Ecrit des Curés* too, we find: 'Ils auront permis aux Chrétiens tout ce que les Juifs, les Païens, les Mahométans et les Barbares auraient en exécration' (Cognet, p. 423). As Ferreyrolles comments, in *Pascal et la raison du politique*:[2] 'La nature est renversée chaque fois que les jésuites autorisent ce que les païens interdisent... C'est-à-dire que les jésuites justifient des conduites que la raison, sans l'aide de la grâce, suffit à condamner.'

But it is 'lois ecclésiastiques' which are, above all, contrasted with the Jesuit morality. Its teaching on duelling is 'contre les édits de tous les Etats chrétiens, et contre tous les Canons de l'Eglise', and has as its grounding 'ni lois, ni Canons, ni autorités de l'Ecriture ou des Pères, ni exemple d'aucun saint, mais seulement ce raisonnement impie' (xiv. 263). Or, following the statement that homicide is against civil and pagan laws and so all the more against Christian ones, the Church's perspective is introduced in its most emotive register: 'Elle [cette chaste épouse du fils de Dieu] considère les hommes non seulement comme hommes, mais comme images du Dieu qu'elle adore. Elle a pour chacun d'eux un saint respect qui les rend tous vénérables, comme rachetés d'un prix infini, pour être faits les temples du Dieu vivant' (xiv. 265–6). This is then enhanced by synecdoche in the case of the man potentially dispensed of the sin of homicide by the Jesuits, who, with their authorization, 'tue et damne celui pour qui Jésus-Christ est mort' (xiv. 270). The condemnation now becomes explicit. This tendency, reinforced by extreme examples on the one hand and evangelic absolutism on the other (biblical quotation and paraphrase are extensively used in letters xii–xiv) underlines the simple dichotomous structure which is employed, and in which the position of the polemicist holds sway most effortlessly by virtue of its rigidity and simplicity.

We see it again in the conclusion to the fourteenth letter: 'Car enfin, mes Pères, pour qui voulez-vous qu'on vous prenne: pour des enfants de l'Evangile, ou pour des ennemis de l'Evangile? On ne peut être que d'un parti ou de l'autre, il n'y a point de milieu' (xiv. 271). The 'milieu' that is occupied in different ways by the 'esprits géométriques', deists, and Jesuits (and arguably by the majority of Christians) is squeezed out in favour of the absolute option. Even Rome seems to be placed in this middle ground in one fragment of the *Pensées*, referring to the placing of the *LPs* on the Index: 'Si mes lettres sont condamnées à Rome ce que j'y condamne est condamné dans le ciel' (L 916). And finally in the last stage of the debate (the sixth *Ecrit des Curés*) the same pattern emerges, as the Jesuits are accused of neither condemning nor supporting the *Apologie pour les Casuistes*: 'Criminelle neutralité! Est-ce donc là tout le fruit de nos travaux que d'avoir obtenu des Jésuites qu'ils demeureraient dans l'indifférence entre l'erreur et la vérité, entre l'Evangile et l'Apologie?' (Cognet, p. 447). It could furthermore be argued that the counter-polemic is thereby pushed into isolation, since, as the grounds for its argumentation have been removed by Pascal from the outset, it lacks a ratifying framework. The increasingly dramatic use of this appositional writing will culminate in the sixteenth letter, on the eucharist, where once again quotations are diametrically opposed, a résumé of Arnauld's *Fréquente Communion* being countered by a passage from the Portuguese Jesuit Mascarenhas beginning: 'Que toutes sortes de personnes, et même les prêtres, peuvent recevoir le Corps de Jésus-Christ le jour même qu'ils se sont souillées par des péchés abominables' (xvi. 310), leading finally to the violent: 'Il n'importe que les tables de Jésus-Christ soient remplies d'abominations, pourvu que vos églises soient pleines de monde' (xvi.

310). (It is worth noticing the preponderance of antiphrastic irony in this letter, evident to a greater degree than elsewhere in the series.) Finally the devotion of the Port-Royal nuns to the sacrament is placed symmetrically alongside the Jesuit accusation of Port-Royal's lack of eucharistic orthodoxy:

Pendant que ces saintes Vierges adorent nuit et jour Jésus-Christ au Saint-Sacrement, selon leur institution, vous ne cessez nuit et jour de publier qu'elles ne croient pas qu'il soit ni dans l'Eucharistie, ni même à la droite de son Père; et vous les retranchez publiquement de l'Eglise pendant qu'elles prient dans le secret pour vous et pour toute l'Eglise. (xvi. 321–2)

A similar use of sarcasm is found in the disputed sixth *Ecrit des Curés*,[3] where the Jesuits are invited to 'rentrer dans une vie de retraite plus conforme à des religieux, pour y pratiquer les exercices de la pénitence, dont ils dispensent si facilement les autres' (Cognet, p. 455).

It is the voice of Christ the judge, the apocalyptic resolution, founded 'sur les règles de sa vérité éternelle et sur les saintes ordonnances de son Eglise' (xvi. 322) that answers these accusations. All that is implicit in the earlier letters is rendered explicit, and functions increasingly by appeal to evangelic injunction and indeed to eschatology. The oxymoronic apostrophe to 'saints et pieux calomniateurs' (xvi. 323) seals the condemnation, and encapsulates the irony.

It also becomes increasingly important after the eleventh letter for the polemicist to take account of the *Réponses*: he speaks of them at the beginning of this letter, and at the end of the thirteenth; and it is their use of detail which to some extent forces him into his consideration of detail in the trio of letters xii–xiv. But whereas the method may seem characteristic of the 'doctrine de l'Ecole', the material initially remains largely Pascal's, deflected through the replies, rather than introducing any defensive arguments in response to new aggressive material emanating directly from them.

[3] The tone of this passage (and cf. x. 191) could indeed be thought to lend some internal support to arguments for Pascal's part in the authorship of the *Ecrit* (always allowing for the fact that Nicole is also assigned a hand in both pieces of writing (see n. 4)).

The same is not entirely true of the next two letters. The fifteenth is still very wide-ranging, within the general accusation of lying, taking on board both moral and doctrinal questions; but more importantly it represents another partial break in the series, because it again addresses itself to an attack on the methods of argument. Just as the Jesuits have attacked the polemicist's 'raillerie', so he attacks, by exposing it, their 'calomnie', and from this exposure the underlying theology is then adduced and negated. Their earlier equation ' "raillerie" = heresy' is thus matched by his 'calumny = casuistry', and so in effect a new subject for accusation has arisen out of the very terms of the dispute, (and the mode of argument is in both cases made to point to the underlying theology). It is in this context too that we see the polemicist juxtaposing two languages, by showing the amended, indeed inverted, significance which the Jesuits are able to give to a particular action:

Il ne faut plus dire de vous... Comment ces bons Pères voudraient-ils calomnier leur ennemis, puisqu'ils ne le pourraient faire que par la perte de leur salut? Mais il faut dire au contraire : comment ces bons Pères voudraient-ils perdre l'avantage de décrier leurs ennemis, puisqu'ils le peuvent faire sans hasarder leur salut? (xv. 280)

These terms are taken up again at the end of the letter: 'Ils commettent des crimes tels que la calomnie, non pas contre leurs maximes, mais selon leurs propres maximes' (xv. 296) (as well, vitally, as at the end of the sixteenth *LP*).

The ground is again shifted in the sixteenth letter, although it still contains a mixture of detail (tentatively attributed to Nicole by Cognet)[4] and generality, and, at least initially, of moral and doctrinal questions. It deals most substantially however with sacramental theology, a central issue in any challenge to orthodoxy, and in it broad accusations levelled by the Jesuit writings are countered by a detailed examination of the Jansenist position in the *LPs*. The roles thus seem to have been reversed. But the polemicist regains control in two ways. He first reintroduces the idea of the linguistic emptiness of Jesuit accusation: 'il faut que tous ceux qui combattent vos relâchements soient hérétiques'

---

[4] Cognet, p. 297 n. 2.

(xvi. 309) (a further example of antiphrastic irony); but then, secondly, he forces the argument back onto the practice of 'relâchements', that is the question of the reception, rather than the definition of the eucharist, thereby reawakening the accusation of spiritual corruption. He thus recovers on two fronts: by the first of these ploys, he reintroduces the idea of a linguistic perversion so acute as to offend common sense—by demonstrating its linguistic aberration the polemicist again finds a means of puncturing not just the arguments but the means of argumentation of the Society; and then, by the hyperbolic application of the linguistic tendency to render everything heretical that is not explicitly in accord with the Society, he demonstrates how the Scriptures (xvi. 311), the Council of Trent (xvi. 316), and the Fathers (xvi. 316) also contain heresy. He thereafter 'translates' the Jesuit position into what he sees as acceptable terms (xvi. 319). Secondly, the sixteenth *LP* turns the attack made by the Jesuits on heresy back on the Society by taking up again the question of the morality of those who receive the sacrament, bringing together a statement of Jansenist eucharistic orthodoxy and Jesuit moral poverty (xvi. 319) and so returning once more to the polemicist's privileged area of criticism. Only then does he return to the business of replying to the 'quatre grandes preuves' given by the Jesuits of the eucharistic heresy of Port-Royal.

Even if it could still be argued that these two letters (xv and xvi) show Pascal at his weakest in the series, since they show him following rather than leading, at the same time the global assault on calumny of the fifteenth letter, the violently antithetical writing, and the counter-attack on eucharistic reception, all take attention away from specific aspects of the Jesuit accusation, which are made thereby to appear to serve only as examples, *inter alia*, of general tendencies. Even more damaging, because attacking the grounds of the argument, are the successive demonstrations in these two letters of how the Jesuits employ two self-subverting systems: a moral justification of lying, and a semantic doctrine of meaninglessness. Their accusations of heresy are rendered invalid by the latter, and morally unacceptable by the former. They fail, yet again, on grounds of ideology and pragmatism.

Finally, in the fifteenth and sixteenth *LPs* the polemicist presents his adversaries by virtue of their flexibility as their own worst enemies: 'Qu'il est avantageux, mes Pères, d'avoir affaire à ces gens qui disent le pour et le contre! Je n'ai besoin que de vous-mêmes pour vous confondre' (xv. 287). (Similarly, in the *Pensées*, the apologist remarks: 'En vérité, il est glorieux à la religion d'avoir pour ennemis des hommes si déraisonnables' (L 427).) The Jesuit texts are shown to contain within themselves such potential for self-contradiction that they are easily employed for their own negation: so in the fifteenth letter: 'Je n'ai à montrer que deux choses : l'une, que cette maxime ne vaut rien; l'autre, qu'elle est du P. Bauny. Et je prouverai l'un et l'autre par votre propre confession... Vos réponses s'entre-détruisent' (xv. 287). Further specific examples are then adduced in order to demonstrate the principle. However the terminus, and indeed revelation of the grounding, for this self-subversion again occurs in the later parts of the sixteenth letter, in which the very system is shown to work against itself: 'tant le mal est contraire à soi-même, et tant il s'embarrasse et se détruit par sa propre malice' (xvi. 323). (This was illustrated satirically earlier in the series by the episode of Jean d'Alba, who used the writings of Bauny to justify stealing pewter from the Jesuit Collège de Clermont (vi. 110–13).) The self-defeating evidence which the polemicist draws from the Jesuits is thus now placed in an ideological context; it again functions satirically, but also definitionally, since 'D'autant... que vous avez mis votre espérance en la calomnie et au tumulte... cette iniquité vous sera imputée' (xvi. 324).

Such demonstrations have also illustrated Pascal's powers of recovery: his mastery lies in his manipulation of broad sweeps of argument; in the perception of the tactics which will destroy not the detail but the whole infrastructure of the adversaries' position; and in the imposition of the 'esprit de synthèse' on disparate and hostile material. As Miel points out, 'on ne peut jamais dire que Pascal échoue, parce que l'échec peut toujours être transformé en réussite'.[5] Morel too summarizes helpfully (in fact, in connection

---

[5] J. Miel, in *débat* following D. Jaymes, 'La Méthode d'ironie dans les *Provinciales*', p. 208.

with another part of the series) Pascal's achievements in these letters: 'Pascal [fait] porter ses efforts et son talent sur l'essentiel : systématisation radicale, mise en ordre des arguments, ordonnance convaincante de l'ensemble'.[6] And finally Descotes, assessing Pascal's handling of the two types of response (Annat/ Nouet and Pirot), remarks: 'dans les deux cas, la cause était perdue. Pascal avait prévu la manœuvre et mis au point le dispositif argumentatif approprié'.[7]

Nevertheless the fifteenth and sixteenth letters, containing no reference (unlike the previous three) to the material preceding the eleventh letter, still function to some extent as a bridge passage back to the opening, doctrinal, emphasis. Even if in this defensive material, as we have seen, Pascal has found the means of turning the argument to his own advantage, they still lead indirectly, by conceding attention to the charge of heresy, to the bringing together again of the original *question de fait* and *question de droit*. The fundamental *question de droit* having been expressed in the eleventh letter in terms of the relationship of polemics to the credibility of Christianity, the last two letters now return to the political domain, and examine the original doctrinal *question de fait*. This reinforces the 'reflecting' view of the *LPs* too, whereby the central letters' attention to morality is contained within the outer letters' attention to doctrine. At the same time the whole terminology of the series has been 'renversé' by the eleventh letter, and the new perspective which has ensued will prevail until the end of the series. In the letters preceding the eleventh the illusion of the unimportance of the political issues was superficially maintained; thereafter however, and once the Jesuit 'renversement' has been convincingly proved and illustrated, the role of it in the creation of a political supremacy becomes clear. The relationship is thus established whereby the 'renversement' is shown to bring about the conditions governing the political workings of the Society; indeed it is the condition *sine qua non* of their efficacity. It is only when the debate has been fully rehabilitated, therefore, that Pascal returns to the doctrinal detail, enabled thereby to show its dependence on, and functioning

[6] 'Pascal et la doctrine du rire grave', p. 216.
[7] 'Fonction argumentative', p. 59.

through, a far more profound and wide-ranging system of perverted values. Before attending to the concluding letters, it is necessary to return to the later parts of the counter-polemic.

12

The Later Réponses

IN the replies to the eleventh to seventeenth letters, much of the familiar material recurs; the emphasis on moral questions and 'impostures' is however only maintained in the first three. In the reply to the twelfth *LP*, questions of accuracy and detail predominate. The accuracy of Pascal's accusations is challenged in terms of *questions de fait*, with the question of anonymity clearly still rankling: 'Encore qu'il soit difficile de vous connaître, *il n'est pas malaisé de découvrir les faussetés* que vous avez commises, puisque les plus simples en sont capables, et que ceux qui n'ont pas assez d'étude pour pénétrer dans les questions de droit, ont assez de lumière naturelle pour juger des questions de fait' (*RLP* 210). Here too 'lumière naturelle' is appealed to in judging the issues; and here again distinctions are opposed to generalizations. Vasquez is quoted *in extenso* on the subject of 'l'aumône et le superflu' (the principal subject of the first part of the twelfth letter) with the comment: 'Ce qui vous trompe, Monsieur, ou plutôt ce qui vous sert à tromper les autres, c'est la subtilité de cet auteur, qui distingue le nécessaire et le superflu en plusieurs manières selon lesquelles il règle l'obligation des riches' (*RLP* 217), and the more fundamental point is remade that: 'Ce sont des questions de droit, qui se sont élevées dans l'Ecole depuis plusieurs siècles, et que les théologiens n'ont pas encore décidées. S'il en fallait attendre le bout, nous ne sortirions jamais d'affaire' (*RLP* 219). Both parties in fact accuse the other of being too general, since the polemicist had also objected in the twelfth letter (apropos the Jesuit claim that Vasquez imposes on the rich the obligation to give alms not 'de leur superflu' but 'de leur nécessaire'): 'Vous avez oublié de marquer l'assemblage des conditions qu'il déclare être nécessaires pour former cette obligation... et qui la restreignent si fort, qu'elles l'anéantissent presque entièrement' (xii. 221). Indeed, he qualifies the occasions on which the rich are thus obliged by Vasquez as 'des rencontres si rares, qu'elles n'arrivent presque jamais' (xii. 222), exactly the terms which the Jesuits had in turn attributed to the *cas-limite* examples of moral ambiguity which were quoted against them (e.g. *RLP* 82). We thus find the reflecting polemics exploiting identical modes of argument to different ends, although the polemicist's adoption of the Society's terms is in fact short-lived and, we must assume, at least partially ironic. He duly returns thereafter to a more familiar line later in the twelfth letter, where he insists that his adversaries use detail for the purposes of obfuscation: 'Voilà, mes Pères, comment il faut traiter les questions pour les démêler, au lieu de les embrouiller, ou par des termes d'Ecole ou en changeant l'état de la question' (xii. 228); and again, with reference to duelling, in the fourteenth: 'Il est bien question de savoir si ce cas-là est rare! il s'agit de savoir si le duel y est permis. Ce sont deux questions séparées' (xiv. 263). It is thereby shown by him how the two types of question can in fact be distinguished, but in his hands the reality of the first is the more commonly denied by the absolute simplicity of the second.

The thirteenth *Réponse* moves to the charge against the polemicist of changing ground (on the matter of homicide): 'Vous pouvez bien changer le sujet de la dispute, parce que vous n'y trouvez pas votre avantage. C'est la méthode ordinaire des hérétiques, que vous n'avez pas mal étudiée' (*RLP* 237). The very style of argument is thus again deemed to betoken heresy, and a list is then provided of questions of detail which the polemicist has 'forgotten' to reply to, concluding with the image: 'Vous ressemblez à ces mauvais débiteurs, qui font tous les jours de nouveaux procès, de peur de payer de vieilles dettes' (*RLP* 245). The polemicist has of course also levelled the same reply in the twelfth *LP*: 'vous essayez en vain d'éluder en détournant la question' (xii. 233); and he will in turn accuse the author of the *RLPs* of not replying in the fourteenth *LP*: 'C'est par ce même principe qu'ils autorisent les duels, comme je l'ai fait voir par tant de passages sur lesquels vous n'avez rien répondu' (xiv. 263).

This sense of a *dialogue de sourds* is nowhere stronger than in the thirteenth *RLP*. Further points are then made concerning the difference between 'spéculation' and 'pratique' (a distinction which the polemicist denies in the thirteenth *LP*), reinforced by a further accusation against the Jansenists, this time of stealing money (from the Collège de Sainte-Pulchérie), with the jibe: 'Les Jésuites, dites-vous, approuvent les crimes dans la spéculation, et les condamnent dans la pratique; et les Jansénistes commettent les crimes dans la pratique, et les condamnent dans la spéculation' (*RLP* 251–2). (The polemicist defends the Jansenists against such accusations in xvi. 299–300.) The question of 'opinions probables' is then taken up again and illustrated by a quotation from St Ignatius, but now with reference to the counter-charge of heresy: 'Quand il leur [= to the Society of Jesus] recommande l'uniformité de sentiments et de doctrine, il ne leur ôte pas la liberté des opinions probables, mais il leur défend sévèrement les opinions hérétiques et dangereuses' (*RLP* 260–1).

The fourteenth *Réponse* reintroduces the question of the *Cinq Propositions*, and then develops a clever but over-obscure argument to show that if the polemicist adopted an even more rigorist line he would necessarily find himself on the side of the Jesuits; although we again recognize here the same kinds of tactic as in the *LPs* ('je ne me veux servir que de vos propres armes pour vous combattre' (*RLP* 279)), the complexity of the ploy detracts significantly from its satirical efficacity. Where the *Réponse* does carry conviction is in its appeal (also transferred from the *LPs*) to common sense: 'n'avez-vous pas raison de nous dire que vous voulez nous *remettre dans les principes les plus simples de la religion et du sens commun?* Vous auriez grand besoin, Monsieur, qu'on vous y ramenât' (*RLP* 293). The point is illustrated by the simple need on occasion to decide rapidly on a course of action: it would, for example, scarcely be possible to have long judicial arguments 'au coin d'un bois quand un voleur vous surprend et vous demande la bourse' (*RLP* 293), an example taken up and embroidered on by Morel (p. 54). Morel's reply concludes with a reaction to the fourteenth *LP*, in which he accuses the polemicist of having no argument, but rather a series of exclamations: 'qu'une amplification continuelle, que des redites ennuyantes, que des exclamations réitérées, et qu'un éternel retour à ce qu'ils [Jesuits] vous nient, et que vous ne prouvez point' (p. 56).

The fifteenth *Réponse*, replying to the fifteenth *LP*'s attack on

Jesuit calumny, uses as a motif the slogan 'Mentiris impudentis-
sime: vous mentez très imprudemment', which runs through the
whole letter, and is taken up from the accusation of Valérien
Magni, quoted in the fifteenth *LP*. (Anaphora is indeed one of the
more common rhetorical devices in the *Réponses*: in the *VIᵉ
Imposture*, on the subject of passages described by Pascal as
'décisions horribles, injustes et extravagantes', each of a series of
parallel passages in the writings of St Thomas Aquinas, St
Antoninus, and others is introduced by the phrase: 'Que sera-ce
de les voir dans. . .'; and in the enumeration of orders sympathetic
to the Jesuits, again in the fifteenth *Réponse*.) The matter of the
Cinq Propositions is now revived, and the theme of opposition to
papal authority introduced. Once again the Jansenists are accused
of changing ground:

> Avant la Bulle du Pape c'était un crime de vous disputer les cinq
> Propositions, et ceux qui les tenaient suspectes étaient des Semipéla-
> giens. . . qui s'efforçaient de détruire les plus anciennes vérités. . . Après
> la Bulle, c'est un outrage de vous les imputer, et ceux qui vous les
> reprochent sont des calomniateurs insignes. (*RLP* 307)

> Il n'y a que la haine que vous portez aux Jésuites qui ne change jamais.
> (*RLP* 308)

The end of the *Réponse* contains a plea for retraction: 'C'est le sujet
de mes vœux, c'est l'attente publique, c'est l'intérêt de l'Eglise,
c'est la réponse que j'ai résolu de faire désormais à toutes vos
injures' (*RLP* 323).

At this point the series is interrupted by the *Réponse d'un
théologien aux propositions extraites des lettres des Jansénistes par
quelques Curés de Rouen*. This goes over a great deal of the ground
already covered, without introducing any new material or emphasis. The following *Réponse à la plainte que font les Jansénistes de
ce qu'on les appelle hérétiques*, however, deals predominantly with
the *Cinq Propositions*, and does so in a good deal of detail. It
constitutes in fact the major Jesuit reply on the serious points
arising from them. Its writer is identified as Annat.

The Pope, in condemning the Propositions, it is explained, 'ne
condamne pas les caractères avec lesquels on les écrit; ni la voix
avec laquelle on les prononce, mais le sens de ceux qui les écrivent
ou qui les prononcent, c'est-à-dire le jugement qui répond à la

propre signification de la voix et des caractères' (*RLP* 346). If the Jansenists refuse to condemn them, 'ils soutiennent les cinq Propositions au sens auquel le Pape a déclaré qu'elles sont hérétiques' (*RLP* 347), and 'leur évasion ordinaire par la distinction de la question de droit et de la question de fait ne peut pas les sauver' (*RLP* 348). The *question de fait* is here interpreted as follows: the Jansenists know that what is condemned is the doctrine of Jansenius, 'et n'ignorent point qu'elle a du rapport aux cinq Propositions; et que dans ce rapport, les cinq Propositions ont un sens conforme à la doctrine de Jansénius. Nous sommes donc d'accord de ce fait' (*RLP* 348). Then it is again insisted that the Jansenists acknowledged the existence of the *Cinq Propositions* before the condemnation, and 'ceux qui ne les y trouvent plus, n'ont qu'à reprendre les yeux qu'ils avaient avant qu'elles fussent condamnées' (*RLP* 350). The complementary charge of change of ground in this context is found in the *Pensées*: 'Il y a six mois que c'était *totidem*; à présent c'est le sens' (L 955). And of course the polemicist has challenged the Jesuit moral maxims in the same way:

tandis que votre théologie accommodante passe pour une sage condescendance, vous ne désavouez point ceux qui la publient, et au contraire vous les louez comme contribuant à votre dessein. Mais quand on la fait passer pour un relâchement pernicieux, alors le même intérêt de votre Société vous engage à désavouer des maximes qui vous font tort dans le monde. (xii. 220)

The only *question de droit* that therefore remains to be solved is whether the Pope was mistaken to condemn the Propositions and an incoherence in the Jansenist position is suggested whereby (assuming a consistent belief in papal authority): '[les] Jansénistes... s'efforcent de justifier le mépris qu'ils font de l'autorité du Pape Innocent, par des raisons qui détruisent aussi celle du Pape Célestin, en laquelle néanmoins ils ont fondé leur principale défense' (*RLP* 356). And a similar point is made in *La Bonne Foi des Jansénistes* on the matter of the Church's infallibility: if the Jansenists refer to the Church at the time of Augustine and Basil as authoritative, they must also concede the authority of the present Church (pp. ix–xi).

The *Réponse* then juxtaposes in two columns the 'propositions hérétiques' (that is the *Cinq Propositions*), and 'propositions de Jansénius' with references to volume, book, and chapter, and headed by the information: 'Il ne faut pas être docteur en théologie pour connaître leur conformité' (*RLP* 357). The two vital quotations from Jansenius on the fourth and fifth propositions, followed in each case by the respective 'proposition hérétique', are:

(4) ['l'erreur des Massiliens' was] 'qu'ils pensent que nous avons quelque reste de notre liberté originelle, par laquelle l'homme corrompu pourrait pour le moins croire s'il voulait; *non toutefois sans le secours de la grâce intérieure, dont le bon ou le mauvais usage est laissé au franc-arbitre et au pouvoir d'un chacun.*

(4) Les semi-pélagiens admettaient la nécessité de la grâce intérieure prévenante pour chaque action, même pour le commencement de la foi. Mais en cela ils étaient hérétiques, qu'ils voulaient que cette grâce fût telle que la volonté humaine peut lui résister, ou lui obéir.

(5) Jésus-Christ est mort... *non pas pour ceux qui manquant à la foi et à la charité meurent dans l'iniquité*... Jésus-Christ n'a pas prié son Père pour leur salut (des infidèles ou des justes qui ne persévèrent pas) *non plus que pour le salut du diable.*

(5) Cela est semi-pélagien de dire que Jésus-Christ est mort ou a répandu son sang généralement pour tous les hommes.
Jésus-Christ est mort seulement pour les prédestinés.

The conformity is indeed clear; but the condemned propositions are differently and, most importantly, more generally worded. It is perhaps useful finally to juxtapose a passage from the *Pensées* at this point:

M. Arnaud [*sic*], et ses amis, proteste qu'il les condamne en elles-mêmes [*Cinq Propositions*], et en quelque lieu où elles se trouvent, que si elles sont dans Jansénius il les y condamne.
Qu'encore même qu'elles n'y soient pas, si le sens hérétique de ces propositions que le pape a condamné se trouve dans Jansénius, qu'il condamne Jansénius.
Mais vous n'êtes pas satisfaits de ces protestations, vous voulez qu'il assure que ces propositions sont mot à mot dans Jansénius. Il a répondu qu'il ne peut l'assurer, ne sachant pas si cela est, qu'il les y a cherchées et une infinité d'autres sans jamais les y trouver. (L 955)

In the last part of this *Réponse* there occurs a description of the Jansenists in terms of (partly biblical) animal imagery. The Jansenists, it is claimed, '[font] ores le loup, ores le renard': by claiming that the *Cinq Propositions* are orthodox, 'c'est faire le loup, et se déclarer contre le troupeau'; to say they condemn them, 'en quelque lieu qu'elles se trouvent', 'c'est faire le renard par la restriction mentale et l'exception qu'ils font du sens de Jansénius, qui est néanmoins celui que l'Eglise a condamné' (*RLP* 372). The image ends: 'ils savent encore faire la brebis, par cette innocence et sainteté de vie dont ils se vantent, et qu'ils tâchent même de confirmer par des miracles' (*RLP* 372), a subject on which the piece concludes, and to which we shall shortly return.

The series then ends with the *Réponses* to the sixteenth and seventeenth *LPs*. As with the last two letters, there is now a change of circumstantial detail: the *Réponse* to the former is addressed to 'Messieurs de Port-Royal'; and that to the latter identified as being by 'le P. Annat, de la Compagnie de Jésus'.

The sixteenth *Réponse* begins with an appeal to Port-Royal to silence the 'inconnu': 'il fait dès sa première Lettre le plaisant à vos dépens' (*RLP* 378). (It is curious to note that Morel had earlier appealed to the polemicist against his alleged masters, whom he accuses of exploiting him: 'Jugez je vous prie, mais sans passion, où l'animosité de ceux que vous servez s'emporte' (p. 10).) The *Réponse* then returns to the accusation of complicity with Geneva, and suggests the real reason for hostility against the Jesuits is not 'leur théologie morale'; rather 'ils ne vous sont odieux que parce que vous n'aimez pas trop le Saint Siège qui les approuve, ni l'Eglise qui les emploie, ni la Foi qu'ils enseignent' (*RLP* 386). The accusation of heresy also takes a new impetus in this letter through the use made of 'incriminating' material. The Jansenists, it is proposed, should go to England (or Holland, or Switzerland), because 'la Gazette de Londres du 3 de Janvier 1656... vous a par tout rendu ce témoignage, *que votre doctrine en beaucoup de choses est la même que celle des Eglises réformées*' (*RLP* 396). This is then reinforced by the example of two Jansenists who have become Calvinists, notably one Masson, who 'ne trouve point de meilleure défense pour justifier sa perfidie, que de dire qu'étant disciple de Jansène, il n'a point changé de parti en prenant celui de Calvin, qu'il n'a fait que déclarer extérieurement ce qu'il était déjà dans l'intérieur de son âme' (*RLP* 398). The *Fréquente Communion* is then attacked on (among others) the question of the 'présence locale' in the sacrament; and then quotations are introduced from the *Chapelet secret du Saint-Sacrement*, the work of Agnès Arnauld, which suggest among other things that Christ withholds himself in the Sacrament from the sinful, leading the writer in turn to conclude that Port-Royal denies the fundamentals of sacramental doctrine (*RLP* 414–15).[1]

This *Réponse* constitutes the writing in which the Jesuits proceed the furthest onto their privileged territory of attack, the accusation of heresy. It is furthermore now principally with the sacramental dimensions of the accusation that the counter-polemic is dealing, seeking thereby to emphasize the additional areas of alleged conformity between Port-Royal and Protestantism, over and above those primarily identified in the *Cinq Propositions*. And at an entirely textual level, it would be possible to see Pascal's return to the detail of the *question de fait* and *question de droit* controversy as mirroring the Jesuits' return to detail in response to Pascal's incursions onto their vulnerable territory. Historically, however, there is unlikely to be a direct cause-and-effect relationship, since, as Cognet ponts out,[2] this *Réponse* was not published until the *recueil* of 1657. The publication of the Bull of Alexander VII may well however have prompted what is after all a return to the original defensive position of the letters, completing the albeit uneven alternation of defence and attack in the two series of polemic and counter-polemic. The *Réponse* concludes by asserting that the Jansenists' persistent claims to orthodoxy simply demonstrate duplicity, since the evidence negates it (again taking up a tactic from the *LPs*): 'vous êtes contraires à vous-mêmes... vous ne publiez jamais une hérésie que vous n'ayez votre apologie toute prête; vous mettez en même lieu la vérité et l'erreur, le poison et le remède, et par un artifice commun à tous les ennemis de la Foi vous employez une partie de

---

[1] Both works had already been attacked in the *Port-Royal et Genève d'intelligence*.
[2] Introduction, p. lviii; and p. 326 n. 1.

vos ouvrages à défendre l'autre' (*RLP* 417). After this letter then, in which the intensity and specificity of attack are considerable, both sides return to the *question de fait*.

The last *Réponse*, the seventeenth, draws attention to this return to earlier matters, although attributes a different motivation to it:

Le Secrétaire [= Pascal] a fait premièrement le *scholastique* dans ses quatre premières Lettres, disputant contre la censure de la Sorbonne. Et puis voyant qu'il avançait peu en voulant heurter contre un jugement soutenu par l'autorité du Pape et des Evêques, il a passé dans la *morale des Jésuites*, qui lui a fourni la matière des douze suivantes. Mais étant encore chassé de ce champ-là par la conviction de ses faussetés, il repasse à la *scholastique*. (*RLP* 422)

The Catholic view on 'grâce efficace' is then succinctly put—'elle nous laisse le pouvoir d'y résister', against the Calvinist: 'elle ne nous laisse autre liberté que la *liberté de contrainte*' (*RLP* 424). But it is to the *Ecrits sur la Grâce* that we have to turn to find Pascal's elaboration of this distinction (and associated discernment of 'orthodoxy') most fully developed.

One remaining question needs to be considered here (although not strictly speaking intrinsic to the *LPs*), that of miracles. An independent section of the *Pensées*, related only tangentially to the apologetic project,[3] is devoted to the subject, as, in particular, are two contemporary counter-polemical statements. These are the *Rabat-Joie des Jansénistes* and the *Défense de la Vérité Catholique touchant les miracles*.[4] I have not however dealt with the reply to the first of these, attributed to Antoine Lemaistre.[5]

If we first turn to the *Pensées*, and begin with generalities, we find a miracle defined by Pascal as 'un effet qui excède la force naturelle des moyens qu'on y emploie' (L 891). Miracles are also directly related to truth: 'La vérité…est la fin principale des

---

[3] J. Mesnard writes: 'Cette réflexion sur les miracles n'aboutit en définitive ni à un écrit polémique ni à un écrit apologétique', *Les Pensées de Pascal* (Paris, 1976), 39.

[4] *Rabat-Joie des Jansénistes*: see Appendix I. xii. *Défense de la vérité catholique touchant les miracles, contre les déguisements et artifices de la réponse faite par MM. de Port-Royal à un écrit intitulé 'Observations nécessaires'*: see Appendix I. xxiii.

[5] *Réponse à un écrit publié sur le sujet des miracles qu'il a plu à Dieu de faire à Port-Royal*: see Appendix I. xii.

miracles' (L 832, cf. L 856), and so are not arbitrary manifestations of supernatural power, displays of divine fireworks,
rather they exist in order to point to something beyond themselves. Indeed, Pascal is at pains to point out that miracles are, in
one sense, subsidiary supernatural phenomena, and to emphasize
the qualifying considerations which should surround both their
verification and interpretation.

Furthermore, and fundamentally, miracles serve doctrine: 'Les
miracles sont pour la doctrine et non pas la doctrine pour les
miracles' (L 840), and lead men to Christ: 'Ceux qui suivent J.-C.
à cause de ses miracles honorent sa puissance dans tous les
miracles qu'elle produit' (L 855). Men are only the instruments
through which miracles are worked by God, whose role therein is
primary: 'Ce ne sont point des hommes qui font ces miracles par
une vertu inconnue... c'est Dieu même, c'est l'instrument de la
passion de son fils unique' (L 854). Miracles, like prophecies, are
thus not absolute reasons for believing, but nor do they make it
absurd to believe; and those who believe because of them do so by
'la grâce et non la raison' (L 835). The general principle that
informs the willingness to believe miracles when they are true
(that is, apparently authentic) is that God will not lead men into
error (the opposite of Descartes's 'mauvais génie' hypothesis). A
reciprocal duty is evinced between God and man whereby, on the
one hand, men will receive the belief that is handed down to them
in various ways, and on the other, 'Dieu doit aux hommes de ne
les point induire en erreur' (L 840). Miracles will therefore, if
accepted in themselves as authentic, lead to truth and not error:
'Jamais en la contention du vrai Dieu, de la vérité de la religion
il n'est arrivé de miracle du côté de l'erreur et non de la vérité'
(L 839), since 'ou Dieu a confondu les faux miracles ou il les a
prédits' (L 873).

If, then, miracles are the work of God, it will be nothing less
than an 'endurcissement surnaturel' which prevents man from
believing them. Thus of the miracles of Christ during his life-
time, which verified his status (L 846), Pascal writes that 'il n'y a
point d'impie qui ne s'y rende' (L 840) because they demonstrate
Christ's communication with God, and not just his 'autorité
privée' (L 840)—(although the Jews 's'aveuglaient en jugeant des

miracles par l'Ecriture' (L 892)). Those in later times who refuse to believe true miracles are accorded the same scorn: 'ceux qui refusent de croire les miracles d'aujourd'hui pour une prétendue contradiction chimérique, ne sont pas excusés' (L 841). The times when assent may safely be witheld from miracles are then, 'dans le vieux Testament quand on vous détournera de Dieu; dans le nouveau quand on vous détournera de J.-C.' (L 852). Pascal expresses his hatred for those who are sceptical towards miracles: 'Que je hais ceux qui font les douteux des miracles', but in the same fragment concedes that 'Quoi qu'il en soit l'Eglise est sans preuve s'ils ont raison' (L 872).

More particularly, the problem of miracles and error is re-sumed systematically in fragment L 830, interestingly enough in the form of a series of questions addressed to Barcos, with some replies.[6] The main points to emerge are, first, a reaffirmation that it is God who works miracles, 'seul auteur et opérateur des miracles', and secondly the assertion that miracles point to some-thing beyond themselves, and therefore cannot be performed 'pour confirmer une erreur'. Thus the performer (and his sect presumably if it is implicated) holds a purely instrumental posi-tion between the actual worker that is God and the greater truth to which the miracles point; miracles could be seen as providing a kind of mirror, a reflecting object for God to look at himself, and for man to look at the reflection. Thus if, hypothetically, miracles had been achieved by heretics, they would have been, in the reply of Barcos, 'marques de l'Eglise, parce qu'ils n'étaient faits que pour confirmer la vérité que l'Eglise enseigne, et non l'erreur des hérétiques' (L 830), an argument that will saliently be used against Port-Royal. Developing this point, miracles have been accorded a validating quality against error: 'Jamais l'Eglise n'a approuvé un miracle parmi les hérétiques. Les miracles, appui de religion. Ils ont discerné les Juifs. Ils ont discerné les chrétiens, les saints, les innocents, les vrais croyants' (L 903), since God does not lead men into error, and will thus not allow a heretical miracle

---

[6] The fragment opens thus: 'Les points que j'ai à demander à M. l'abbé de Saint-Cyran sont ceux-ci principalement'. As Saint-Cyran (i.e. Duvergier) died in 1643 it is highly unlikely that he is the addressee; and much more probable that the answers were provided by his nephew and successor as abbot, Barcos.

to be credible. Men 'seraient induits en erreur si les [false] faiseurs (de) miracles annonçaient une doctrine qui ne paraît pas visiblement fausse aux lumières du sens commun, et si un plus grand faiseur de miracles n'avait déjà averti de ne les pas croire' (L 840). The idea of a diabolic miracle is also presented, but here again the overseeing power of God is put forward as a guarantee of truth: 'Jamais signe n'est arrivé de la part du diable sans un signe plus fort de la part de Dieu, au moins sans qu'il eût été prédit que cela arriverait' (L 903). The prediction of false miracles also plays its part in the discernment of Christ over and against the Antichrist: 'les miracles de J.-C. ne sont pas prédits par l'Antéchrist, mais les miracles de l'Antéchrist sont prédits par J.-C.' (L 834). Or again, later in the same fragment, 'Moïse a prédit J.-C. et ordonné de le suivre. J.-C. a prédit l'Antéchrist et défendu de le suivre'.

The case of schismatic miracles is also considered in this context, but easily dismissed by Pascal because of the visible erroneousness of schism. A hierarchy is therefore established:

Le schisme est visible, le miracle est visible, mais le schisme est plus marque d'erreur que le miracle n'est marque de vérité; donc le miracle ne peut induire à erreur.
Mais hors le schisme l'erreur n'est pas si visible que le miracle est visible, donc le miracle induirait à erreur. (L 878, cf. L 903)

Thus the enemies of the Church, the 'injustes persécuteurs de ceux que Dieu protège visiblement' (L 859), are without miracles; and although the Church 'a toujours eu contre eux des miracles, ils ont tous eu le même intérêt à les éluder' (L 858). Calvinists and Jesuits are both named in this category: Jesuits, it is implied, are no better than heretics, although they remain within the confines of the Church, since they, like heretics, are held to deny 'les trois marques de la religion: la perpétuité, la bonne vie, les miracles. Ils détruisent la perpétuité par la probabilité, la bonne vie par leur morale, les miracles en détruisant ou leur vérité, ou leur conséquence' (L 894). And it is in turn the authenticity ('vérité') and implications ('conséquences') of the Port-Royal miracles that will be challenged by the counter-polemic.

The final point to mention is the need for miracles, since it is, in

Pascal's view, not automatically necessary for there always to be miracles. They are, as we have seen, subservient to doctrine, and so presumably once right doctrine has been established and is prevailing, they have fulfilled their role. However, when tradition is placed into question or even suppressed, truth must reassert itself supernaturally: 'Les miracles ne sont plus nécessaires à cause qu'on en a déjà, mais quand on n'écoute plus la tradition... et qu'ainsi ayant exclu la vraie source de la vérité... alors... la vérité doit parler elle-même aux hommes' (L 865).

The first more specific counter-polemical work which addresses itself solely to the question of miracles is the *Rabat-Joie des Jansénistes*, a brief, but sharply argued and carefully documented anonymous piece, attributed to Annat, and subtitled: 'Observations nécessaires sur ce qu'on dit être arrivé à Port-Royal, au sujet de la Sainte Epine. Par un docteur de l'Eglise Catholique'.[7] (The subtitle, abbreviated to *Observations nécessaires*, is largely preferred in later discussion of the work). It appeared, according to Cognet, in August 1656, the same month as the eleventh *LP* and the eleventh *Réponse*.

The major point to emerge from the text is, almost inevitably, the question of discernment; and the first general expression of this takes the form of an emphasis on the role of episcopal authority in the exposition of relics, accompanied by a reminder of the caution which the Church has insisted should surround the publication of any miracles reputedly associated with them. Thus the relics of the saints, and especially of Christ, 'sont dignes d'une vénération toute particulière', and the miracles which God has operated through them are therefore a sign of his approval. However, 'plusieurs abus se sont glissés sur le fait des reliques et des miracles', and therefore: 'l'Eglise, conduite par l'esprit de Dieu, a jugé nécessaire d'apporter diverses précautions pour empêcher ces abus, et pour conserver la véritable religion en sa première pureté' (p. 1). There follows an example of just such precaution being exercised (by the Bishop of Padua), before the

---

[7] Pascal's niece Marguerite Périer was suffering from a lachrymal fistula. Her cure took place at Port-Royal on 24 Mar. 1656. The writings on miracles date from later in 1656 and 1657.

events at Port-Royal are described, and the evidence of disobedience and lack of authority which they provide explained and
condemned.

There remains however the possibility that the cure attributed
to the Holy Thorn did in fact happen, in other words that a
miracle has taken place, and the second part of the *Rabat-Joie*
explores the significance of this hypothetical phenomenon. The
argument here is developed in two parts: first of all, the hierarchy
of signs is established (as by Pascal in the case of false doctrine and
of schism) between the status of apparent miracles and that of
doctrine endorsed by authority. Thus: 'premièrement c'est non
seulement une fausseté, mais aussi un blasphème, de dire que
Dieu fasse des miracles pour autoriser des erreurs condamnées par
son Eglise, et pour justifier ceux qui les soutiennent avec obsti-
nation contre l'autorité de la même Eglise' (p. 6). If miracles do
happen, therefore, 'il ne s'ensuit pas que ces miracles soient une
preuve de la saine doctrine, ou de la vertu des personnes qui
demeurent en ce lieu' (pp. 6–7). The existence of miracles 'chez
les infidèles' (illustrated by examples) is evinced as proof of this.
Such evidence then leads the writer onto his second argument
namely that 'les signes et les miracles sont ordinairement em-
ployés pour la conversion de ceux qui n'ont pas la vraie foi' (p. 9).
This simple premise then allows the development of the implications of the Port-Royal miracles to be taken in a diametrically
contrary direction to that claimed by the Jansenists, thereby
reversing their purported significance. The way in which this is
effected is by proposing that the nature of the relic associated with
the miracle points to the potential universality of salvation
achieved by the Redemption. It is deemed apposite that the relic
should be taken from an instrument of the Passion (the Crown of
Thorns), since 'les sectateurs de Jansénius dénient que ce divin
Sauveur ait offert son sang et sa mort pour le salut de tous les
hommes... et même ils osent soutenir avec une étrange impiété
que Jésus-Christ n'a non plus prié pour le salut des pécheurs qui se
perdent par leur impénitence, que pour le salut des démons' (p.
10). The result of the miracle, if true, should then be to bring the
Jansenists to a state of humility and obedience, in particular to
papal authority, and to a recognition that Christ died for all men.

In the mean time, nevertheless, and in conclusion, the faithful are urged to show extreme caution in making pilgrimages to the place of the miracle: 'Visitez de pensée et d'affection le sacré Mont de Calvaire... et cela suppléera très abondamment à vos pèlerinages du Port-Royal' (p. 12).

The second anti-Port-Royal work is the *Défense de la vérité catholique touchant les miracles*, attributed to Annat or Morel, which takes up many of the same themes, and in the same terms as the *Rabat-Joie*. The work is divided into an introduction and two parts: in the first, the writer states that 'nous parlerons des miracles en général, et nous rechercherons pourquoi Dieu a fait celui qui est arrivé à Port-Royal' (p. 2); and in the second he will reply explicitly to Antoine Lemaistre's *Réponse* to the *Rabat-Joie des Jansénistes*. I shall attend exclusively, and briefly, to the first part.

It begins with the definition of a miracle, in terms very close to those employed by Pascal, if slightly fuller, and supported by quotation from Augustine and Aquinas, as 'un effet qui est contre le cours ordinaire de la nature, et qui surpasse le pouvoir de toutes les créatures, tant corporelles que spirituelles; et par conséquent qui ne peut être produit que par la Toute-Puissance de Dieu' (p. 3). It is thereafter insistently asserted that miracles cannot support false doctrine, heresy, or schism (again now a familiar theme). Once the general points have been made, it is then hypothetically supposed, for the purpose of developing the argument, that the Port-Royal miracle is authentic, and the implications explored. The possibility of miracles being worked by those in error is accorded (with no diminution of error automatically ensuing), and the provisional negative conclusion reached that: 'bien qu'ils [Jansenists] fussent tout éclatants en miracles, ils n'en seraient pas pour cela moins hérétiques, tant qu'ils demeureront obstinés à soutenir leurs erreurs, contre l'autorité de l'Eglise' (p. 16). The putative questioner is allowed to persist, however, in his enquiry, so that a more elaborate hypothesis can be advanced for a miracle being worked on this occasion. The reasons are again familiar: 'Dieu a voulu, par une conduite toute particulière de sa miséricorde, faire éclater la vertu de la Passion de Jésus-Christ, en se servant d'un instrument de cette Passion, pour opérer un miracle devant les yeux de ceux-là mêmes qui s'obstinent à impugner le mérite et l'effet de la Passion du même Jésus-Christ' (p. 17). The aim is again to effect their humble submission to the Church. Finally, the timing is considered, and the miracle is identified as a last means of persuasion. It is therefore deemed appropriate that it should have taken place at Port-Royal, and that it should have affected a blind *pensionnaire*, 'pour inviter les Jansénistes à faire réflexion sur leur aveuglement intérieur' (p. 18). The first part then concludes with an address to the Jansenists who are in possession of the relic.

In the absence of any explicit reaction by Pascal to these arguments, it is clearly more difficult to relate them to the dispute as a whole. However the general points which emerge show how, in common with other polemical topics, and perhaps to a greater degree than most, the question of miracles is characterized by its ambivalence. The agreed acknowledgment of their subsidiary place in the establishment of theological certainty (witness the perhaps telling questionnaire addressed by Pascal to Barcos) may be seen as a consideration which detracts from their argumentational value, endowing them *per se* with too neutral a status. They are only a vehicle for the mediation of truth, whereas the polemical effort is concerned with that truth as it is mediated. Furthermore in Pascal's terms, the close attention which the two works considered give to Port-Royal specifically, and thus to the doctrinal elements of the dispute, place them in a somewhat peripheral position to the *grandes lignes*, and to the preferred emphasis, of the *LPs* as they were evolving at the time.

The replies to the *Lettres Provinciales* as a whole demonstrate amply what we shall not be surprised to find, that two opposing polemics will be related both by their contrasts and their similarities. It is almost as if the intensity of conviction expressed by both parties unites them at one level. What, in more detail, underline this parallelism are the appeals to orthodoxy and common sense, and the tactical astuteness which identifies the strengths and weaknesses of both positions as complementary or contrasting ploys pass from writer to writer. What divide are the exploitation by Pascal of moral problems against the exploitation by the Jesuits of doctrinal ones; the identification by Pascal of orthodoxy in the patristic/lay terms of 'doctrine de la foi' and by the Jesuits in the scholastic/clerical terms of 'doctrine de l'Ecole'; and the understanding of common sense by Pascal with reference to the Christian response to *cas-limites*, and by the Jesuits with reference to the Christian response to ordinary moral difficulties. But it is more broadly the fact that both are working within the same basic credal framework, the intra-Christian nature of the dispute, that endows the two polemical series with their common aspects; and it is the tensions inherent in that system—between grace and free will, the world and the Gospel, antiquity and actuality—that endow the particular positions with their potential for disputatious use. In other words, polemic can only have this combination of referential and formal similarities with interpretative and thematic oppositions because it operates within a system whose primary feature (here the Christian revelation) is at the most fundamental level conceded by both parties.[8]

[8] D. Descotes writes in 'Le Rapport des parties dans les *Provinciales*': 'il faut... qu'au moins sur un domaine restreint [les adversaires] aient trouvé des points d'accord, et formé un état de la question' (p. 12). To some extent this is the case, although as I suggest in Ch. 2, the areas of agreement remain largely unexpressed. Maingueneau (*Sémantique de la polémique*) suggests a more radical incompatibility, writing of 'une grammaire de l'interincompréhension', though again without I think denying the basic framework: 'Chacun ne fait que traduire les énoncés de l'autre dans ses propres catégories...L'incompréhension n'est pas un raté du système d' "échanges", elle en est la condition de possibilité' (pp. 23–4).

13

Letters XVII and XVIII
Closure and Continuity

THE last letters complete the process of defictionalization by mirroring the first series: the *LPs* began with a correspondence between two individuals (Montalte and the 'ami provincial'), and they conclude with two letters (and the beginning of a third) addressed by Pascal (still for obvious reasons not specifically identified) to Annat. At the same time, the representative status of the two later participants is different each from the other. The protection of the individuality of the first person of the *LPs* has, as we have seen, brought to it a particular combative intensity and flexibility by virtue of its autonomy: 'Personne ne répond de mes Lettres que moi, et... je ne réponds de rien que de mes Lettres' (xvii. 333). In the letters preceding the seventeenth, and in a different way in the last two, it stands alone against the Society, although united with the tradition and authority, as it sees it, of the universal Church. Annat on the other hand, as a spokesman, is required to answer for the whole company, since 'vos règles... vous défendent de rien imprimer sans l'aveu de vos supérieurs' (xvii. 332); and is furthermore the King's confessor. Yet it is the Jesuits who are portrayed as isolated, deprived both of individual intensity and of universally recognized corporate authority; they are represented as no more than an ungrounded amalgamation of disparate voices, uniting only in a political aim.

At one level, the actuality of the dispute of which the *LPs* and their replies are the major popular documents makes inevitable this eventual emergence of the two principal adversaries; the series have as their starting-points a conflict of opinion which (and however much the intervening contributions deflect, rehabilitate, or introduce material) still remains to be settled. Since both polemics seek to resolve or prevail in a given controversy, the *LPs* and the *RLPs* work towards closure, effected by the identification of a specific (if unspecified)epistoler and a named addressee/respondent, battling it out in the long-postponed terms of their original and particular dispute.[1] The givenness of the context does not allow an absolute freedom of development or universality of appeal to exist coherently alongside the maintenance of the terms which dictated the initiation of the polemical enterprise. Thus two opposing Christians attend, in the last two complete exchanges, to *questions de fait*, but which now concern consciences. The correspondence finally revolves around the original accusations of heresy which, albeit on the Jesuit side inflated by their various intervening polemical publications, still remain, unanswered, as the theological *raison d'être* of the series. And in addition they now explicitly implicate the writer of the *LPs* in directly personal terms: 'Il est temps que j'arrête une fois pour toutes', writes Pascal, 'cette hardiesse que vous prenez de me traiter d'hérétique, qui s'augmente tous les jours' (xvii. 328), leading him to challenge the Jesuits to provide evidence on a factual level: 'Prouvez donc... que je suis hérétique... Prouvez par mes écrits que je ne reçois pas la Constitution [*Cum Occasione*]. Ils ne sont pas en si grand nombre; il n'y a que 16 Lettres à examiner, où je vous défie... d'en produire la moindre marque' (xvii. 329). But if the last stage thus brings Pascal into exclusive correspondence with an individual, it is at the same time clear that the issues discussed in the last two *LPs* are still deemed to be of wider interest and significance; and the use of such phrases as 'Que tout le monde apprenne' (xviii. 363) underlines this continuing emphasis. So the narrowing down to one epistolary 'destinataire' only conceals the continuing appeal to the judgement of as wide a public as possible.

The issues of the dispute have not been resolved by the appearance of the *LPs* and their replies. What however have emerged are the accusations which complement the defences, accusations which have in turn provoked new defences, and further counter-accusations; and what has been changed is the

---

[1] The apologetic fragments of the *Pensées*, by contrast, work towards an opening out, as the text moves away from specificity of speaker/addressee. In this respect too the two works, while addressing themselves to many of the same problems, point in opposing directions.

broader perspective in which the questions are studied. The two polemics, albeit not forming an exactly interlocking sequence, exhibit a contrapuntal interplay of defence and attack; and the sense in which they are a *dialogue de sourds*, while not always making this interplay clear, does not *pour autant* diminish their complementarity. At the same time, the linear progression of the *LPs* has provided the means for a development not of degree but of kind to take place; so that although the terms of the argument remain superficially the same (hence the complementary/reflecting quality of the first three and last two letters), their potential for interpretation has been altered radically in favour of the Jansenist position. The whole theological infrastructure that has been built up over the series now lies beneath the terms of the conclusion, whose deeper significance is thus revealed, even if the specific accusations of the Jesuits will still be made to seem obscure or incoherent in their detail:

Si vous conveniez de part et d'autre du véritable sens de Jansénius...les jugements... toucheraient ce qui serait véritablement en question. Mais la grande dispute étant de savoir quel est ce sens de Jansénius...il est clair qu'une Constitution qui ne dit pas un mot touchant ce différend... ne décide rien de ce qui est en dispute. (xviii. 355–6)

As the original questions of theology now finally come to the surface again, the initial accusations, frivolously dismissed in the first two letters, are taken up with all the force with which the intervening letters have endowed them: 'Je trouve d'une extrême importance de détruire ces fausses impressions... pour montrer qu'en effet il n'y a point d'hérétiques dans l'Eglise' (xvii. 333).

If the problem has not been solved, nor has either side 'won'. What might seem to be a defeat for Pascal, in so far as he has been brought back onto the issues from which he had moved away, is none the less only a pyrrhic victory for the Jesuits. He has 'mené le jeu', and now resolves what he insists on presenting as a simple problem, with the more difficult and substantial questions resolved, by implication to his advantage, in the intervening material. As Sellier remarks: 'Si l'auteur des *Provinciales* a perdu en ce qui concerne la théologie de la grâce, il a gagné en théologie morale' (*IL* 323). But it is also a pyrrhic victory for Pascal, who retreats from the discussion, with the Jesuits just perhaps beginning to embark on a course of argument that Port-Royal would have found more embarrassing. It is noteworthy too that Pascal in the last two letters comes closest to the kind of discursive argument that is more characteristic of his adversaries; and indeed historical circumstances had also turned against Pascal's position. As Cognet puts it: 'Malgré leur retentissement dans l'opinion, les *Provinciales* aboutissent à un échec'.[2]

The defensive questions involved in the dispute concerning the *Cinq Propositions* are, then, confronted head on and discussed explicitly and seriously (but now only those, and none of the circumstantial accusations). Yet the reductive phrase of the first letter: 'Voilà comment s'est terminé la question de fait, dont je ne me mets guère en peine... Ma conscience n'y est pas intéressée', which serves simply as a pretext for the satirical development in its and the following pieces, spans across to the mirroring statement in the seventeenth: 'Quand je vis que vous ne disputiez plus que pour savoir si elles étaient *mot à mot* dans Jansénius ou non, comme la religion n'y était plus intéressée, je ne m'y intéressai plus aussi' (xvii. 337). And again: 'Votre dispute me touche peu, comme elle touche peu l'Eglise' (xvii. 338–9). There are however vital differences. First, as the original distinction is reintroduced, it is now underpinned by the full amplitude of importance and implication attached to the overriding, composite *question de droit* which we may now understand in its final, but still tacit, formulation: '(How) is Christianity believable; and (how) does the interaction of ethics, spirituality, and doctrine affect its credibility?' Such an understanding furthermore carries with it the whole argumentation of the central series of letters, both accusatory and defensive. *Question de droit* is now not only endowed with meaning, it is at the centre of the whole web of resonances which have gradually accrued to it. The change of perspective, 'le changement de langage', has in the *LPs* endowed a meaningless phrase with meaning. In the interim, the struggling Jesuits have shifted their accusation of heresy around, thereby implying a loss of centre, a failure to find meaning: 'vous avez seulement changé

[2] L. Cognet, *Le Jansénisme* (Paris, 1968), 72. See also Duchêne, *IL* 233.

leur hérésie selon le temps' (xvii. 338). And thus, it can also be argued, the debate has been resolved in Pascal's favour by this clarification. At the same time, perhaps for this very reason, the term *question de droit* is itself now abandoned in favour of the broader *question de foi*. Secondly, these later phrases of dismissal function now as doctrinal and not just satirical pretexts, as they prelude the exposition and fuller historical examination both of the *question de fait* in the remainder of the seventeenth letter (seriously and systematically illustrated from previous examples of this kind of disagreement within the Church, whence will emerge the distinction between 'témérité' and 'hérésie') and of the original *question de droit/foi* in the eighteenth.

First of all, though, this *question de droit/foi* is, in the seventeenth letter as in the first, extended as far into the realm of the *question de fait* as possible, now in the light of historical parallels ('N'est-ce donc pas ici une question de fait de même nature que les pré-cédentes?' (xvii. 347)), and accompanied by the accusation that the Jesuits acted in the opposite way: 'vous avez essayé de détourner la question du point de fait pour la mettre en un point de foi' (xvii. 349) (just as Pascal was accused in the *Réponse à la douzième lettre*: 'Vous ne répondez point à la question de fait, en quoi vous péchez contre votre devoir' (*RLP* 211)). In addition, the 'resolution' of the *question de fait* in the seventeenth letter identifies the initial satire for what it was (although Duchêne insists as well on the difference in historical circumstances be-tween the two phases: 'La légèreté avec laquelle était présentée l'affaire d'Arnauld dans la première *Provinciale* n'est plus de mise maintenant qu'il s'agit d'une accusation générale d'hérésie' (*IL* 233)); it is as if Pascal is showing that he could have dealt with the problem seriously all along, but has been taunting his opponents throughout. Despite the similarity between the terms of dis-missal therefore between the first and seventeenth letters, the later piece does contain an exhaustive examination of the dispute surrounding the *question de fait*, the central part of which concludes: 'La question demeure donc toujours dans ce point de fait... Et ainsi on n'en peut faire une matière d'hérésie' (xvii. 349); and later, 'il est bien de foi que ces propositions sont hérétiques, mais... il ne sera jamais de foi qu'elles soient de Jansénius' (xvii.

353). In this way both sides have now claimed in their defence that what is in play is less than a *question de droit/foi* or 'doctrine de la foi', Pascal by stressing here that accusations against the Jansensists are a *question de fait*, the Jesuits by insisting all along that their exploration of moral dilemmas is a 'doctrine de l'Ecole'. And both sides, in attacking, have claimed that the other is erring at a fundamental, that is heretical, level.

The reply to this letter takes Pascal into the concluding phase of his campaign. The central issues have re-emerged from triviality, and in their emergence many related issues have also been exposed. The specific *question de droit/foi* that was trivialized and dismissed in the first letter will now be restored to its full significance in the current debate. It is furthermore Pascal who, in this final letter, establishes what is to be examined, by implication from the previous *Réponse*: 'N'était-ce que l'erreur de Calvin que vous vouliez faire condamner sous le nom du sens de Jansénius? Que ne le déclariez-vous plus tôt?' (xviii. 357). Pirot considers this eighteenth letter 'une raillerie des Jansénistes pour se moquer du Père Annat, de ce que depuis tant d'années qu'il lit leurs livres, il n'a pas compris en quoi leur doctrine est différente de celle des écrivains Catholiques' (p. 186). Thereafter the doctrinal position(s) attributed to Jansenius and Augustine on grace and free will are rapidly elucidated (xviii. 358–61), in distinction to Protestant teaching and to Molinism, and in parallel with the first two *Ecrits sur la Grâce*. (And this is the most sustained treatment by Pascal in the polemical medium which the theology of grace will receive.)[3] The fundamental questions of doctrinal orthodoxy thus return to the centre of the dispute and are confidently restated.

The debate is thus presented rhetorically by Pascal as having run its course. The *question de fait* and the semantic disputes remain in play, but as the taunt of the party that has won the argument: 'N'est-ce pas malgré vous un point de fait pour lequel il serait ridicule de prétendre qu'il y eût des hérétiques dans

---

[3] Sellier (*Pascal et saint Augustin*, p. 340) nevertheless writes: 'Il suffit de souligner les affirmations fondamentales de ces pages lumineuses pour mettre en relief la conception pascalienne de l'accord entre la grâce et le libre arbitre'.

l'Eglise?' (xviii. 364). If the *question de fait* remains to be resolved, the means for its resolution are stated in the simplest of terms: 'Ce n'est que l'examen d'un livre qui peut faire savoir que des paroles y sont. Les choses de fait ne se prouvent que par les sens' (xviii. 376). Such a procedure has already been followed in the thirteenth letter: 'C'est une question de fait qu'il sera bien facile de décider... il ne faut, pour en être éclairci, qu'ouvrir le livre même où vous renvoyez' (xiii. 238–9), as is mentioned in the eighteenth: 'Que ne preniez-vous la même voie que j'ai tenue dans mes lettres pour découvrir tant de mauvaises maximes de vos auteurs, qui est de citer fidèlement les lieux d'où elles sont tirées?' (xviii. 368). But of course if this simple expedient had been proposed at the outset, rather than just mentioned in passing ('Son livre [the *Augustinus*] n'est pas si rare, ni si gros que je ne le pusse lire tout entier pour m'en éclaircir, sans en consulter la Sorbonne' (i. 7)), much of the potential for satirical elaboration would have been pre-empted. The holding back of the introduction of a methodology has allowed the development of the major series of satirical letters. Now that that has been exhausted the questions which began the debate are given a straight answer. The *question de fait* is taken seriously.

It is right that this should be the level at which the writing tails off into incompleteness, since the *question de fait/droit* controversy is capable of identification as a kind of leitmotiv of the whole series, never being endowed *per se* with much satirical sparkle, or intellectual or spiritual emphasis (the abbé Maynard writes of 'ce misérable thème du *fait* et du *droit*'),[4] but rather carrying as a vehicle in its passive defensive status the active and aggressive challenge that the letters *in toto* present to the Society of Jesus. And they too, less far and less glamorously, have moved from the original terms out onto their territory, so that two different views of the Church have been allowed to emerge on the strength of a quickly soluble dispute about wording. Or perhaps, rather than emerging from it, they had already been concentrated into it.

It is appropriate too that the series should end, in the eighteenth letter, on the simple erection of an epistemological system,

---

[4] *Les Provinciales et leur réfutation*, i. 52.

differentiating means of knowing in a way that recurs throughout
Pascal's writing (from the *Préface* of the *Traité sur le Vide* to the
Pensées), and which stands here as some sort of conclusion:

S'il s'agit d'une chose surnaturelle, nous n'en jugerons ni par les sens, ni
par la raison, mais par l'Ecriture et par les décisions de l'Eglise. S'il s'agit
d'une proposition non révélée et proportionnée à la raison naturelle, elle
en sera le premier juge. Et s'il s'agit enfin d'un point de fait, nous en
croirons les sens, auxquels il appartient naturellement d'en connaître.
(xviii. 375)

Yet while apparently providing the means of resolving, unam-
biguously, different questions on their various levels, this hierarchization, standing where it does, implicitly recognizes that
such questions are imbued with a potential for development that
endlessly defeats a neat epistemology. The fact that Pascal has
taken the Jesuits into a hyperbolic affirmation and recognition of
Jansenist orthodoxy which is entirely of his own making—'L'on
saura... par votre propre confession, qu'il n'y a pas le moindre
soupçon d'erreur dans ceux que vous en avez tant accusés' (xvii.
363)—revives in this final letter an ironic status, by echoing the
statements of simple resolution which characterize the first letter,
and indeed recalling certain of the motifs: 'si vous n'en voulez pas
aux syllabes, mais à la chose qu'elles signifient, vous devez être
satisfait' (xviii. 366); 'vous trouvez que ce n'est rien de condamner
les erreurs, si on ne condamne les personnes à qui vous les voulez
imputer' (xviii. 367).

Something more of this co-existence of continuity with inter-
ruption/conclusion is implied in a somewhat opaque fragment of
the *Pensées*, apparently not denying the probability that the battle
of the *Provinciales* has been fought before and will be fought
again, and yet within the terms of its opening paradox retaining
the hierarchy of nature and grace as it stands: 'La grâce sera
toujours dans le monde et aussi la nature; de sorte qu'elle est en
quelque sorte naturelle. Et ainsi toujours il y aura des Pélagiens et
toujours des catholiques, et toujours combat' (L 662).[5] Or as
Derôme puts it: '[les] deux courants... existent depuis l'origine

---

[5] The fragment continues: 'Parce que la première naissance fait les uns et la
grâce de la seconde naissance fait les autres'.

dans le sein du christianisme, celui des réguliers, des ascètes, des parfaits... et celui du plus grand nombre, le courant séculier'[6] (perhaps, however, thereby missing the vital attractiveness of Jansenist absolutism to the secular spirit). The writer of the *LPs* proposes an apparently simple solution, superficially, to the problem addressed by the polemic, whilst recognizing it at the deepest level as insoluble. And the structure of the work reflects this contradiction. The simple mirroring proposes a conclusion to the letters, because a return to the beginning, but co-existing with their incompleteness. The 'changement de langage' of the eleventh letter has introduced a mirror image, and one further-more in which the previously distorted reflection is corrected. The deforming vision of the Jesuits, supported by the deceiving fiction of Montalte's indifference, have been replaced by a cor-rected angle of vision as Pascal confronts the Society with its true image, the real *imago primi saeculi*. And yet, on the page, the series shows nothing of a concluding character, trailing off as it does after the ominous ending of the eighteenth letter into notes for the unfinished nineteenth, with the same issues waiting to be taken up again in subsequent writing. The *LPs*, like the comedy that they are, both propose an artificial resolution to a particular set of circumstances, but also give to understand that the broader dilemma will not change.

The tripartite epistemology has of course been emerging throughout the series; already in the first letter we find the distinction between 'mémoire', 'intelligence', and 'conscience'. (The conclusion's simplicity is perhaps, too, adumbrated in the promise of the first letter: 'C'est ce que je vous dirai en peu de mots, après m'en être parfaitement instruit' (i. 4).) It also takes up the distinction sketched out in the fourth letter: 'Ce n'est pas ici un point de foi, ni même de raisonnement; c'est une chose de fait : nous le voyons, nous le savons, nous le sentons' (iv. 63); and develops the need expressed in the twelfth: 'Voilà, mes Pères, comment il faut traiter les questions pour les démêler, au lieu de les embrouiller, ou par des termes d'Ecole ou en changeant l'état de la question' (xii. 228). The first clear distinction however

---

[6] *Lettres Provinciales*, i, Introduction, p. cxx.

appears in the seventeenth letter, where the two sorts of question now stand clearly (if zeugmatically) defined, as do the appropriate areas of reference for their resolution: 'il n'y a que Dieu qui ait pu instruire l'Eglise de la foi. Mais il n'y a qu'à lire Jansénius pour savoir si des propositions sont dans son livre' (xvii. 343), since 'Dieu conduit l'Eglise, dans la détermination des points de la foi, par l'assistance de son esprit, qui ne peut errer; au lieu que, dans les choses de fait, il la laisse agir par les sens et par la raison, qui en sont naturellement les juges' (xvii. 343).

This bipartite (but subdivided) division prepares for the more clear-cut tripartite division in the eighteenth letter, which in turn announces the crucial statement of the theory of three orders: 'D'où apprendrons-nous donc la vérité des faits? Ce sera des yeux, mon Père, qui en sont les légitimes juges, comme la raison l'est des choses naturelles et intelligibles, et la foi des choses surnaturelles et révélées' (xviii. 374). What the later tripartite model achieves is both elegant and convincing, and its qualities can themselves be divided into three:

(1) It has a clarity and simplicity which have been held back throughout the series. The first letters took the *fait/droit* distinction not as a pretext to the elaboration of an epistemology, but of a counter-attack. Now, however, having proposed a destructive way of coping with the dilemma (the letters on 'la morale relâchée'), a theory is provided which, with equal simplicity, turns to a constructive one; but the impression is therefore given that it has simply been delayed, and that the Jesuits have been strung along and implicated on the way.

(2) It unites constructively the perspectives of orthodoxy and (common) sense to which the destructive writing has appealed: 'tant s'en faut que la foi détruise la certitude des sens, que ce serait au contraire détruire la foi que de vouloir révoquer en doute le rapport fidèle des sens' (xvii. 374). Both are satisfied by the terms of the solution, and dissatisfied by the Jesuits: 'Vous allez chercher des moyens si éloignés de cette simplicité, que cela frappe nécessairement les plus stupides' (xviii. 368).

(3) It concedes a third (middle) kind of knowledge, but, vitally, excludes the current questions from it. This is why a tripartite

epistemology is provided to resolve a dilemma arising from the bipartite distinction between 'fait' and 'droit'.

Davidson in fact suggests that the series is concluded by a bipartite division:[7] '*Questions de fait* have to be judged in the light of sense experience. . . *Questions de foi* have to be decided . . . in the light of Scripture and of decisions handed down by the Church. The intermediate order of *raison* seems to have no relevance to the problems of the *Provinciales*'. The role for *raison*, if understood as 'doctrine de l'Ecole', is, I would suggest, that fulfilled by the Society of Jesus; but, by the terms of the seventeenth and eighteenth letters, this 'doctrine de l'Ecole' that has been their concern is indeed made peripheral to the dispute. In the light of the tripartite epistemological division of the eighteenth letter, the original problems of the series are situated at the first (faith/authority) and third (fact/senses) levels, and are shown to arise from a confusion between the two. The central letters of the *LPs* have also introduced into the debate however the tendency of the Jesuits to confuse the first and second (reason/nature) levels, as they seek to resolve problems on an intellectual plane, whose true resolution lies in the acceptance of authority. Thus the moral questions, which Pascal himself initiated, are, in the manner in which the Jesuits treated them, excluded from the paradigm; and the doctrinal questions, which the Jesuits promoted, are dismissed because resolved by it. In its elaboration of a methodology, the work provides the formula for its own dissolution.

A final parallel with the *Pensées* may be drawn. The need to establish an epistemological hierarchy, to determine the kind of question that is being asked, is the note on which the series is abandoned. This discernment of the level of enquiry appropriate to a particular question is, of course, also a differentiation vital in the apologetic project to the conversion of the unbeliever. He too must recognize the legitimate domains of the senses, the intellect, and the heart; and just as the overstretching of reason (the error of the 'doctrine de l'Ecole') is the epistemological misemphasis of which the Jesuits are deemed to be guilty, so does it constitute the

---

[7] *Audience, Words, and Art*, p. 133.

overriding impediment to belief that characterizes the erroneous seeker of the apologetic fragments. We are in this respect too therefore left with both a solution and a problem. Pascal has identified in the *LPs* the types of question that are for him really and not just apparently in play; and he has proposed a method for answering them on their respective levels. The elegance of Pascal's model is here indisputable, but its more systematic application to broader questions of belief—and most notably in so far as the role of reason is concerned—remains to be demonstrated. The interaction between the two higher orders of knowledge has received only a destructive treatment in the polemical context of the *Lettres Provinciales*; it will be in the *Pensées* that the exact, if more complex, rights and limits of all three in the apologetic domain will be more fully articulated.

Conclusion

THE *Lettres Provinciales* constitute an attempt at the construction of a variety of ideological frameworks within which two related disputes are made soluble and, indeed, superficially resolved. Much of the subtlety of the work lies in the deflected terms of debate which are employed to this end—Pascal erects an analogous model (morality) to the one presented at the outset (doctrine), argues the issues on that territory, and then suddenly swings back to the original area of dispute. The universality of interest of the letters lies in the centrality of the substance and structure of the arguments deployed, both to Pascal's thought and writing as a whole, and to the claims and traditions of Christianity.

Dismantling and rebuilding are the means by which Pascal establishes the terms of the problem he is concerned to resolve, so that what appears to be the rehabilitation of the dispute is in fact its demolition and reconstruction. Thus the lesson of the *LPs* is as much a lesson in argumentation as it is in orthodoxy. The establishment of a 'doctrine de la foi' (theology), a *question de droit* (methodology), a perspective (metaphysics), a language (semantics), and finally of a hierarchy (epistemology) has been Pascal's principal concern. Theologically, he persuades by his appeal to the traditions of evangelic simplicity, particularly because, on one reading, the material he is attacking is shown as calling out for reform and a return to the fundamental Christian tenets. Methodologically, he is able to prevail above all by the dictation of the underlying direction of the argument, rather than in the manipulation of detail. It is by his (initially unchallenged) introduction and gradual development of what he sees as the essentials at issue that is he able to capture, and retain, the tactical advantage. He dominates the argument because, at the deepest level, he dictates its terms.[1] Metaphysically, he proposes a dualistic clash,

---

[1] Descotes writes: '[Les Jésuites] ont fait dans la querelle l'expérience de ce que coûte, dans un combat, l'erreur de rester à la traîne de l'ennemi, et celle de se laisser dicter une tactique' ('Le Rapport des parties dans les *Provinciales*', p. 32).

with a simple choice of referent (transcendent or immanent), whose outcome is dictated in advance by the context of the dispute, but whose very polarization would in fact be contested by his adversaries. Semantically, he works through the ideas of meaninglessness and private meaning to a consonance of the common sense and transcendent understanding of denotations; and epistemologically he negates the terms of the original argument, tacitly evolves new terms to assess the problems to which he then attends, and then proposes a simple method of judgement in conclusion that maintains all the preceding material within a rigid categorization.

Furthermore the whole polemical effect of these particular structures, with their associated focuses, is contained as much in the presentation of the *problématique* as in its solution; it is by the engagement of the reader in the terms of the dilemma that Pascal predicts, indeed determines, his acknowledgement of its outcome—just as it will be in the *Pensées*. All the fictional aspects further promote this end: the entertaining vein in which the problem is articulated in the first part of the work induces in the reader a readiness to embrace seriousness when it is shown to be appropriate in the later parts, as the pathos of these letters invites association; the demonstrated jungle of case ethics provided by the eager Jesuit father implants a desire for the simplicity of absolute values; and the provision of points of identification guides the reader in the process of discovery.

At the same time, one whole category of reader is left without, or deprived of, an associative focus, and that is the believer living in the world or, put another way, the intra-Christian majority. It is to such figures that the 'doctrine de l'Ecole' with its attendant apparatus addresses itself: to detail in matters of moral *questions de fait*; to the needs of those who 'vivent ès villes, ès ménages, en la cour, et qui par leur condition sont obligés de faire une vie commune quant à l'extérieur'[2] in terms of perspective; to some accommodation with their language in terms of semantics; and to the whole middle area, epistemologically, which deals with the

---

[2] François de Sales, *Introduction à la vie dévote*, in *Œuvres complètes* (Bibliotheque de la Pléiade; Paris, 1969), 23.

complexities engendered by the theory and practice of belief. It is just this exclusion which ensures the polemical success of the letters, catering as they do for the non-Christian onlookers and for the fervent adherents. Pascal's appeal is successful at the two extremes, both of which have their privileged point of reference in the text, of secular straightforwardness and orthodox rigidity. Curiously enough, it is more likely that the arguments of the *Provinciales* will stand some chance of exciting the indignation of a majority of nominally non-Christian readers than that of a nominally Christian one. The former will find itself able to respond in terms of simple common sense; but the latter will not encounter any tolerance of its foibles or imperfections. The Pascalian epistemology leaves unanswered the question to which the Society of Jesus attends, simply by suppressing it.

Thus, in the light of a critical reading, we see how the terms which ensure the *LPs* their victory are the same as those which define their defeat, since they reveal the fact that the major force of their destructive thrust has finally prevailed not by answering but by negating a principal aspect of the broader *problématique* as it has been exposed, that of the middle order of knowledge and experience. That the Jesuits are deemed to have dealt with it wrongly or inadequately is indisputable; it is equally indisputable that they have thereby failed to attend theologically/doctrinally to the full implications of their (tacit) epistemological hierarchy. But Pascal's simple moral absolutism, whilst at first sight compelling, ends up by drawing attention to the range of questions it leaves unanswered. What, perhaps inevitably, arises from a more distanced, objective reading of these negative texts is the *opposite* critique to that which each party had originally levelled at his adversary. Port-Royal was accused of defective doctrine, the Jesuits of corrupt morality; and these remain the primary accusations. But at the same time we are made strongly aware that Pascal offers no *modus vivendi*, and that the Jesuits subvert their own *modus credendi*. The dilemmas arising from the interplay of ethics and doctrine are thereby, once again, found to lie at the root of the dispute.

What the two polemics taken together do provide, largely because they are bound to propose hyperbolically simplified emphases, is a vivid articulation of one of the central dilemmas which Christian allegiance proposed in the seventeenth century; and they do so in a form which makes of that statement the primary contemporary illustration of a *modus disputandi*.

Appendix I
Replies to the Lettres Provinciales

(i) *Réponse et remerciement d'un Provincial à Monsieur EAABPF-DEPA sur le sujet de ses lettres et particulièrement de la cinquième.* Dated by Cognet April–May 1656. BN D. 9580 (missing November 1985); BPR LP 382 (3)

(ii) *Lettre de Philarque à un de ses amis, sur le sujet des plaisantes Lettres écrites à un Provincial.* Dated by Cognet April–May 1656. BPR LP 383 (4)

(iii) *Lettre d'un Provincial au secrétaire de Port-Royal.* Dated by Cognet April–May 1656. BN shelfmark illegible; BPR LP 382 (5)
Works (i)–(iii) described by Cognet as 'libelles... très médiocres... que [les jésuites] n'ont jamais reconnus pour leurs' (p. xlviii).

(iv) There also exists in the BPR collection an incomplete *Lettre écrite à un abbé par un Docteur, sur les sujets des trois lettres écrites à un Provincial par un de ses Amis* (LP 382 (2)), which is presumably earlier than the above (February 1656?). There is apparently a complete version at Besançon. The BPR edition runs to 8 pages only.

(v) There also exists a work not mentioned by Cognet dated 1656, the *Justification du Procédé des Catholiques contre les Jansénistes tirée de Saint-Augustin.* BN D 3740

(vi) *Réponses aux Lettres Provinciales publiées par le Secrétaire de Port-Royal contre les PP de la Compagnie de Jésus, sur le sujet de la Morale des dits Pères* (*RLP*) (Liège, 1657 and 1658). BN D 46086, D 89990 (1657); BN D 12353 (1658). Described by Cognet as 'le recueil officiel de leurs réponses' (p. xlviii). Attributed to Jacques Nouet, SJ (pencil note in BN D 46806: 'Par le P. Jacques Nouet'). For list of contents see Appendix II. Pagination differs in the two editions. They both contain the pieces identified below by the letters RLP; many of these are also published separately.

(vii) *Première Réponse aux Lettres que les Jansénistes publient contre les Jésuites* (RLP) (?1656)

(viii) Abbé Léonard de Marandé, *Considérations sur un libelle de Port-Royal.* Dated by Cognet as 20 March 1656. BN 4° Ld⁴ 228; BPR LP 382 (42).

(ix) *Lettre écrite à une personne de condition sur le sujet de celle que les*

jansénistes publient contre les jésuites (RLP). Reply to the 8th *LP*.
Described by Cognet as 'fort médiocre' (p. 1).

(x) *Lettre écrite à une personne de condition sur la conformité des reproches et des calomnies que les jansénistes publient contre les Pères de la Compagnie de Jésus avec celle que le ministre Du Moulin a publiées devant eux* (RLP). Cognet dates as contemporary with ninth *LP* (3 July 1656). Bodleian 3. △. 487.

(xi) *Réponse aux lettres que les jansénistes publient contre les jésuites* (RLP). BN D 4411 (1–11); Bodleian 3. △. 487. Initially attributed to P. Pinthereau, then to Nouet. However 'il est probable que les réponses aux *Provinciales* sont elles aussi des œuvres collectives, où d'autres, et en particulier le P. Annat, tinrent une place fort importante' (Cognet, p. lii). There is a MS attribution to Annat in the BN copy. Cognet dates it as August, 1656. The work consists of six *Impostures* attributed to the author of the *LPs* followed by six *Avertissements aux jansénistes*.

(xii) *Rabat-Joie des Jansénistes*. Attributed to Annat, and dated by Cognet as August 1656. BNLd⁴ 242, Ld⁴ 242B; BL 860. l. 18 (8); BPR LP 382 (57). The reply by A. Lemaistre, *Réponse à un écrit publié sur le sujet des miracles qu'il a plu à Dieu de faire à Port-Royal*, is dated by Cognet as August–November 1656; he does not consider Pascal had any part in it (p. liii). It is to this that the *Défense de la vérité catholique* (see below, xxiii) is in turn a reply.

(xiii) *Réponse à la onzième lettre des jansénistes* (RLP). Attributed to Nouet. Dated by Cognet as August 1656. BL C. 37. f. 5 (12).

(xiv) *Réponse à la douzième lettre* (RLP). Attributed to Nouet. Dated by Cognet as September 1656. This is also answered by a *Réfutation de la Réponse à la douzième lettre*, attributed to A. Lemaistre or to Nicole (BL C. 37. f. 5 (14)).

(xv) *Continuation des impostures que les jansénistes publient dans leurs lettres contre les jésuites* (RLP) Attributed to Nouet. Dated by Cognet as September 1656.

(xvi) *Réponse à la treizième lettre* (RLP). Attributed to Nouet. Dated by Cognet as October 1656. BL C. 37. f. 5 (16).

(xvii) *Réponse à la quatorzième lettre* (RLP). Attributed to Nouet. BL C. 37. f. 5 (18).

(xviii) *Seconde Partie des Impostures* (RLP). Dated by Cognet as October 1656. He comments that it 'se perd dans le détail' (p. lvi).

(xix) *Réponse générale à l'auteur des lettres qui se publient depuis quelque temps contre la doctrine des jésuites*, 'par le prieur de Sainte-Foy, Prêtre Théologien' (Lyons, ?October 1656). BPR LP 382 (1). Sainte-Foy is a pseudonym. Attributed to P. Andoche Morel.

Considered by Cognet to be 'la meilleure... des réponses aux *Provinciales*' (p. lvi).

(xx) *Réponse à la quinzième lettre* (RLP). Attributed to Nouet. Dated by Cognet as December 1656. BL C. 37. f. 5 (20).

(xxi) P. Annat, *La Bonne Foi des Jansénistes en la citation des auteurs reconnue dans les lettres que le secrétaire de Port-Royal a fait courir depuis Pâques.* BN D 4406, D 6192. Dated by Cognet as Jan. 1657. He comments: 'La pièce est médiocre... Elle n'ajoute rien aux Impostures du P. Nouet' (p. lviii).

(xxii) Annat, *Réponse à la plainte que font les jansénistes de ce qu'on les appelle hérétiques* (RLP). Dated by Cognet as after 17 Mar. 1657. BN D 3773.

(xxiii) *Défense de la vérité catholique touchant les miracles, contre les déguisements et artifices de la réponse faite par MM. de Port-Royal, à un écrit intitulé: 'Observations nécessaires sur ce qu'on dit être arrivé à Port-Royal au sujet de la Sainte Epine'* [i.e. the *Rabat-Joie des Jansénistes*], par le Sieur de Sainte-Foy, docteur en théologie [François Annat]. (NB this pseudonym is also used by Andoche Morel, cf. above xix. Cognet attributes the work to Annat or Morel (p. 328 n. 1). Sommervogel (*Bibliothèque de la Compagnie de Jésus*) lists it under Annat.) BN Ld⁴ 248, Ld⁴ 248A; BL [Sainte-Foy] 860. l. 18 (7).

(xxiv) *Apologie pour les Casuistes contre les calomnies des jansénistes* (mid-December 1657). By P. Georges Pirot. BN D 4414; Bodleian 3. △. 488 (1659). The *Ecrits des Curés* are a reply to this. See Cognet, pp. lxv–lxx.

Appendix II
Details of the Réponses aux Lettres Provinciales

Réponses aux *Lettres Provinciales* publiées par le Secrétaire du Port-Royal contre les P P. de la Compagnie de Jésus, sur la Morale des dits Pères. *Numbering according to 1st edn.* (BN D 46086 : A Liège. Chez Jean Mathius Horius à l'enseigne du Paradis Terrestre. MDCLVII. Avec la permission des supérieurs) *and 2nd edn.* (BN D 12353). *Details given in parentheses appear on the title-page but not in the table of contents. In the* Deuxième Réponse *each* Imposture *is followed by an* Avertissement.

TROISIEME REPONSE

Bibliography

PRIMARY TEXTS

PASCAL, *Les Provinciales ou les lettres écrites par Louis de Montalte à un provincial de ses amis et aux RR. PP. Jésuites*, ed. L. Cognet (Paris, 1983).

——*Œuvres complètes*, ed. L. Lafuma (Paris, 1963).

Réponses aux Lettres Provinciales publiées par le Secrétaire du Port-Royal contre les PP. de la Compagnie de Jésus, sur la morale des dits Pères (Liège, 1657).

See also Appendix I

SECONDARY TEXTS

ABERCROMBIE, N., *The Origins of Jansenism* (Oxford, 1936).

BAADER, H. (ed.), *Onze études sur l'esprit de la satire* (Tübingen and Paris, 1978).

BAIRD, A., *Studies in Pascal's Ethics* (The Hague, 1975).

BAUDIN, E., *Etudes historiques et critiques sur la philosophie de Pascal* (Neuchâtel, 1946–7), 3 vols.

BAUDRY DE SAINT-GILLES D'ASSON, A., *Journal*, ed. E. Jovy (Paris, 1936).

BENICHOU, P., *Morales du grand siècle* (Paris, 1948).

BERGSON, H., *Le Rire* in *Œuvres* (Paris, 1959).

BRUNSCHVICG L., *et al.*, Pascal, *Œuvres*, 14 vols. (Paris, 1904–14); *Lettres Provinciales*, ed. F. Gazier, vols. 4–7.

CARREYRE, J., 'Jansénisme', in A. Vacant and E. Mangenot (eds.), *Dictionnaire de Théologie Catholique* (Paris, 1903–50).

COGNET, L., *Le Jansénisme* (Paris, 1968).

CRUICKSHANK, J., *Pascal: Pensées* (London, 1983).

DAVIDSON, H., *Audience, Words, and Art* (Ohio, 1965).

DEROME, L. (ed.), Pascal, *Lettres écrites à un Provincial*, 2 vols. (Paris, 1885–6).

DESCOTES, D., 'Fonction argumentative de la satire dans les *Provinciales*', in H. Baader (ed.), *Onze études sur l'esprit de la satire*, pp. 43–65.

——'Le Rapport des parties dans les *Provinciales*' in J. -J. Demorest and L. Leibacher-Ouvrard (eds.), *Pascal, Corneille*, pp. 11–36.

DEMOREST, J. -J., and L. LEIBACHER-OUVRARD (eds.), *Pascal, Corneille: Désert, retraite, engagement* (Paris, Seattle, and Tübingen, 1984).

DUCHENE, R., *L'Imposture littéraire dans les Provinciales de Pascal*, 2nd edn. (Paris, 1985).

FERREYROLLES, G., *Blaise Pascal: Les Provinciales* (Paris, 1984).

——*Pascal et la raison du politique* (Paris, 1984).

GOLDMANN, L., *Le Dieu caché* (Paris, 1959).

JAYMES, D., 'La Méthode d'ironie dans les *Provinciales*', in *Méthodes chez Pascal* (Paris, 1979), 203–11.

——'Pascal's Ironic Silence in *Les Provinciales*', in J. -J. Demorest and L. Leibacher-Ouvrard (eds.), *Pascal, Corneille*, pp. 37–56.

KRAILSHEIMER, A., *Pascal* (Oxford, 1980).

KUENTZ, P., 'Un discours nommé Montalte' in *Revue d'histoire littéraire*, 71 (1971), 195–206.

LE GUERN, M. (ed.), Pascal, *Les Provinciales* (Paris, 1987).

LE GUERN, M. -R. and M., *Les Pensées de Pascal: De l'anthropologie à la théologie* (Paris, 1972).

LEPRUN, J., 'La Parabole de la seconde *Provinciale*', in *Méthodes chez Pascal* (Paris, 1979), 241–52.

LEWIS, P., 'Dialogic Impasse in Pascal's *Provinciales*', *Canadian Review of Comparative Literature* (Winter 1976), 27–38.

MAINGUENEAU, D., *Sémantique de la polémique* (Lausanne, 1983).

MARIN, L., 'Pascal: Text, Author, Discourse . . .', *Yale French Studies*, 52 (1975), 129–51.

MAYNARD, M. -U., *Les Lettres Provinciales . . . et leur réfutation* (Paris, 1851), 2 vols.

MESNARD, J., *Les Pensées de Pascal* (Paris, 1976).

MIEL, J., *Pascal and Theology* (Baltimore and London, 1969).

MOLINIER, A. (ed.), Pascal, *Lettres Provinciales* (Paris, 1891), 2 vols.

MOREL, J., 'Pascal et la doctrine du rire grave', in *Méthodes chez Pascal* (Paris, 1979), 213–22.

NELSON, R., *Pascal, Adversary and Advocate* (Harvard, 1981).

PARISH, R., 'Mais qui parle? Voice and Persona in the *Pensées*', *Seventeenth Century French Studies*, 8 (1986), 23–40.

PLAINEMAISON, J., 'La "méthode géométrique" contre la "doctrine des équivoques" dans les *Provinciales*', in *Méthodes chez Pascal* (Paris, 1979), 223–9.

REISLER, M., 'Persuasion through Antithesis: An Analysis of the Dominant Rhetorical Structure of Pascal's *Lettres Provinciales*', *Romanic Review*, 69 (1978), 172–85.

REX, W., *Pascal's Provincial Letters: An Introduction* (London, etc., 1977).

SEDGWICK, A., *Jansenism in Seventeenth-Century France: Voices from the Wilderness* (Charlottesville, 1977).

SELLIER, P., *Pascal et saint Augustin* (Paris, 1970).

SOMMERVOGEL, C., *Bibliothèque de la Compagnie de Jésus* (Brussels, Paris, and Louvain, 1890–1960), 12 vols.

STEWART, H. (ed.), *Les Provinciales de Blaise Pascal* (Manchester, 1951).

TOPLISS, P., *The Rhetoric of Pascal* (Leicester, 1966).
WOLFE, P., 'Langage et vérité dans les *Provinciales* XI à XVI', in J. -J. Demorest and L. Leibacher-Ouvrard (eds.), *Pascal, Corneille*, pp. 79–88.

Index